1986

C0-AWP-663

3 0301 00089592 6

HAROLD PINTER

Harold Pinter. Photo by Ivan Kyncl.

HAROLD PINTER

Critical Approaches

Edited by STEVEN H. GALE

Rutherford • Madison • Teaneck
Fairleigh Dickinson University Press
London and Toronto: Associated University Presses

LIBRARY
College of St. Francis
JOLIET, ILLINOIS

© 1986 by Associated University Presses, Inc.

Associated University Presses
440 Forsgate Drive
Cranbury, NJ 08512

Associated University Presses
25 Sicilian Avenue
London WC1A 2QH, England

Associated University Presses
2133 Royal Windsor Drive
Unit 1
Mississauga, Ontario
Canada L5J 1K5

The paper used in this publication meets the minimum requirements of the American National Standard for Permanence of Paper for Printed Library Materials Z39.48-1984.

Library of Congress Cataloging in Publication Data
Main entry under title:

Harold Pinter: critical approaches.

Bibliography: p.
Includes index.
1. Pinter, Harold, 1930–   —Criticism and interpretation—Addresses, essays, lectures.   I. Gale, Steven H.
PR6066.I53Z667 1985   822′.914   83–49346
ISBN 0-8386-3215-7 (alkaline paper)

Printed in the United States of America

822.9
P659gal

To
Kathy, Shannon, Ashley, and Kristin
with all my love

119,771

Contents

A Chronology of Pinter's Writing and First Performances

The Caretaker is staged at the Arts Theatre, London, April 27.

"The Black and White" (prose version) is published in *The Spectator,* July 1.

Night School is televised by Associated Rediffusion Television, July 21.

The Birthday Party becomes the first Pinter play performed professionally in America, Actors Workshop, San Francisco, July 27.

The Dwarfs is broadcast on the BBC Third Programme, December 2.

The Hothouse is finished.

1961   "Harold Pinter Replies" (essay) is published in *New Theatre Magazine,* January.

A Slight Ache is staged as part of a triple bill, *Three,* at the Arts Theatre Club, London, January 18.

"Afternoon" (poem) is published in *Twentieth Century,* February.

"Writing for Myself" (essay) is published in *Twentieth Century,* February.

The Collection is televised by Associated Rediffusion Television, May 11.

A Night Out is staged at the Gate Theatre, Dublin, September 17.

1962   *The Servant* is filmed in November in London.

The screenplay of *The Caretaker* (*The Guest*) is written.

"Between the Lines" (essay) is published in *The Sunday Times* (London), March 4.

The Collection is staged at the Aldwych Theatre, London, June 18.

"The Examination" is read by Pinter on the BBC Third Programme, September 7.

1963   "Tea Party" (short story) is written.

The Lover is televised by Associated Rediffusion Television, March 28.

The Caretaker (film) is shown at the Berlin Film Festival, June 27.

The Lover and *The Dwarfs* are staged at the Arts Theatre Club, London, September 18.

The script is written for *The Pumpkin Eater,* and the script for *The Compartment* (later published as *The Basement*).

"Filming *The Caretaker*" (interview) is published.

1964   *The Homecoming* is written.

"Writing for the Theatre" (essay) is published in *Evergreen Review,* August–September.

"Applicant," "Dialogue for Three," "Interview," "That's All," and "That's Your Trouble" are broadcast on the BBC Third Programme, February–March.

"Tea Party" is read by Pinter on the BBC Third Programme, June 2.

The Pumpkin Eater is shown.

1965   "Tea Party" (prose version) is published in *Playboy,* January.

The Homecoming begins a pre-London tour in March; staged at the Aldwych Theatre, London, June 3.

Tea Party is televised by BBC-1 in England and throughout Europe, March 25.

1966   *The Quiller Memorandum* is shown in November.

Accident is written.

Langrishe, Go Down is published.

1967   *Landscape* is written.

"Two People in a Room: Playwriting" (essay) is published in *The New Yorker,* February 25.

The Basement is televised on BBC-TV, February 28.

"Beckett" (essay) is published in *Beckett at Sixty.*

Accident is shown in February.

1968   *Silence* is written.

Mac (memoir) is published.

A film version is made of *The Birthday Party,* shown in New York, December 9.

Landscape is broadcast on the BBC Third Programme, April 28.

The Basement is staged at the Eastside Playhouse, New York, October 19.

Poems is published.

1969   *The Go-Between* is completed.

Night is staged in a collection of one-act plays, *Mixed Doubles,* at the Comedy Theatre, London, April 9.

Landscape and *Silence* are staged at the Aldwych Theatre, London, July 2.

"Pinter People" is televised on NBC's *Experiment in Television.*

1970   *Old Times* is written.

"All of That" (poem) is published in *The Times Literary Supplement* (London), December 11.

The film script of *The Homecoming* is completed.

1971   *The Go-Between* is shown at the Cannes Film Festival.

Old Times is first staged at the Aldwych Theatre, London, June 1.

"Speech: Hamburg 1970" (essay) is published in *Theatre Quarterly,* July–September.

"Pinter on Beckett" (essay) is published in *New Theatre Magazine,* May–June.

"Poem" (poem) is published in the *New York Times Magazine,* December 5.

1972   The film adaptation of *Remembrance of Things Past (À la recherche du temps perdu)* is written.

Monologue is written.

1973   The film version of *Butley* is made.

The Homecoming (film) is shown.

Monologue is televised, April 10.

"Pinter on Pinter" (essay) is published in *Cinebill,* October.

1974   "An Unpublished Speech" is published in *Theatre Quarterly,* August–October.

No Man's Land is written.

Butley (film) is shown.

1975   The film version of *The Last Tycoon* is made.
No Man's Land is staged at the Old Vic, London, April 23.

1976   *The Last Tycoon* is shown on November 18.

1978   *Betrayal* is staged at the National Theatre, London, November 15.

1980   *The Hothouse* is first performed at the Hampstead Theatre, London, April 24.
Family Voices is broadcast on BBC III Radio, January 22.

1981   *The French Lieutenant's Woman* (film) is shown.
Family Voices is staged at the National Theatre, London, February 13.

1982   *Victoria Station* and *A Kind of Alaska* are first performed as part of a triple bill with *Family Voices* at the National Theatre, London, October 14.

1983   *Players* is presented at the National Theatre, London, September 7.

1984   *One for the Road* is published in *The New York Review of Books*, May 10.

N.B. Full bibliographical information on published works is included in Steven H. Gale, *Harold Pinter: An Annotated Bibliography* (New York: G. K. Hall, 1978). Additional published short essays and correspondence are also listed in this volume.

Preface

In December, 1980 after a Special Session at the Modern Language Association Convention in Houston where I chaired a panel on "Comedy in Contemporary British Drama," Leonard Powlick and I struck up a conversation that led to my wondering if anyone was going to do anything special to commemorate the twenty-fifth anniversary of the first production of a Harold Pinter play. Len and I agreed that this would be a worthwhile project, and we tentatively decided to put together a proposal for a volume of original essays by leading Pinter scholars to celebrate the event.

Over the next several months I became sidetracked by other projects, but in the early spring of 1981 Len wrote to me to find out whether I was still interested in the project. I was, and with this stimulation I began trying to contact potential contributors. Although I was not able to contact everyone whom I wanted to invite to submit an essay for consideration, I was gratified by the response. Everyone thought that the idea was a good one, and most were eager to participate. A few had too many commitments already and could not write a new article at the time, but this was made up for by the scholars who heard about the volume and approached me to find out if it would be possible for them to submit something. As soon as I had a reasonable list of contributors, and abstracts of their essays, I put together a proposal, and in January, 1983 Fairleigh Dickinson University Press accepted the volume for publication. Unfortunately, Len's commitments had grown so that he was no longer able to continue as a coauthor of the project, but I am happy to say that he was able to offer some valuable advice at several stages of the development of the book, and that he was able to find the time to write an essay, which is included in the volume, commenting on Pinter's career.

Although it was obviously too late to publish *Harold Pinter: Critical Approaches* to celebrate the twenty-fifth anniversary of *The Room*, the press decided that Pinter is important enough in twentieth-century literature to deserve such a volume and that a collection of seventeen original pieces by many of the leading contemporary drama scholars in America and Britain was so attractive that the volume should be published.

Nevertheless, there was some dissent. One reviewer, not connected with Fairleigh Dickinson, recognized most of the names in the table of contents and, without having seen any of the essays, suggested that the volume might be limited, for all of these Pinter scholars must surely already have said every-

13

thing that they could say about Pinter's canon and therefore would only repeat themselves. Needless to say, this is not the case. To the contrary, whereas seven of the authors included have written books on Pinter (and three have authored more than one book on the subject), there are a couple of promising young scholars included who have published little or nothing on Pinter previously. Moreover, the authors of all of the articles included have, in fact, built upon their own and others' scholarship. Thus, the critics herein included expand on what they have already said, or explore entirely new areas, or go into more detail about a specific topic than they have heretofore.

There remains a question of why another volume should be published on an author who is himself still publishing new works every other year or so. This does present a problem because there is necessarily a time lag involved, and Pinter has already produced three new short plays since the essays were collected. However, this drawback to writing about a living author (which must be faced by anyone who is willing to accept the challenge of dealing with a contemporary, alive, and changing literature and does not need to hide behind a body of critical responses) is offset by several factors. First, in a quarter of a century Pinter has written a large number of plays, and he has not remained static, either thematically or stylistically. Second, there have been changes in critical approaches to the dramatist, to some extent evolving out of the scholarship that has accumulated to date. Third, for future scholars it will be useful to have reactions from critics who have been able both to see première productions and, paraphrasing Wordsworth, to reflect in tranquillity over a twenty-five year period about what they have seen. A dual perspective is thereby achieved. Some of the essays in *Harold Pinter: Critical Approaches* could only have been written after the critical groundwork was prepared; presumably, they are in turn preparing further groundwork.

As I began collecting the essays for this volume, I had a number of criteria in mind. Primarily, of course, I wanted insightful and well-written articles. In addition, I wanted the pieces to reflect the gamut of critical approaches to Pinter's writing that has evolved over the past quarter century, and I wanted each essay to be able to stand on its own. A quick glance at the table of contents will reveal that the essays cover a wide spectrum of subjects over the entirety of Pinter's career, ranging from his radio and stage plays to his film scripts, from text to performance, and from thematic studies to examinations of individual plays (from *The Room* [1957] to *Family Voices* [1981]).

Acknowledgments

The editor of any collection of original essays such as this requires the assistance and cooperation of a number of people, and I am pleased to be able to say that the help that I received during the initial stages of the project, the solicitation and collection of the essays, and the subsequent editorial tasks made the editing of *Harold Pinter: Critical Approaches* relatively easy.

A great deal of recognition should go to Len Powlick, who helped me devise the proposal in the first place and who then continued to provide me with advice after he had to withdraw from the editing aspect of the project. Naturally, I want to thank all of the contributors, who graciously agreed to be included in this volume, who sent me their manuscripts in a timely manner, and who responded to my suggestions immediately, and with good cheer. Among the contributors, I would like to single out two, however. Al Wertheim and Kathy Burkman were especially helpful, freely supplying me with good advice at all stages of the development of the manuscript. Furthermore, there are also a number of people who deserve thanks who were invited to submit articles for consideration, but whose work does not appear in this volume. Even when time constraints would not allow them to be contributors, many scholars gave me helpful advice and either informed me of others who might be considered for inclusion or contacted others to let them know of the project. Two of the essays that were finally included came to me in this way.

I would also like to acknowledge the help and encouragement given to me by Professor Harry Keyishian, Director of the Fairleigh Dickinson University Press, and to thank Professor T. J. Ross for his sympathetic reading of the manuscript and useful suggestions for some minor revisions. Furthermore, Julien Yoseloff at Associated University Presses was particularly helpful and understanding as we worked through the actual production process, and Katharine Turok's attention to detail during the copy editing helped us all.

Additional help in terms of typing and duplicating was provided me by Teresa Plew and her staff (primarily Sharon Campbell), and by Pat Martin.

Finally, as always, I acknowledge the help, love, and encouragement given to me by my family during the whole process. Without all of the support of my wife and three daughters, this volume would not have come about. I can never fully repay them for their understanding and their sacrifices.

15

Introduction

In 1957 Harold Pinter was a young actor using the stage name David Baron. While Pinter was engaged in a repertory stand in Torquay, Devon, Henry Woolf, a friend and fellow actor, telephoned him to see whether he would be willing to write a play for production at Bristol University, where Woolf was teaching in the Drama Department. Woolf needed the play in six days. Pinter responded that there was not enough time to write a play, but he began working on one anyway; it took him four days to write *The Room*.

The Room was originally performed in the old Drama Studio, a converted squash court, on 15 May 1957. The following January it was presented at the Festival of University Drama, and the drama received its professional premiere at the Hampstead Theatre Club on 21 January 1960. In the meantime, the playwright's second play, *The Birthday Party*, became his first play to be staged professionally when it was mounted at the Arts Theatre in Cambridge on 28 April 1958. The play's producer, Michael Codron, had been so impressed by Harold Hobson's *Sunday Times* (London) review of the Festival of University Drama presentation of *The Room* that he had immediately asked Pinter to write a full-length play.

Since that time Pinter has written twenty-two plays, a number of revue sketches, essays, a memoir, poetry, and thirteen film scripts. He has also been recognized as the major playwright writing in English today, though the first reviews of his plays suggested that such a thing would never be possible.

Critical reaction to Pinter's work has not always been favorable, as in the case of the disastrous first run of *The Birthday Party*, in spite of that promising review by Hobson. Sometimes even when it is positive it is positive for the wrong reasons[1]; some critics who have jumped on the Pinter bandwagon demonstrate little understanding of his work. However, each piece in this collection makes a reasoned argument independent of the other essays, and, at the same time, the essays taken together present a fuller picture of the dramatist's canon and a better understanding of what he tries to do and how he tries to do it. This is accomplished in part by the variety of approaches to and readings of the plays—which is also indicative of the richness of Pinter's texts—and it is especially true when an individual play is dealt with in more than one article. Interestingly, several of the authors in *Harold Pinter: Critical Approaches* contradict one another. While I do not completely agree with some of the interpretations presented in this volume, many of the points of disagreement are not mutually exclusive, and the arguments expounded are carefully defined and evidence is offered to support the conflicting views. In part, of course, this circumstance in itself reflects the complexity and multilayered character of Pinter's writing. In some cases, in fact, it seems that Pinter's concept that something can be both true and false at the same time is applicable, for there are instances when the critics persuasively demonstrate opposing points of view where both interpretations may, indeed, be valid.

The structure of *Harold Pinter: Critical Approaches* was arrived at rather arbitrarily. Essentially, the articles are arranged in chronological order according to the date of the subject play's premiere production, although there is also a categorical distinction involved. After the introductory essays the first set of articles (through Arnold P. Hinchliffe's piece) tend to deal with individual plays, and the concluding articles consider broader aspects of Pinter's work. There is an index, but no bibliography (a full-length annotated bibliography already exists). As editor, I have corrected spelling and punctuation errors that crept in unnoticed, and I tried to standardize somewhat, but, aside from minor suggestions, I have followed the practice of British editors and not intruded, letting the author's words speak for themselves.

Bernard F. Dukore's "My, How We've Changed," leads off the volume. It is an overview of Pinter's career, commenting on how the dramatist's writing has changed, and how attitudes toward his work have changed as well—in effect, how his presence has altered the nature of the theatre. Leonard Powlick's "'What the Hell Is *That* All About?': A Peek at Pinter's Dramaturgy" discusses the concept that there is a physical image from which each of Pinter's plays derives and which is central to the meaning of the particular drama. He also notes affinities between Pinter and Franz Kafka and Samuel Beckett. Francis Gillen's "Harold Pinter's *The Birthday Party*: Menace Reconsidered" is a reassessment of the nature of menace in *The Birthday Party* that analyzes the menace specifically as it is related to Stanley's "search for self-identity" instead of focusing on the menacers and the sources of menace as is traditionally done.

Martin Esslin in "Harold Pinter's Work for Radio" writes about an interesting and deserving but little-explored topic, drawing on his own experience as the former Head of the British Broadcasting Corporation Radio Drama Department to provide a historical account of Pinter's work on BBC radio. Esslin also includes a comparison of the radio, television, and stage versions of several of Pinter's scripts to show how the dramatist's techniques and mastery of language (and silence) are even more important on radio than on the stage. Albert Wertheim's "Tearing of Souls: Harold Pinter's *A Slight Ache* on Radio and Stage" treats the difference between writing for radio and the stage, too, through a comparison of the presentations of *A Slight Ache*, one of Pinter's minor masterpieces, in two different media. Wertheim utilizes an unpublished BBC radio interview with Donald McWhinnie and Pinter.

Scott Giantvalley traces the history of textual changes in *The Dwarfs* in

"Toying with *The Dwarfs*: The Textual Problems with Pinter's 'Corrections.'" An interesting phenomenon is that Pinter's publishers may not be aware that there are textual changes between printings of some of the dramatists plays,[2] but Giantvalley demonstrates how changes in moving from the radio version to the stage version of the drama have created a lack of consistency that affects character development and Pinter's patterns of imagery. This essay demonstrates how textual scholarship can shed interpretive light on the plays. Austin E. Quigley is a critic noted for his linguistic analysis of drama, yet in "Design and Discovery in Pinter's *The Lover*" Quigley presents a fairly traditional explication, with some structuralist overtones, as he delves into the dramatic structure of *The Lover*. This examination relates the play's structure to the thematic content of movement and change more explicitly than has been attempted before. Christopher C. Hudgin's "Intended Audience Response, *The Homecoming*, and the 'Ironic Mode of Identification'" explains why there are widely divergent reactions to *The Homecoming*. Taking the writings of Walter J. Ong and Hans Robert Jauss on audience response as his starting point, Hudgins states that Pinter imagines a particular audience at which his plays are directed, and that this fictionalized audience must be willing to and be intellectually capable of recognizing themselves in his "negative examples," leading to a parallel emotional identification. Therefore, it is the responsibility of the audience, he posits, to recognize themselves in the characters and to react to events on stage accordingly. A. R. Braunmuller relates Beckett's *Happy Days* and *All That Fall* to *Silence* in "Pinter's *Silence*: Experience without Character." With some deconstructionist criticism as a subtext, Braunmuller explores the language embodied in the different styles of the three dialogues to explain why it does not seem to be related to the characters' experiences in spite of their attempts to define themselves through it.

Over the years there has been an ever increasing interest in Pinter's films. At first there were but a few articles dealing with individual movies. Now there are more articles being written, plus dissertations on the subject, and several full-length studies of his cinematic canon are reportedly under way. In December 1978 there was a Special Session on "The Films of Harold Pinter: Focus on Adaptations/*The Proust Screenplay*" at the MLA Convention in New York City. Thomas P. Adler's "Pinter/Proust/Pinter" is another example of this growing interest in Pinter's screenwriting. I first heard a shorter version of this paper read at the Seventh Annual Conference on Literature and Film in Tallahassee, Fla., in January, 1982. I was impressed by it, and I asked Professor Adler if he would expand it for this collection. Beginning with *The Proust Screenplay*,[3] Adler compares Pinter's theory of memory with that of Marcel Proust and then analyzes the film script in relation to a number of Pinter's plays in order to determine what is Proustian and what is Pinterian about the various works. Enoch Brater's "Parallel Lives in Pinter's Screenplay of *The French Lieutenant's Woman*" discusses the way in which Pinter has adapted the John Fowles novel (Pinter's most successful film script to date), relating it to his earlier adaptations for film, and pursuing its links with the dramatist's recent work for the threatre.

Arnold P. Hinchliffe gives fairly straightforward, though brief, thematic explications of *Betrayal, The Hothouse,* and *Family Voices* in "After *No Man's Land*: A Progress Report." Katherine H. Burkman defines Pinter's concept of the family in terms of ritual patterns and archetypes, with Freudian overtones, in "*Family Voices* and the Voice of the Family in Pinter's Plays." Lucina Paquet Gabbard's book on Pinter was a psychological study; in "The Pinter Surprise" she examines the kinds of reversals that the playwright utilizes and their effects. Pinter's theatrical success, she contends, is based on his ability to use the element of surprise as he reverses the well-made-play technique of exposition and explanation of character. Pinter's technique is effective and believable, she contends, because the reversals are related to the nature of his characters. William F. Dohmen employs a thematic approach in "Time after Time: Pinter Plays with Disjunctive Chronologies." In this article he traces the treatment and the various uses of time in Pinter's works, and the development of his concept of the relationship between the characters' pasts and their presents. John Fuegi's "The Uncertainty Principle and Pinter's Modern Drama" was also read, in a slightly different version, at the 1982 Tallahassee conference. It is a comparison of traditional dramatic patterns —showing how they do not reflect the actual random nature of the universe that has been established by modern science—with Pinter's patterns in *The Caretaker* and *The Dumb Waiter*, showing that his are more realistic, less absurd, than those which appear in conventional dramas. Steven H. Gale's "Chronological Index to *Harold Pinter: An Annotated Bibliography*" is a supplement intended to make that bibliography more useful for scholars.

Certainly, as mentioned above, Pinter is the major English-language playwright of his generation, and possibly of the past several centuries, given the power, range, amount, and influence of his works. *The Caretaker, The Homecoming, Landscape,* and *Old Times* are already considered classics of the modern theatre. In a sense, then, the essays in this volume are a summing up of his more than twenty-five years of playwriting to date, and also of critical reactions to his dramaturgy. Neither this volume nor any of the individual essays, however, is trying to give the answer to what Pinter and his works are all about. Rather, as in the dramatist's plays, the attempt has been to provide a wide range of possibilities and to include representative examples of some of the diverse critical approaches that have been applied to Pinter's writing.

Steven H. Gale

Notes

1. See the "Introduction" to my *Harold Pinter: An Annotated Bibliography* (Boston: G. K.

Hall, 1978) for a more extended discussion of this.

2. See my *Butter's Going Up: A Critical Analysis of Harold Pinter's Work* (Durham, N. C.: Duke University Press, 1977) for further discussion.

3. A project that Pinter has described as the most difficult task that he has ever undertaken—see ibid., p. 247.

HAROLD PINTER

1

"My, How We've Changed"

BERNARD F. DUKORE

Has it really been twenty-five years since Harold Pinter wrote his first play?[1]
To some of us who saw those first or early productions or read their first
published editions, or both, who in effect grew up with him—though we may
have been adults at the time, as of course he was—the quarter-century
anniversary comes as a surprise. To some, not all: the passage of twenty-five
years surprised me when I became aware of it, but fortunately it did not
surprise this book's editor, who had the foresight to plan for it. Nor, I suspect,
did recognition of this anniversary surprise Pinter. A writer whose preoccupations include time would very likely have been alert to its milestones in his
own life. If he were not, interviewers have been there to remind him. "Harold
Pinter, who began his career in the theatre as actor, has been writing plays for
22 years," says Mel Gussow, for instance, at the beginning of his narrative
that precedes a 1979 interview with the playwright shortly before the American premiere of *Betrayal*. Almost at the start of the interview is this exchange
(Pinter speaks first):

> "Well, I would say that we all change. (Pause) Damn it ... in terms of age
> ... when did I write 'The Birthday Party'? I think it was 1957."
> "When you were in your 20's, and then the next plays when you were in
> your 30's, and the last three when you were in your 40's."
> "That's right. And now I'm hitting 50. (Laugh)"[2]

Gussow does not record whether the laugh was joyfully spontaneous or
whether it was, in Samuel Beckett's terms, bitter (laughter at what is not
good) or mirthless (laughter at unhappiness).[3] In any case, it really has been a
quarter of a century since Pinter wrote his first play. Although the last statement is partly an intimation of mortality for both Pinter and those of us who
were there at the beginning, now that much older, its intent is a reminder of
how long Pinter's plays have been part of our dramatic and theatrical consciousness.

119,771

LIBRARY
College of St. Francis
JOLIET, ILLINOIS

"My, how you've changed!" is a common exclamation when one sees a person after an absence of many years—despite one's recognition of the sameness of that person's features. The exclamation rewords what Edmund Spenser called "The ever-whirling wheel/Of change; the which all mortal things doth sway."[4] Put that way, the expression is classic, not cliché, as the former phrase might seem. To anyone familiar with Pinter's full-length plays, a recollection of their titles should alone suffice to indicate that his work has changed since his first such play,*The Birthday Party* (written in 1957, immediately after and in the same year as his first play): *The Caretaker, The Homecoming, Old Times, No Man's Land,* and *Betrayal.* So, too, and especially, are there substantial changes between Opus One, *The Room,* and his most recent play, *Family Voices,* both short works. Nevertheless, elements of early Pinter inhere in recent Pinter, just as, say, elements of early Eugene O'Neill inhere in late O'Neill. As in Pinter's first two plays, his most recent work has a person sequestered in a house (in the first, only a room). As in the first, someone (or two in *The Birthday Party* and *Family Voices*) comes (or come) to visit that person (in *The Room,* a delegate from the father; in *Family Voices,* the mother and sister themselves, or so they say, according to a character who says that someone else told him). In both first and latest plays, the man who conveys information about relatives is named Riley. But whereas *Family Voices* provides a fuller background for the sequestered man than *The Room* or *The Birthday Party* do for their sequestered people—which constitutes a significant difference—the additional information does not provide clarification. Apart from the fact that the latest play was written for radio rather than for the stage, it fundamentally differs from the first play, as the title indicates, in that it is a work for voices, structured somewhat like a sonata (though for three vocal instruments, not one or two), while the first is a work of dramatic action whose structure builds to a climax of physical violence and blindness. Whatever threads of ideas or techniques weave through one's life and writings, the concerns—and therefore the ways in which one dramatizes them—of a person in his twenties (when Pinter wrote his first two plays) differ from those in his thirties (when he wrote *The Homecoming*), his forties (when he wrote *Betrayal*), and now his fifties (he wrote *Family Voices* in 1980, the year he turned fifty, and because its first performance, on BBC radio, was on 22 January 1981, one may reasonably infer that he completed the play as he approached his fiftieth birthday, 10 October 1980).

Because we have absorbed Pinter's plays and methods into our dramatic and theatrical experiences, we too have changed. Even among his detractors, one does not encounter today either the type or amount of adverse criticism that greeted the first London production of *The Birthday Party* (virulent and nearly unanimous). Most of his current detractors grant him the respect due someone who has earned the esteem and captured the admiration of so many theatregoers and playreaders. Still, the quintessential Pinter disturbs some people as much as the quintessential Pirandello used to. By substituting Pinter's name for Luigi Pirandello's, one may apply the latter's partial parody of his champions and antagonists to the English playwright. This semispoof occurs in the First Choral Interlude of *Each in His Own Way*:

ONE OF THE FRIENDS OF PIRANDELLO. If you want to sleep, why don't you stick to the other plays? With them you can just lean back in your seat and take what is sent you across the footlights. But with a comedy of Pirandello's you have to be on your pins. You sit up straight and dig your finger nails into the arms of your chair as though you were going to be knocked down by what the author has to say! You hear a word ... any word at all ... "chair" for instance! Now with most people that word means "chair," but with Pirandello you say "A chair? ... No sir! He isn't going to get away with that! I'm going to find out what's under the chair!"

ONE OF THE ADVERSARIES. Yes, yes! That's right! Pirandello gives you everything except a little sentiment! But not a bit of sentiment!

OTHER ADVERSARIES. That's it! That's it! Not a bit of sentiment ... and you've got to have sentiment!

ONE OF PIRANDELLO'S FRIENDS. If you want sentiment go and find it under the chair that fellow is talking about.

THE ADVERSARIES. But let us have done with these spasms, this nihilism ... this delight he takes in denying everything![5]

For sentiment—which in the context of this passage is a comic non sequitur that reflects the adversaries' inflexible, preoccupying notion of an essential characteristic of acceptable drama—one certainly does not go to Pinter, who like Beckett (in Pinter's italicized tribute to him) *"hasn't got his hand over his heart."*[6] As for views about a chair, Pinter in the second act of *The Homecoming* has characters offer some about a chair's companionpiece, a table:

LENNY. Well, for instance, take a table. Philosophically speaking. What is it?

TEDDY. A table.

LENNY. Ah. You mean it's nothing else but a table. Well, some people would envy your certainty, wouldn't they, Joey? For instance, I've got a couple of friends of mine, we often sit round the Ritz Bar having a few liqueurs, and they're always saying things like that, you know, things like: Take a table, take it. All right, I say, *take* it, *take* a table, but once you've taken it, what are you going to do with it? Once you've got hold of it, where are you going to take it?

MAX. You'd probably sell it.

LENNY. You wouldn't get much for it.

JOEY. Chop it up for firewood.

I have no way of knowing whether Pinter drew on Pirandello's play when he composed that passage, whether he is familiar with *Each in His Own Way*, or whether one of the intended levels of meaning in that quotation is sly mockery of his interpreters. Even if the parallel passages are merely coincidental, however, they reveal a parallel awareness both of multifaceted meanings and of the comic aspect of people who attempt explications of what they take to be symbols or meanings, including perhaps (dare I say it?) every contributor to this book. Nevertheless, we admiring contributors delight in what his adversaries mistakenly consider to be his spasms, nihilism, and denial; and we are by no means tired of what they erroneously call his tearing down.

In one important sense, the "we" who have changed include Pinter's detractors as well as his friends, and this change has affected our attitude toward the drama. What Bernard Shaw said about Henrik Ibsen and old-fashioned nineteenth-century dramatists holds for Pinter and old-fashioned twentieth-century dramatists:

When Mr [Charles] Charrington produced Ibsen's Doll's House at the Royalty in 1889, he smashed up the British drama of the eighties. Not that the public liked Ibsen: he was infinitely too good for that. But the practical business point is not how people like Ibsen, but how they liked [H. J.] Byron, [Victorien] Sardou, and Tom Taylor after Ibsen. [...] In short, a modern manager need not produce The Wild Duck; but he must be very careful not to produce a play which will seem insipid and old-fashioned to playgoers who have seen The Wild Duck, even though they may have hissed it.[8]

Would the laborious exposition and trite symbolism of plays like W. Somerset Maugham's *The Constant Wife* or Arthur Miller's *All My Sons* seem quite so laborious and trite, and the plays themselves so old-fashioned, had not Pinter accustomed us to a different type of drama? In contrast to these works, the exposition in his usually casts doubt rather than dispels it, raises questions rather than gives answers, and the plays' symbolism is usually subtle and highly implicit, lacking simple one-to-one correspondences—as I once put it, he deliberately refuses to cross his *t*'s and dot his *i*'s. Like Ibsen's plays, Pinter's have not invalidated earlier superior works of their respective centuries, like Nikolai Gogol's *Inspector General* or Miller's own *Death of a Salesman*, but they have (to use Shaw's term) smashed up the ordinary popular plays. In the 1890s, as Shaw said in a passage deleted from the quotation, plays by the old-fashioned writers still made more money in London than those by Ibsen, but newer writers whose plays had more in common with Ibsen's than with the others were becoming increasingly popular and the others decreasingly so. The London revival of *All My Sons* in 1981 drew audiences, though the house was relatively small when I attended, as it was when acquaintances attended at different times. Meanwhile, works by such writers as Simon Gray (some directed by Pinter), which clearly have more in common with his than with old-fashioned plays, draw full houses. So, for that matter, do the comedies of Alan Ayckbourn, who explicitly states that Pinter was "enormously influential" and that Pinter's language had "an immediate effect" on him.[9] Those twenty-five years since Pinter wrote his first play have made a difference. The theatre is no longer the same. We theatregoers are no longer the same. Through Pinter, we too have changed.

Notes

1. This essay was completed in early April 1982.

2. Mel Gussow, "Harold Pinter: 'I Started with Two People in a Pub,'" *New York Times,* 30 December 1979, sec. 2, p. 5. Here and elsewhere in this essay, three periods, unless bracketed, do not represent ellipses but are in the quoted passages.

3. Samuel Beckett, *Watt* (London: John Calder Jupiter Books, 1963), pp. 46–47. Between the bitter and mirthless laughs, according to Beckett, is the hollow—laughter at what is untrue—which in this instance is inapplicable.

4. Edmund Spenser, *The Faerie Queene*, bk. 2, canto 6, stanza 1.

5. Bernard F. Dukore and Daniel C. Gerould, eds., *Avant-Garde Drama: A Casebook* (New York: Thomas Y. Crowell, 1976), p. 297.

6. *Beckett at 60: a Festschrift* (London: Calder and Boyars, 1967), p. 86.

7. Harold Pinter, *The Homecoming* (New York: Grove Press, n.d.), p. 52.

8. Bernard Shaw, *Our Theatres in the Nineties* (London: Constable, 1948), 1: 164–65.

9. Ian Watson, *Conversations with Ayckbourn* (London: Macdonald Futura, 1981), p. 107.

2
"What the Hell Is *That* All About?": A Peek at Pinter's Dramaturgy

LEONARD POWLICK

About ten years ago, while attending a very good university theatre production of *Old Times*, I observed in its purest form what I have come to see as a very common reaction to the plays of Harold Pinter. The man sitting to my left was middle aged, middle class, and (as I gathered from overhearing snatches of his conversation) decidedly middle brow. When the curtain rose, he settled in for what he apparently had expected to be a usual evening's entertainment in the theatre, but as the first act progressed, he grew restless. *This,* obviously, was not what theatre was supposed to be like. He gradually calmed down, however, and by the time act 1 was half gone, he was caught. I could feel the tension coming from him as he strained forward in his seat so that he could hear every word, see every gesture. A couple of times I even overheard him humming some of the tunes that Deeley and Anna sang to each other. Throughout the rest of the play, he continued to respond physically to what was happening on the stage. At the end, after the final curtain call (he had applauded enthusiastically), and as the houselights were coming up, he sank back in his seat, let out a breath, and said to his wife: "What the hell was *that* all about?"

Last week, at the premiere showing in our town (at the largest of the shopping mall "cinemas") of *Betrayal,* the same reaction was evident on the faces of the middling-sized crowd that had come out to see the performance of Academy Award–winner Ben Kingsley. Glancing around after the film was over, I was certain that a good many of them were thinking the same thing: "What the hell was *that* all about?" In fact, I would even venture to say that many of us—critics, scholars, theatre professionals, serious theatregoers— have had nearly the same reaction, even though we would not put it quite so bluntly. "Hmmm," we have said to ourselves or to a companion upon coming out of the theatre in which we have just seen *No Man's Land* for the first time. "Very interesting." We then would add a few stock phrases from our store of stock phrases labeled "Pinter," and resolve to ourselves to reread the script first thing in the morning.

The fascinating thing about all of these reactions is that, despite not being able to verbalize what the play—or film or video drama—was "about," audiences had responded to it; they had *felt* it; it had affected them emotionally. The work had communicated with them, even if not on a cognitive level, touching them somewhere beneath the surface of their psyches. The resonances of the words, actions, and images had set up a reverberation deep within them that had moved them, though they were unable to explain why. The work had, to use Kenneth Burke's term, "danced."

This results in an interesting situation, for despite Pinter's (deserved) reputation for being a "difficult" playwright (some might even say "obscure"), his plays are extremely popular. Despite the fact that for twenty-five years audiences have been saying about his plays "What the hell is *that* all about?", those plays have had long, successful runs in England, the United States, Canada, Europe, and elsewhere. Pinter has become not only the most important playwright working in the English language, but also one of the most popular and successful, a phenomenon not to be expected in an age when many artists are producing for other artists.

Even though he has been accused of deliberate obfuscation,[1] Pinter does care about his audiences and about communicating with them. His theatrical experience—both as an actor and as a director—has given him an acute sense of what "works" in the theatre. He said in 1961:

I think I certainly developed some feeling for construction which, believe it or not, is pretty important to me, and for speakable dialogue. I had a pretty good notion in my earlier plays of what would shut an audience up; not so much what would make them laugh. That I had no idea about.[2]

He has, of course, learned what makes audiences laugh, as is clearly evident in nearly any performance of his subsequent plays (although there was much that was humorous even in the pre-1961 plays, particularly *The Dumb Waiter* and *The Birthday Party*; Irving Wardle had to have *some* reason to call them "*comedies* of menace.")[3]. But beyond that, Pinter's plays contain more than just effective technique; he is more than just suspense and curtain lines. There is in Pinter's work a crucial element that accounts both for his importance as an artist and for his ability to affect his audiences: that is his ability to zero in on one basic metaphor, basic because it strikes all of us somewhere in the center of our being. Peter Hall speaks of this quality when he says, "Anyone who has lived in a family and has been with that family at, say, Christmas, and understood that this is an opportunity for murder, *must* understand *The Homecoming.*"[4] By "understand," of course, he does not necessarily mean to recognize on a cognitive level. We can "understand" with our guts as well as our minds.

If we cannot at once verbalize our reactions to the plays but have nonetheless reacted to them, we have recognized nevertheless in the plays, sub-

liminally, situations we have known, dilemmas we have found ourselves
enmeshed in, nightmares we have dreamt, and so on. Pinter's plays are
meaningful for us because, if we have lived any length of time at all, we
have lived many of those same, or similar, situations—even if we cannot
immediately recognize them.

Pinter says that the idea for his plays come to him as monetary inspirations,
sometimes verbally and sometimes as visual images:

"What invariably happens ... is that an image or a couple of sentences come
to me. I go on from there."[5]

"The germ of my plays? I'll be as accurate as I can about that. I went into a
room and saw one person standing up and one person sitting down, and a few
weeks later I wrote *The Room*. I went into another room and saw two people
sitting down, and a few years later I wrote *The Birthday Party*. I looked
through a door into a third room, and saw two people standing up and I wrote
The Caretaker."[6]

Q. "Could you retrace the genesis of *Old Times*?"
A. "... I was lying on the sofa ... reading the paper and something flashed
    through my mind. It wasn't anything to do with the paper."
Q. "Something to do with the sofa?"
A. "The sofa perhaps, but certainly not the paper. I rushed upstairs to my
    room...."
Q. "What was the thought?"
A. "I think it was the first couple of lines of the play. I don't know if they
    were actually the *first* lines. [Quickly.] Two poeple were talking about
    someone else."[7]

"I remember when I wrote *No Man's Land,* I was in a taxi one night coming
back from somewhere and suddenly a line, a few words came into my mind. I
had no pencil. I got back to the house and wrote those lines down. I can't
remember exactly what they were, but it was the very beginning of the play,
and I didn't know who said them."[8]

Q. "What was the initial image for *Betrayal*?"
A. "Two people in a pub ... meeting after some time."[9]

And one can see in the finished plays the fleshing out of these seeds. Pinter
has, indeed "gone on from there," and one can pretty well discern where in
the play that seed has sprouted. The visual images remain intact, and the
verbal ones have become solidified:

—In *The Room*, the play opens and closes with a tableau of one person standing and one person sitting down. At the opening, it is Bert who is sitting at the
table while Rose serves his meal. At the end their positions have reversed and
it is Rose sitting in her chair with Bert standing over her.

—Similarly, *The Birthday Party* opens and closes with a scene of Meg and

Petey sitting at the kitchen table.

—*The Caretaker* ends with a tableau of two men standing in a room: Aston firm in his insistence that Davies must leave, Davies pleading that he be allowed to stay.

—The seed for *Old Times*—the opening conversation between Deeley and Kate about Anna—culminates in the final tableau, a key image made even more important by the explicit lighting direction:

Lights up full sharply. Very bright.
DEELEY *in armchair.*
ANNA *lying on divan.*
KATE *sitting on divan.*

(London: Methuen [1971], p. 75)

This is the scene that Anna had earlier described as one she remembered, after commenting that "There are things I remember which may never have happened but as I recall them so they take place" (p. 32).

—*No Man's Land* establishes in the first few lines of the play the relationship that will culminate in the final attitude of Spooner envying Hirst his security, Hirst envying Spooner his freedom.

—Finally, the opening scene of *Betrayal*—"two people at a pub ... meeting after some time"—is the scene from which the rest of the play springs. Had it not been where it is, but been played in correct chronological sequence, the remainder of the play would be merely banal soap opera. The first image of Jerry and Emma in the pub—obviously uncomfortable after not seeing each other for such a long time—is one of the most painful scenes in all of Pinter's plays and is crucial to the experience of the play.

To this list one can add other images not commented on by Pinter: the "family portrait" at the end of *The Homecoming,* Beth and Duff sitting at the table in *Landscape,* the final scene of Flora, Edward, and the Matchseller in *A Slight Ache,* the narrator addressing an empty chair in *Monologue.* In each case the image is composed of several people (only one in *Monologue*) in a precise spatial relationship. The simple spatial relationship contains within it, however, powerful psychological relationships, and Pinter takes it as his dramaturgical task to explore those psychological relationships.

"Pinter has the firmest grasp of psychological verities and the metaphysic that lurks behind them," Charles Marowitz pointed out back in 1967, before most of Pinter's major works had been written.[10] Since then, Pinter has gone on to prove Marowitz's assertion many times over. Gaston Bachelard has pointed out that "All great, simple images reveal a psychic state," [11] and it is in the elucidation of the psychic state implicit within those spatial relationships between his characters that Pinter has developed a unique form of dramaturgy. As a director, and thus one who searches for the physical image within the play-text, Peter Hall noted that quality in Pinter's work: "... what stirs the audience is not the mask, not the control, but what is underneath it: that's what moves them, that's what terrifies and moves them. In that sense, Pinter's is a new form of theatre.... It's a reaching toward a kind of imagery—an emblem in silence."[12]

This approach to playwriting could be described as the actualizing of fleeting impressions: taking a momentary occurrence and fleshing it out until it adequately explains itself, until it becomes psychologically satisfactory. For an analogue one is tempted to look to Tom Stoppard's *After Magritte* with its opening tableau and subsequent exploration. But *After Magritte,* as clever and entertaining as it is, is merely an attempt to show how the seemingly absurd opening scene might *logically* have come about, and so any resemblance is merely superficial. The real analogues come from two of Pinter's spiritual and artistic mentors, Franz Kafka and Samual Beckett. All of Kafka's works of course function in much the same way: K., Joseph K., Gregor, and so on all attempt to come to an accommodation with their private situation—a situation represented by a grand image: a trial, a castle, a transformation into a bug. But this desire of the author's to flesh out momentary occurrences, to turn, as Beckett says, "... a disturbance into words,"[13] is most manifest in a short parable entitled "Passers-by":

When you go walking by night up a street and a man, visible a long way off—for the street mounts uphill and there's a full moon—comes running toward you, well, you don't catch hold of him, not even if he is a feeble and ragged creature, not even if someone chases yelling at his heels, but you let him run on.

For it is night, and you can't help it if the street goes uphill before you in the moonlight, and besides, these two have maybe started that chase to amuse themselves, or perhaps they are both chasing a third, perhaps the first is an innocent man and the second wants to murder him and you would become an accessory, perhaps they don't know anything about each other and are merely running separately home to bed, perhaps they are night birds, perhaps the first man is armed.

And anyhow, haven't you a right to be tired, haven't you been drinking a lot of wine? You're thankful that the second man is now long out of sight.[14]

In this short piece, an inexplicable event—a man running headlong down a street in the night—is explained away in such a manner that the narrator, although irritated by the obvious discomfort of not knowing what to do, is able to accept his lack of action. Similarly, Beckett's Sam says of Watt:

... if Watt was sometimes unsuccessful and sometimes successful ... in foisting a meaning where no meaning appeared, he was most often neither the one, nor the other. For Watt considered, with more reason, that he was successful, in this enterprise, when he could evolve, from the meticulous phantoms that beset him, a hypothesis proper to disperse them, as often as this might be found necessary.[15]

In Pinter's dramaturgy, however, the phantoms are not dispersed, they are confronted. The central images of the plays, he says, come to him out of the blue, intact as images. He is then compelled to write a play creating a psychological context for them. Beckett, in *Proust,* says of "involuntary memory" that "In extreme cases, memory is so related to habit that its word takes flesh."[16] In Pinter's case, it is a momentary, amorphous image, rising out of the depths of the involuntary memory that then becomes the central image of the play: the *image* takes flesh, since we are dealing not in prose as Proust (whom Beckett is discussing), and Kafka, and Beckett himself (at the time he wrote *Proust*) are doing, but in the visual medium of theatre. The image becomes the driving force of the work, and the play becomes that image expanded and examined in all of its dimensions. Martin Esslin, in commenting on Pinter's way of working, said:

Intuitions of the obsessive intensity that Pinter describes when he talks about his method of work are daydreams, almost hallucinations. Their very realism is part of their menace: it is the clarity of outline of the most frightening nightmares. The dreamer of such dreams may not be aware of their inner consistency, yet on closer analysis they will be bound to reveal to the dispassionate observer such a consistency, which is no more and no less than the structure of the dreamer's personality itself. That is why the work of artists of Pinter's stature can also, though not solely or even mainly, be open to a psychoanalytic approach. Not to yield any revelations about the author's personality and problems, but to explain the impact of the work on audiences. It is not the private, personal element in such works of art that exercises that appeal, but precisely the element which the author *shares* with the rest of mankind.[17]

As the surrealists and expressionists demonstrated early in this century, dreams can legitimately communicate as works of art. Pinter's "dreams" or "daydreams," while welling up from within his subconscious, have a universality that communicates to an audience, even when the individual members of that audience have not shared the experience that prompted that particular image. But the *feeling* gets through. How many members of the audience have not felt fear, desperation, loneliness, or anxiety about their own temporality? Thus the audience shares the fear of Rose and Stanley, the desperation of Davies and Edward, the longings of Deeley and Hirst and Spooner, and the desperation of Disson and Max. Even if they have not been able to say exactly what the play was about, they've been able to share with Pinter and his characters one of those paradigmatic moments in a human life when an entire stage of one's being is captured in one great frozen image, forever caught within one's subconscious and ever likely to pop to the surface, usually when least expected.

This is a new form of theatre, as Peter Hall has pointed out. Its fascination lies in part in the fact that what we see on the surface is only one very small part of the play. A member of the audience could ask with Len of *The Dwarfs*, "What have I seen, the scum or the essence?"[18] The major part of the play, and that part which makes Pinter's plays such unforgettable experiences, occurs underneath the surface of the play in the glimpses we share into the private worlds that Pinter has given us. In *The Poetics of Reverie*, Gaston Bachelard says:

The correlation between the dreamer and his world is a strong correlation. It is this world experienced through reverie which refers most directly back to the being of the solitary man. The solitary man directly possesses the worlds which he dreams.... The man of reverie and the world of his reverie are as close as possible; they are touching; they interpenetrate. They are on the same plane of being; if the being of the man must be linked to the being of the world, the *cogito* of reverie will be expressed in the following manner: I dream the world, therefore, the world exists as I dream it.[19]

Harold Pinter dreams worlds, and as he dreams them they come into existence. This, to a great extent, explains the strangeness of his plays, as well as their familiarity. We are not used to seeing plays produced in such a manner. We, along with Watt and Kafka's nocturnal stroller, want an explanation of what we have experienced; we, too, want to turn "a disturbance into words"; for us, too, "to explain [is] to exorcise."[20] But the experience of the play is too complex for simple explanations. Even within the play, the characters are unable—or unwilling—to verbalize what is behind the emotional phenomena. Thus it is not surprising that we find ourselves in a situation in which we have experienced something, but are unable to say what it "means." The play has worked on us, but Pinter has not given us an explanation sufficient to "disperse ... the meticulous phantoms." Like Kafka's stroller, we must create our own explanations.

The world of Pinter's plays is a private world—a dream world—even though it is grounded in everyday reality. We have entered into that private world and shared it with the characters. Thus, "What the hell was *that* all about?" begs the question. We have *felt* what it was about, and in time might come to *know* what it was about. But, in the meantime, the question is irrelevant, for we have been there.

Notes

1. See, for example, Alrene Sykes: *Harold Pinter* (St. Lucia: Queensland University Press, 1970), p. 25.

2. Harold Pinter, "Writing for Myself," *The Twentieth Century* 168 (February 1961): 173.

3. Irving Wardle, review of *The Birthday Party, Encore* 5 (July–August, 1958), 30–40.

4. Quoted in Eleanor Blau, "Does *Betrayal* Reveal a New Pinter?" *New York Times,* 4 December 1979, sec. C., p. 7.

5. Interview with Mel Gussow, *New York Times,* 30 December 1979, p. 5.

6. Pinter, "Writing for Myself," p. 173.

7. Interview with Mel Gussow, *New York Times Magazine,* 5 December 1971, p. 127.

8. Interview, with Gussow, 30 December 1979, p. 5.

9. Ibid.

10. Charles Marowitz, "'Pinterism' is Maximum Tension through Minimum Information," *New York Times Magazine,* 1 October 1967, p. 36.

11. Gaston Bachelard, *The Poetics of Space,* trans. Maria Jolas (Boston: Beacon Press, 1969), p. 72.

12. Peter Hall, "Directing Pinter," *Theatre Quarterly* 14, no. 16 (November 1974): 9–12.

13. Samuel Beckett, *Watt* (New York: Grove Press, 1959), p. 117.

14. Franz Kafka, *The Complete Stories,* ed. Nahum N. Glatzer (New York: Schocken books, 1971), p. 388.

15. Beckett, *Watt,* pp. 77–78.

16. Samuel Beckett, *Proust* (New York: Grove Press, 1957), p. 18.

17. Martin Esslin, *Pinter: A Study of His Plays* (London: Eyre Methuen, 1978), p. 53.

18. *Three Plays by Harold Pinter* (New York: Grove Press, 1962), p. 104.

19. Gaston Bachelard, *The Poetics of Reverie,* trans. Daniel Russell (New York: Orion Press, 1969), p. 158.

20. Beckett, *Watt,* p. 78.

3

Harold Pinter's *The Birthday Party*: Menace Reconsidered

FRANCIS GILLEN

Nothing has occurred since the first production of Harold Pinter's *The Birthday Party,* on 28 April 1958, to alter Martin Esslin's estimate of the play as a "wholly individual, wholly original creation."[1] Translated into over a half-dozen languages including Czech, French, German, Portuguese, Japanese, Polish, and Turkish, and performed around the world, it has entered the repetory of living theatre. Linked with Pinter's other "comedies of menace," *The Room, The Dumbwaiter*, and sometimes *A Slight Ache,* the play portrays the fate of a failed individual, Stanley, who has sought refuge in a shabby, seaside resort run by the mothering Meg and her ineffectual husband, Petey. There he has found shelter and safety of a sort, until two mysterious envoys, Goldberg and McCann, descend upon him, reduce him to a catatonic, infantile state, and, by the end of the play, lead him away. Critical speculation about the play has dealt largely with the exact nature of the menace posed by the pair of invaders. Most frequently they are seen as forces of society and convention who, at the price of the surrender of his inner being, will grant Stanley "a new, prosperous and socially approved life."[2]

Goldberg:	You'll be reoriented
McCann:	You'll be rich
Goldberg:	You'll be adjusted
	. . . .
McCann:	You'll be a success
Goldberg:	You'll be integrated
McCann:	You'll give orders
Goldberg:	You'll make decisions[3]

Other interpreters of the play see Goldberg and McCann as representatives of death or of the inevitable loss of childhood security, as projections of Stanley's own Oedipal guilt, or as representatives of specific groups or organizations from which Stanley has defected. Still others prefer the ubiquity of leaving the threat as something unspecified in Stanley's past, thus linking him more closely with the auidence. For, "like Oedipus, we all seem to carry within us the sense of secret guilt and a suspicion that sooner or later someone will come around to collect on debts outstanding."[4] Whether assigning a specific or a more general nature to the threat, all of these readings have in common the view that the menace in the play resides primarily in Goldberg and McCann. Arthur Ganz has been the notable exception, writing that the "disintegrating lassitude that Stanley has lapsed into at the beginning of *The Birthday Party,* for example, is hardly preferable to the bumptious certainties and brutish sentimentalities of Goldberg and McCann."[5] But surely Ganz goes too far in that direction and is not in accord with the dramatic impact of the play as performed when he goes on to claim that Goldberg and McCann are vital forces who appear "not, like the organized assassins they appear to be, to remove Stanley from the living but to do no less than to raise him from the dead."[6] What I propose is to reconsider the menace represented by Goldberg and McCann, not to deny its threatening force or dramatic impact but to place that threat against the background of Stanley's search for self-identity. Such an exploration will show, I believe, that what Pinter is presenting in the play are alternative but equally impossible contexts for the discovery of the self, the one personal and the other social and dehumanizing. If so, then the real terror of the play is not just that Stanley is destroyed as he is led away at the end of the play, but that he is also destroyed if he remains, that if "It's no good here" and no good out there in the world of Monty, then truly, as Stanley remarks to Lulu, "There's nowhere to go" (p. 36).

If Stanley has been reduced to an object by the close of the play, "a washed and walking corpse,"[7] he is also an object at its opening to the extent that his presence at this dilapidated boarding house fulfills Meg's needs to have a man-child to satisfy in a nonthreatening manner her mothering, sexual drives. "I'd much rather have a *little* boy" (p. 21, italics mine), the childless Meg tells her husband, Petey, when he relates a newspaper account of the birth of a baby girl. Meg's vocabulary, with its diminutives, and her games, such as making Stanley say "please" and "sorry," telling him to eat his cornflakes like a good boy, and admonishing him for saying a bad word like "succulent" to a married woman, all emphasize her pleasure in this role. If Goldberg and McCann seem to offer him no future, Meg denies him a present outside the confines of her house and her view of him. To others, she refers to his social identity in the past as one might refer to that of a dead person: "He used to work. He used to be a pianist" (p. 41). And Stanley plays the role Meg desires of a sometimes agreeable, sometimes petulant or naughty child. What Meg in turn offers Stanley is what Rose and many other mother figures offer in Pinter's plays, an open and totally uncritical affirmation of his existence, an affirmation that is prelogical and presocial. Whether or not Stanley's story about being a concert pianist who had had one successful concert and had been locked out of his next is true or not, clearly Stanley feels rejected by and

afraid of the external world with its categories, such as "successful." There
are no such judgments here in Meg's boarding house, as her extremely in-
accurate version of what Stanley had told her about his career makes clear.
The external world does not matter. Meg offers a purely subjective, personal
affirmation of his identity. As Steven Gale has noted, Meg "has no true grasp
of the meaning of most words and so, although she talks and listens, she says
and hears nothing which bears on life as a meaningful experience."[8] Stanley's
security in this purely personal assurance of another person is essentially, and
appropriately here, a child's reaction to the world, implying no firm grip on
external reality. "Dog won't hurt me?" the child asks and is reassured by the
parent's response. As the child matures, however, such assurance may con-
tend with the child's own intuitions or experiences and, though a frightened
adult may still want reassurance, he or she also confronts the objectivity of
the snarling dog and the limits of such subjective reassurance. Mothers and
nuns may indeed worship images, as W. B. Yeats wrote, but one part of the
process of maturing lies in the realization that images, however comforting,
may be shattered by experience. As changing, growing beings we relate to the
world in a number of ways, subjectively *and* objectively, and we require multiple assurances of our complex identity: in Stanley's case, personal (Meg),
sexual (Lulu), and social (Goldberg and McCann). It is the devision of
these assurances into separate and mutually exclusive natures, not simply the
menacing figures of Goldberg and McCann, that ultimately destroys Stanley.

Stanley's dissatisfaction with the limits of the identity affirmed for him by
Meg is seen in his complaints about lack of sleep, sour milk, tea like gravy,
and the room's pigstylike condition. When Stanley demands of Meg, "Tell
me, Mrs. Boles, when you address yourself to me, do you ever ask yourself
who exactly you are talking to? Eh?" (p. 31), he is asking to be recognized for
an identity outside the purely personal context of their relationship. Lacking
any other context herself, though, Meg immediately relates Stanley's question to the child-man she perceives him to be: "Didn't you enjoy your break-
fast, Stan?... Stan?..." (p. 31). Frustrated, Stanley shows himself as a cruel
child, almost as adept as Goldberg and McCann in terrorizing a victim as he
tells Meg that the two strangers she spoke of have come to take her away in a
wheelbarrow and a van.

Lulu's entrance provides the audience's first objective view of Stanley as
she urges him to wash himself, get out of the house and into the world:
"Come out and get a bit of air. You depress me, looking like that" (p. 36).
His later attempts to shave suggest some recognition of the correctness of
Lulu's remarks, but his subsequent denial of his birthday is itself a denial of
time and inevitable change. After Meg gives Stanley his birthday present, a
child's toy drum, to substitute for the piano he no longer plays, his drumbeat,
at first controlled, becomes "erratic" and then "savage and possessed"
(p. 46). What better symbol could there be for the stifled forces inside Stanley that have received no outlet in his existence at this seaside resort. As
Pinter himself noted, "The more acute the experience the less articulate

its expression."[9] Here Stanley's desire for adult recognition and identity, once represented by his story of concert performance, is reduced in scope but magnified in intensity by the "savage and possessed" pounding of the toy drum. He may have thought he had found "a haven of safety and security"[10] but that stifled part of his identity expressed earlier in his complaints to Meg now reaches full, if inarticulate, expression.

If act 1 of *The Birthday Party* demonstrates Stanley's statement "It's no good here," the following acts show why, on the other hand, "There's nowhere to go." Children entering the adult world usually carry with them the confidence gained by a series of controlled but progressively more difficult challenges. Normally, for example, a toy drum would assist the child in gaining the self-confidence to go on to master more complex instruments such as the piano. Clearly this process has been reversed for Stanley, who has moved from the real or imagined piano to the child's drum Meg has given him. If Stanley's confidence was shattered by the rejection he recounts, this sense of impotence has been reinforced by Meg again and again for over a year. One need not necessarily be as specific as William Baker and Stephen Tabachnick are in describing the play as an inverted bar-mitzvah to see its parallels with the puberty rites almost universally associated with coming to adulthood.[11] Such rites usually involve a challenge that the initiate must overcome before being received into the community of the elders. In Pinter's play, however, not only is Stanley so debilitated by Meg's mothering and uncritical assurance that he uses childish tricks to escape instead of meeting the challenge, but there is no real, adult community into which he might, after initiation, be received. The remark of one of John Updike's characters that "a man, in America, is a failed boy"[12] takes on more universal significance here and comes close to expressing on bitter irony of Pinter's play.

Lacking any genuine self-assurance, Stanley's first reactions are to deny the existence of Goldberg and McCann and then to flee. Prevented by McCann, he uses one boyish ploy after another until he is defeated by the superior game-playing skill of Goldberg and McCann. But instead of facing such challenge from the outside, Stanley's next reaction is to flee from the conflict. The first interrogation that takes place is Stanley's as he tries to find a common ground with the two strangers, a connection that McCann skillfully undercuts.

Stanley: Ever been anywhere near Maidenhead?
McCann: No.
Stanley: There's a Fuller's Teashop. I used to have my tea.
McCann: I don't know it.
Stanley: And a Boots Library. I seem to connect you with the High Street.
McCann: Yes.
Stanley: A charming town, don't you think?
McCann: I don't know it.

(P. 49)

Now McCann becomes the interrogator, and Stanley is forced to defend himself, concocting an evidently fabricated story to explain his presence at the boarding house. And just as Davies in *The Caretaker* will turn on the one person who has been kind to him, so Stanley now denies Meg, offering, as boys often do, a sacrifice of a previous friendship as a means of accommodation. "That woman is mad!" (p. 51), he tells McCann. Trying to assert his dominance as he had over Meg by demanding that McCann not call him "sir," Stanley grips the Irishman's arm and is met by superior force as McCann hits his arm savagely. So Stanley tries another common trick boys employ when faced with a hostile pair. By praising Ireland, he asserts his own closeness with McCann, hoping to divide and to ally himself with one against the other. Failing again, Stanley attempts the ruse that he owns the house and they're all booked up. Finally, he blusters that the intruders don't bother him because they are nothing but a dirty joke. As his force dwindles, Goldberg and McCann make him sit—an act that, as Lucina Gabbard notes, implies loss of manhood[13]—and begin the grilling, the most frequently quoted scene from the play in which "The controllers of Stanley's ordeal charge their victim with such a magnificent array of crimes, sins, and *faux pas* that he must have committed some of them."[14] Although the charges appear random and sometimes contradictory (as accusing Stanley of killing his wife and of not marrying), they do fall into the general categories of past and present. Wasting time, getting in the way, forcing Petey out to play chess, lacking cleanliness, treating Lulu like a leper do in some ways mirror his present position and force him perhaps to recognize it. Goldberg's final assertion—"You can't live, can't think, you can't love" (p. 62)—is not far from the truth. If, then, the second group, those which deal with the past, contain the same level of validity, however distorted, what Goldberg and McCann have accomplished is to have taken away both Stanley's present and his past and left him nowhere to go except a future that they or the society they represent control. Without a present or a past, Stanley has no identity and can react now only with physical action and preliterate sounds. He is now indeed the infant boy Meg had desired, and her toast—"he's my Stanley now. And I think he's a good boy, although sometimes he's bad" (p. 65)—contains that irony. Then, amid sentimental talk of childhood, Lulu makes her own excursions into the past, exchanging sexual innuendos with Goldberg, who might have known her when she was a little girl and is the dead image of the first man she had ever loved, perhaps her father. Finally, under cover of the darkness created as they play the child's game of Blind Man's Bluff, a blindness that becomes actual for Stanley as McCann breaks his glasses, Stanley attempts to strangle Meg and to rape Lulu. Act 1 had closed with the mad drumbeat representing the suppressed forces that could find no outlet in the purely personal identity offered by Meg. Now, in an appropriately parallel closing to Act 2, Stanley, who has just been deprived of all but the social identity to which he will be carried by Goldberg and McCann, gives vent to those other frustrated forces by the violently antisocial acts of attempted murder and rape. The submerged violence is the subconscious expression of an identity not allowed in the first case by the purely personal context of his life with Meg, and in this case by the purely social context demanded by Goldberg and McCann.

Act 3 simply makes explicit the implications of the second act as Stanley is led off in a neat business suit amid promises of the success and the objects that success in our culture can bring. It is "a virtual *post-mortem,*" as Ruby Cohn has noted.[15] Again there is a parallel with an earlier part of the play as Goldberg and McCann offer Stanley promises of club cars, spare tires, season tickets, crash helmets, yachts, and animals. Just as the toy drum was the appropriate gift to celebrate Stanley's birth into the world Meg saw for him, so these are the toys of the "adult world" Goldberg sees for him. Having lived for a time with the diminutive name "Stanny," which Meg had given him, now, as Pinter wrote in his poem "A View of the Party,"

Only where Goldberg was,
And his bloodhound McCann,
Did Stanley remember his name.[16]

While in this sense, then, Goldberg and McCann can be seen as representing a challenge that Stanley might have, but failed to overcome, due perhaps to his naïve trust in the boyish games wherewith he had learned to dominate Meg, they also demonstrate that even if he had been successful, there is no community to welcome the initiate. Walter Kerr writes of the pair: "They are emissaries, set on a certain course by an irresistable force outside them, but they are not intimates of the force at work nor are they even capable of thinking about it coherently."[17] Pinter's portrayal of society in *The Hothouse* as a force that moves of its own momentum irrespective of those who might appear to be in charge adds a further dimension to Kerr's picture. In traditional societies the youth who passed the test would then share in the accumulated wisdom of that society. Here there is no wisdom, no common understanding, and so in their absence there can only be force. This bleak irony of the play is compounded by the way in which Goldberg and McCann look back with nostalgia at an idyllic past associated with the very childhood from which they would "rescue" Stanley. Goldberg talks of "golden days" (p. 37), innocent walks past the children's playground with a Sunday-school teacher (p. 53), and "the unashamed expression of affection of the day before yesterday, that our mums taught us in the nursery" (p. 66). When Goldberg seems to be faltering in his determination and is pictured in the stage directions as "walking heavily, brooding" (p. 85), he brings himself back to order with sentimental memories of promises he had made at his father's deathbed:

Do your duty and keep your observations.
Always bid good morning to the neighbors.
Never, never forget your family ...
I knelt down. (He kneels, facing
McCann) I swore on the good book.
And I knew the word to remember—Respect!   (P. 88)

Some of Goldberg's references to the past are obviously apocryphal, growing out of psychological need; some seem almost sardonic in their context. Goldberg has reshaped the past into a series of banalities that in turn enforce the sterile life of second-hand platitudes into which he would force Stanley, but there is also present in these memories a groping for something lost, an irrecoverable golden world buried, ironically, somewhere in that childhood past. It is this world that causes Goldberg's doubts about the present and undercuts, in moments of reverie, his acts. This sense of loss is summed up by the song that McCann sings:

Oh, the Garden of Eden has vanished, they say
But I know the lie of it still.
Just turn to the left at the foot of Ben Clay
And stop when halfway to Coote Hill.
It's there you will find it, I know sure enough
And it's whispering over to me
Come back Paddy Reilly, to Bally James Duff,
Come home, Paddy Reilly, to me.

(P. 71)

Like Stanley himself, Goldberg and McCann seem to need the assurance associated with the uncritical acceptance of childhood, for the present seems to satisfy only as long as there is no reflection. Goldberg's anger when McCann calls him Simey, the name Goldberg's parents had used for him, demonstrates his inability to link his worlds of past and present and his determination to keep that world of affection and light unsullied by the present. For apart from such sentimental reflections and intimations that represent an irrecoverable past, Goldberg has no personal basis on which to act in the present. When he tries to restore McCann's belief and ability to act on the basis of a personally realized world view, he can only come haltingly to a dead end:

And you'll find—that what I say is true.
Because I believe that the world ... (*vacant*) ....
Because I believe that the world ... (*desperate*) ....
BECAUSE I BELIEVE THAT THE WORLD ... (*lost*) ....

(P. 88)

What we find in the play then is the exploration of two equally impossible alternatives—both of which deny an essential part of Stanley's being. The personal and uncritical acceptance offered by Meg would keep Stanley forever a child and deny his social and sexual identity. The alternative forced upon him by Goldberg and McCann, on the other hand, allows no personal identity whatsoever, and merely substitutes other games and other toys. This meaning is reinforced by the parallel endings of acts 1 and 2, in which the submerged forces denied outlet erupt violently, and by the parallel awarding of birthday toys appropriate to each view of Stanley. Ironically, too, after

Stanley has been taken away, Meg reduces all that has happened to a purely personal experience:

Meg: Wasn't it a lovely party last night?

....

It was a lovely party. I haven't laughed so much for years. We had dancing and singing. And games. You should have been there.
Petey: It was good, eh?
Pause
Meg: I was the belle of the ball.
Petey: Were you?
Meg: Oh yes. They all said I was.
Petey: I bet you were, too.
Mey: Oh, it's true. I was.
Pause
I know I was.

(P. 97)

All the violence of the previous evening has already become personal, sentimentalized past. The downfall of Stanley, then, is not merely that he is prey to the menacing figures of Goldberg and McCann, but that between the subjective and social versions of a self nothing offers any full identity. As Pinter put it in his poem: "... Stanley had no home."[18] And this version I find far more discomforting than the recognition that we all have something from the past that will catch up with us or that society robs us of our individuality. Pinter has presented both the personal and the social and found them both devastating. The seemingly senseless exchange between Stanley and Lulu is, in typical Pinter style, the crux of the play:

Stanley: (*abruptly*) How would you like to go away with me?
Lulu: Where?
Stanley: Nowhere. Still we could go.
Lulu: But where could we go?
Stanley: Nowhere. There's nowhere to go. So we could just go. It wouldn't matter.
Lulu: We might as well stay here.
Stanley: No. It's no good here.
Lulu: Well, where else is there?
Stanley: Nowhere.

It is that "Nowhere" which haunts our minds long after we have left the theatre.

Notes

1. Martin Esslin, *The People Wound: The Work of Harold Pinter* (New York: Anchor Books, 1970), p. 87.

2. Bernard Dukore, *Where Laughter Stops: Pinter's Tragicomedy* (Columbia: University of

Missouri Press, 1976), p. 16.

3. Harold Pinter, *The Birthday Party*, in *Harold Pinter Complete Works: One* (New York: Grove Press, 1976), pp. 93–94. All future references to the text are from this edition.

4. James R. Hollis, *Harold Pinter: The Poetics of Silence* (Carbondale and Edwardsville: Southern Illinois University Press, 1970), pp. 42–43.

5. Arthur Ganz, *Realms of the Self: Variations on a Theme in Modern Drama* (New York and London: New York University Press, 1980), p. 193.

6. Ibid., p. 196.

7. Dukore, *Where Laughter Stops*, p. 16.

8. Steven H. Gale, *Butter's Going Up: A Critical Analysis of Harold Pinter's Work* (Durham, N.C.: Duke University Press, 1977), p. 42.

9. Programme Note for *The Caretaker*, quoted in John Russell Brown, *Theatre Language: A Study of Arden, Osborn, Pinter and Wesler* (New York: Taplinger Publishing Company, 1972), p. 41.

10. Lois G. Gordon, *Stratagems to Uncover Nakedness: The Dramas of Harold Pinter* (Columbia: University of Missouri Press, 1969), p. 21.

11. William Baker and Stephen Ely Tabachnick, *Harold Pinter* (New York: Harper and Row, 1973), p. 55.

12. John Upkike, *The Coup* (New York: Alfred A. Knopf, 1978), p. 158.

13. Lucina Paquet Gabbard, *The Dream Structure of Pinter's Plays: A Psychoanalytic Approach* (Rutherford, N.J.: Fairleigh Dickinson University Press, 1976), p. 53.

14. Gale, *Butter's Going Up*, p. 52.

15. Ruby Cohn, "The World of Harold Pinter," in *Pinter: A Collection of Critical Essays*, ed. Arthur Ganz (Englewood Cliffs, N.J.: Prenthice-Hall, 1972), p. 88.

16. Harold Pinter, *Poems and Prose 1949–1977* (New York: Grove Press, 1978), p. 34.

17. Walter Kerr, *Harold Pinter* (New York and London: Columbia University Press, 1967), p. 24.

18. Pinter, *Poems and Prose 1949–1977*, p. 84.

4

Harold Pinter's Work for Radio

MARTIN ESSLIN

Harold Pinter is the epitome of the playwright in the age of the mechanically reproduced media: he is equally at home, equally professional, in his work for the stage, the cinema, television, and radio. Having started his career as a professional actor, Pinter is thoroughly familiar with all the practical problems germane to each of the four different forms in which drama can be written and made accessible to a public in our time.

As far as radio is concerned, this, indeed, was the very first dramatic medium in which Pinter had a chance of working professionally—as an actor. When applying for an LCC (London County Council) grant to enable him to study at the Royal Academy of Dramatic Art in 1948, Pinter first met and impressed the well-known radio producer R. D. (Reggie) Smith, who was acting as an assessor in examining applicants for the LCC. And it was Reggie Smith who gave Pinter his first professional engagement as an actor: on 19 September 1950, not yet twenty years old, Pinter made his acting debut as a "Voice" in a routine, topical radio feature produced by Reggie Smith— "Focus on Football Pools." It was again R. D. Smith who gave Pinter his first chance to act professionally in a classical play. He played Abergavenny in a production of Shakespeare's *Henry VIII* that was recorded on 14 January 1951 and subsequently broadcast on 9 February 1951. Whenever, thereafter, his engagements with touring companies and provincial repertory theatres permitted him to spend some time in London, Pinter sought work in radio. The BBC's correspondence files contain several batches of handwritten letters by Pinter to many radio producers, reminding them of his availability, as well as one set, dating from 1954, in which he informs them all that he has changed his stage name to David Baron.

But the idea that Pinter should work for radio as a playwright did not arise till after the first performance of his first stage play, *The Room,* by the Drama Department of Bristol University in 1957. The BBC's radio drama producer in Bristol, Patrick Dromgoole, suggested a radio performance of *The Room* as early as 31 May 1957. But that play, with its emphasis on the image of the door, clearly was felt to be too visual for a radio performance. Nevertheless, Pinter was approached to write something specially for radio. The record is incomplete, and the recollection of all concerned (including Harold Pinter himself) somewhat hazy. The synopsis of an untitled play, probably called "Something in Common" was submitted in April 1958, but there seems to have been an exchange of critical suggestions and comments between Pinter and the then Assistant Head of the Radio Drama Department, Donald McWhinnie. In a letter, dated 21 May 1958 (BBC Archives), after the failure of *The Birthday Party*, Pinter submitted a new and revised version of this script and added: "... The play has come a cropper, as you know. What else? The clouds. They are varied, very varied. And all sorts of birds. They come and perch at the window-sill, asking for food! It is touching. Thank you for your encouragement...."

McWhinnie took the hint. On 18 July 1958 a contract was issued commissioning a radio play of sixty minutes duration from Pinter; whether this was on the basis of the synopsis that had been under discussion or not, cannot now be ascertained. In any case the completed script, now titled *A Slight Ache,* was delivered by Pinter three months later, on 27 October 1958. Because it takes a long time for a radio play, after it has been accepted, to find a place in the BBC's schedules (which are planned three to six months ahead), *A Slight Ache* was not recorded until the end of July 1959 (with Vivien Merchant as Flora, Maurice Denham as Edward, and directed by Donald McWhinnie) and first broadcast in the Third Programme on the evening of 29 July 1959.

A Slight Ache, which was subsequently staged (in January 1961) and televised, appears in editions of Pinter's plays in its stage version. It is nevertheless a true radio play that can achieve its full impact only in the radio medium. For at the centre of the play stands the mysterious figure of the Matchseller who never speaks and, indeed, never utters the slightest sound. Even when the two other characters in the play refer to his laughing or crying, the radio listener hears *nothing.* This becomes clear from the fact that in the first production nobody was cast in the part of the Matchseller, although, in the *Radio Times,* he was billed as a third character with the name of a fictitious actor in order to make listeners who referred to the cast list during the broadcast keep expecting him to utter some audible sign of life, in order to enhance the suspense of the play.

Pinter, the great master of the pause and the silence, had clearly realized at this early stage of his career that in radio silence is even more effective, even more suggestive, than on the stage. For in radio, silence is, in fact, the ultimate sound effect. In no other medium can the *absence of being*, nothingness, the total and absolute void, be fully represented. Only in radio is it possible to perform the paradoxical feat of actually putting *Nothingness*, that central concept of much contemporary philosophy (Jean-Paul Sartre, Martin Heidegger), onto the stage (albeit only of the listener's imagination); on radio non-being, Death, can thus become a valid and functioning character. Ingmar

Bergman, who wrote a good deal for radio in his early days, for example, introduced the character of Death in his radio play *A Painting on Wood,* the subject of which is a medieval painting of a Dance of Death brought to life. In this play Death is represented by total silence, the absence of any response to the words addressed to Death by the characters to whom he appears. When Bergman later turned this radio script into a film, *The Seventh Seal,* Death had to become visible. But whereas in the radio play Death really was non-being, Nothingness, total silence, in the film he became a man dressed in a black cloak and a tight-fitting skullcap and thus was far less terrifying and, indeed, quite a jolly figure.

A very similar transformation occurs with the Matchseller in stage or television performances of *A Slight Ache,* when he appears as an old man wearing a balaclava helmet (rather similar to that of Bergman's Old Nick) and a woolly coat. In a radio performance the silence that represents the Matchseller is far more frightening and disturbing.

Indeed, one of the main sources of the impact of the play on radio is the element of uncertainty as to whether the Matchseller actually exists in the flesh. He utters no sound, neither laughs, cries, nor is heard breathing. Admittedly, the props he is supposed to be handling can be heard: when he drops his tray, when matches are being placed back onto it, his steps coming up the stairs, the closing and opening of doors as he enters or leaves the room. There is thus a deliberate contradiction in the information the listener is given about the existence of the Matchseller. No *human* utterance comes from him, but there are noises emanating from *things* he might be handling or touching. But such noises might be caused by other influences, or they might exist merely in the imagination of the two characters of the play. That they *see* the Matchseller is made abundantly clear. A visual image is being painted of him, stroke by stroke: "Do take off your balaclava, there's a good chap".... "You are sweating. The sweat's pouring out of you. Take off that balaclava".... "What have you got on, for goodness' sake? A Jersey? It's clogged. Have you been rolling in mud?".... "Oh, you've begun to disrobe".... "Good Christ is that a grin on your face? It's lopsided. It's all down on one side. You are grinning." These visual indicators that occur throughout the play gradually build up an image of the mysterious stranger. And yet that image itself is contradictory, constantly shifting and changing, and Edward and Flora seem each to respond to a different visual image. The radio medium thus allows the mental image before the listener's internal eye to become fluid, exactly as the images in dreams change their shapes from instant to instant.

This, after all, is the main strength of the radio medium, a strength that was firmly grasped by Pinter in his very first venture into radio: that radio deals best with matters that have a purely mental existence—hallucinations, dreams, stream of consciousness, internal monologue, private worlds.

That the Matchseller is a catalyst of the private anxieties and fears of Edward and the sexual fantasies and wish-fulfillment dreams of Flora becomes abundantly clear in the course of the play. Whether the Matchseller actually exists in the flesh or not becomes correspondingly less important. Yet the mystery surrounding that question is an essential element in the play. We are meant to wonder about it, to remain uncertain. For the Matchseller is precisely that element of undefined dread waiting outside the enclosed, seemingly safe space of the characters' private world, which at any moment may intrude into their lives. As in *The Room,* as in *The Dumb Waiter,* as in *The Birthday Party*, the Matchseller is the dreaded Intruder who will invade the safe haven and bring decisive change, in fact, Death. As in *The Room,* as in *The Birthday Party,* that terror announces itself as the onset of blindness. The slight ache of the play's title refers to a pain in Edward's eyes:

FLORA: Have you something in your eyes?
EDWARD: No. Why do you ask?
FLORA: You keep clenching them, blinking them.
EDWARD: I have a slight ache in them.

The Matchseller, whether real or wholly hallucinatory, is, in fact, the materialization of that slight ache in Edward's eyes, which develops into loss of sight, expulsion from the home, carrying the Matchseller's tray into the outer void, Death.

If the Matchseller represents Edward's fear of Death and his eventual death itself, he must, for Flora, Edward's aging but still lusty wife, appear as the fulfillment of a wish for liberation from her marriage to a spent and impotent man, the possibility of a final flowering of her sexuality. That is why, to her, the Matchseller becomes, more and more, an attractive sexual object. He reminds her of the poacher who, in raping her in her youth, accomplished the primeval ritual of her sexual initiation. The absence of the visual element in radio allows the listener to follow the transformation of the Matchseller before Flora's mental eyes from a disgusting object of fear into a vigorous bullock of a sexual athlete. In a stage performance the continued unchanging presence of a balaclava-helmeted old tramp renders that shift of Flora's image of him much harder to accept.

On balance, therefore, it seems safest to assume that, in fact, the Matchseller is a product of the two characters' fevered imaginations rather than a real person and that the play is an extended and complex poetic metaphor, a concertized image of the feelings and emotions of a middle-aged married couple in the face of the actual, imagined, or longed-for death of the male partner.

But, of course, it is precisely the concreteness, the palpability, of such an image that makes it work. Hence radio, that most visual of all the media, must also establish a very solid visual picture of the situation that serves as the objective correlative to the metaphor. Pinter's use of visual indicators that gradually paint the picture in the audience's mind is assured and highly effective. Indeed, the origin of a play like *A Slight Ache* in radio is apparent even when one reads the stage version. Pinter's plays originally conceived for the stage are far less rich in visually descriptive elements in their dialogue:

"The whole garden is in flower this morning. The clematis. The convolvulus. Everything."

. . . .

". . . sit down. There are four chairs at your disposal."

. . . .

"Oh, the sun's shining directly on you. Wouldn't you rather sit in the shade."

. . . .

"Actually the day is cooling. It'll soon be dusk. Perhaps it is dusk."

In each of these passages the scenery and, above all, the light are being sketched in with great accuracy. As the last example, shows, however, radio is able to shift from the external lighting effects to the ones that are inside the characters' minds without any difficulty. "Perhaps it is dusk" annuls the listener's impression that the light is failing and suddenly transports him into the mind of Edward, who is beginning to realize that in fact it is his own—subjective—light, his sight, that is failing.

Light and darkness, seeing and going blind, are the prevailing images of *A Slight Ache*. In the opening scene of the play Edward takes a sadistic delight in killing a wasp trapped in a jam-jar by pouring boiling water on it through the spoon-hole:

EDWARD: Ah yes. Tilt the pot. Tilt. Aah ... down here ... right down ... blinding him ... that's ... it.

And toward the end, shortly before going blind himself, he still boasts about his ability to see:

EDWARD: I was polished. (*Nostalgic*) I could stand on the hill and look through my telescope at the sea. And follow the patch of the three-masted schooner, feeling fit, well aware of my sinews, their suppleness, my arms lifted holding the telescope, steady, easily, no trembling, my aim was perfect, I could pour hot water down the spoon-hole, yes, easily, no difficulty, my grasp firm, my command established. . . .

And as he begins to sink and fail, Edward suddenly sees the Matchseller rocking with derisive laughter about him (which we cannot hear) and looking extraordinarily youthful. But the light has failed: "You want to examine the garden? It must be very bright in the moonlight." Now the visual images have become mere conjecture; Edward can no longer see: "The pool must be glistening. In the moonlight. And the lawn. I remember it well. The cliff. The sea. The three-masted schooner." And after a long pause with his last words uttered, "with great final effort—a whisper," he asks the question the listener has been asking himself too: "Who are you?"

It is after this that Flora invites the Matchseller to come into the garden to have lunch (making us realize that the moonlight Edward was talking about signified the coming of night to him at midday). And she hands Edward the

Matchseller's tray. The last thing we hear is the sound of matches being put on the tray.

It is remarkable, and wholly characteristic of Pinter, that the brilliantly radiogenic quality of *A Slight Ache* is achieved without the use of any of the more spectacular technical devices that constitute the received idea of the perfect radio play—daring shifts of acoustics, the use of powerful sound effects or atmospheric music, bold intercutting of different locales, or sudden shifts of sound perspectives. While fully aware of the nature of the radio medium, Pinter, here as in his other radio plays, mainly relies on the foremost of all the aesthetic potentialities of radio—its ability to bring language into the very center of the dramatic experience and to counterpoint the maximum concentration on the linguistic element with its absolute conterpart, total silence. All of Pinter's work for the stage, television, and the cinema, as well as radio, relies largely on his mastery of the linquistic component, the richness, wit, accuracy of observation, precision of statement, and, above all, the expressive potential of subtle rhythmization of dialogue. In a radio play like *A Slight Ache* this is the only tool at his disposal: all he can use is the stream of language desperately breaking against a barrier of total silence, the nothingness of Death. *A Slight Ache* may be a short chamber play, but it is, in its own right, a masterpiece of compression, a powerful, poetic metaphor as well as a prime example of the unique strengths of the radio medium.

Almost immediately after completion and acceptance of the script of *A Slight Ache,* in the autumn of 1958, Pinter submitted the outline of a new radio play that the BBC commissioned and that he completed by mid-October 1959: *A Night Out.* It reached the Third Programme's schedule to be broadcast on 1 March 1960. The long scheduling delay created the somewhat paradoxical situation that ABC-TV, which works much faster in these matters, was able to televise the same play very shortly after its first radio broadcast (on 24 April 1960) so that considerable confusion arose about whether the play had been written for radio or television, a confusion further compounded by the fact that the published version of the play, divided into three acts, clearly represents the television script. (The "acts" were the sections into which the play had to be broken up to provide the "natural breaks" for commercials prescribed by the British rules for commercial television.) Yet there can be little doubt that *A Night Out* was originally written for radio.

Yet, unlike *A Slight Ache, A Night Out* is a wholly realistic play. It marks, in fact, Pinter's abandonment of the allegorical, metaphoric style of his first phase, when he was still strongly under the influence of Franz Kafka; as such it is close to, but antedates, the play that give Pinter his first great stage success and his breakthrough into world fame, *The Caretaker.*

A Night Out tells the story of a young man of about twenty-eight, Albert Stokes, who lives with, and under the nagging domination of, his mother. When he announces that he is going out for the evening to attend an office party, his mother puts on a great show of distress at being left alone and darkly hints at the moral dangers of his possible contact with girls. At a coffee stall two of Albert's office colleagues, Seeley and Kedge, discuss Albert, for whom they are waiting, as a mother's boy. When Albert comes, he still needs some persuading to go to the party. At the party Gidney, the firm's accountant, who dislikes Albert, incites two of the girls from the typing pool to approach Albert in order to embarrass him. When one of the girls complains that someone has tried to touch her in an indecent manner, Albert is accused and leaves the party in a rage. When he returns home his mother receives him with a stream of nagging complaints, whereupon Albert seizes an alarm clock and strikes her. Thinking he has killed her, he rushes out of the house and is picked up by a prostitute who takes him home. But when the prostitute, in turn, nags him for dropping cigarette ash on her carpet, very much in the manner of his mother, Albert has another temper tantrum, threatens her with her alarm clock, frightens her into tying up his shoe laces, and departs. Back home, he slumps into a chair, relieved at having finally gained his freedom from his mother. But far from being dead the mother reappears and goes on nagging him....

A Night Out is equally effective on television and radio. Yet a comparison of the radio and television versions of the play reveals a number of points in which the radio version—the play as it was originally conceived—has the advantage over the television script. Here again it is the added element of uncertainty, of ambiguity, in radio that yields an extra element of peculiarly Pinteresque chiaroscuro. For example: in the television version of the play it is made abundantly clear that the perpetrator of the sexual assault on Eileen, the girl from the typing pool, was, in fact, Mr. Ryan, the aged employee whose retirement from the firm was being celebrated at the party. A stage direction emphasizes that the camera should give a close-up of Mr. Ryan's hand, resting comfortably on his knee, and then move to his smugly smiling face: "It must be quite clear from the expression that it was his hand which strayed." In the radio version all we get are inarticulate noises from Ryan, who "close to the mike, isolated from the other voices, chuckles, grunts lightly to himself." Mr. Ryan has no articulated dialogue in either play. A gaga old man, he merely nods and smiles in the television version when he is spoken to; in the radio version his presence is indicated precisely by inarticulate chuckles and grunts. But, although we hear him chuckle and grunt to himself when Eileen protests about having been interfered with, that is by no means as conclusive a proof of his guilt as the far more explicit camera movement in the television version. Thus, in the radio version, some doubt must remain as to whether Albert might have been tempted to make a timid sexual approach to one of the girls. Similarly, when Albert hits out at his mother with the clock, the radio version has him uttering an "inarticulate shout" that is followed by "scrape of clock on table. Clock raised," and after a "stifled scream" from the mother we hear "Click of clock close to mike," whereupon the outdoor sounds of the coffee stall are faded in, a cat is heard meowing as Albert utters low moans and sighs. In the television version everything is more—and less—explicit. We see Albert as he "lunges to the table, picks up the clock and violently raises it above his head." And we hear "a stifled scream from the Mother." In order to leave the audience in uncertainty as to what has happened, therefore, the television version has to cut away from the incident quite deliberately. In other words: in that visual version, the audience is clearly told that the writer and director simply did not *want* them to know what happened, whereas in the radio version, they remain uncertain simply because it was impossible to *tell* what happened. Moreover, the menacing crescendo of the clock ticking closer and closer followed by the mother's scream, is far more suggestive and terrifying than the more explicit visual image of Albert raising it above his head.

When Albert, exasperated at the prostitute's nagging, threatens her with her own clock, the radio version can use the exact repetition of the same sound effect as a powerful acoustic leitmotiv. Again we hear the "sudden loud tick of clock close to mike," whereas in the television version we merely see Albert grabbing the clock from the mantelpiece. When Albert finally leaves the prostitute's flat, he throws the clock on the floor and kicks it across the room. In the radio version this leads to another powerfully suggestive effect: as he kicks the clock "the alarm burst and jangles in brief spurts, stops," surely a much more dense and significant touch than the mere sight of a clock being kicked.

This comparison highlights an important aesthetic element peculiar to radio: its ability to isolate, emphasize, and enhance a single, otherwise inconspicuous aspect of reality, thus elevating it onto a plane of high symbolic, poetic, or metaphoric significance. The ability of the eye to perceive a multitude of different quanta of information in the same instant will always tend to make it more difficult for the artist to concentrate his audience's attention on a single point. The unidimensionality of radio, which moves in time alone, thus tends toward a much higher power of concentration, enabling the playwright or director to focus on that aspect of the total picture which he has selected for emphasis. It is this that enables the radio playwright or director to provide, in a medium that by its very nature inclines toward amorphousness, the firm skeleton of a well-defined structure. This radio drama is closely akin to that other purely acoustic medium, music, which also relies on the recurrence and variation of fixed elements, of melody, motif, and rhythm, to give shape to what is essentially formless, a sequence of sounds. In *A Night Out* the radio version certainly uses the symbol of a loudly ticking, and then of a disintegrating, clock as such a thematic signpost. The cluster of associations of the image of a ticking clock is of course particularly apposite to its function in the play: death, the cessation of temporality brought about by a "timepiece" is in itself a neatly ironic touch; there is also, however, the implication of Albert's waiting, through endless hours of boredom and suffering, for his release—the ticking away of the seconds as a cumulative process through which frustration grows into rage.

In the context of Pinter's total oeuvre *A Night Out,* as the title suggests, also constitutes an original variation of his main theme. In the plays that preceded it, it was always a question of an enclosed space, providing safety and reassurance, being invaded by an intruder from outside. Here that situation is reversed: now we have a claustrophobic space from which the protagonist wants to escape, but all he achieves is a disastrous "night out" and at the end he is again trapped inside his stifling, enclosed world. On the other hand, Albert's dependence on his mother echoes Stanley's relationship with Meg in *The Birthday Party,* his fear and guilt about sex and girls, Edward's feelings of inadequacy in *A Slight Ache.* Moreover, the strange parallelism between woman as mother and whore, which dominates later plays by Pinter (*The Lover, The Homecoming*) is here touched upon for the first time. *A Night Out* thus occupies a significant central position within the Pinter canon.

Shortly after the very successful broadcast of *A Night Out* (in which Pinter himself played the small part of Seeley, still being billed as David Baron) the BBC commissioned him to write a third radio play, *The Dwarfs.* The BBC's records also mention the submission of a script entitled *The Dwarfs* by Pinter's agents (Actac Ltd.) even before the proposal to write *A Night Out.* Yet it is by no means certain that this was in fact a play. It might well have been merely the suggestion of a reading from Pinter's very first major literary work, his novel *The Dwarfs,* which has up to now remained unpublished. So, in fact, the radio play *The Dwarfs* and its subsequent stage adaptation represents those fragments of his early writing Pinter wanted to make available to his audience after he had attained a certain degree of prominence as a dramatist.

The Dwarfs (the play, that is) consists of a series of dialogues between three young men, Londoners, who have been close friends in their adolescence but who are now, as they reach maturity, drifting apart. At the end of the play this process is completed. In the radio version the central character is—much more clearly than in the stage version—Len, the one among the three who is undergoing the most acute identity crisis. When the play opens he is working as a porter on the night shift at Euston Station (in the stage version, for some reason, this has become Paddington), and it is he who is plagued by the vision of being surrounded by a nation of "little people," or leprechauns—the dwarfs of the title. These dwarfs represent filth, untidiness, but also warmth, familiarity, the stuffy, closed atmosphere of intimate personal relationships. As Len enters his crisis, which amounts to no less than a complete nervous breakdown, he sees his room changing shape and is filled with nausea (reminiscent of that which overtakes the hero of Sartre's novel of that title); and when he has, at the end, emerged from it, the dwarfs are gone, the world has become clean, antiseptic, and bare. The wild emotional life of adolescence has made way for the ordered, sterile regularity of a bourgeois existence. Mark, who is of "Portuguese" origin (i.e., perhaps of Sephardic Jewish origin and who in the later stage version is an actor, like Pinter), is elegant and sleek; Pete works in the City but is also haunted by visions of people losing their faces in the underground. In one of his long speeches to Mark, during his breakdown crisis, Len discloses to him that Pete thinks him (Mark) a fool.

That is the last straw that brings their friendship to the point of collapse. In all this the play follows the novel very closely, with one exception. In the novel there is a fourth principal character, a girl schoolteacher called Virginia who at first has an affair with Pete but is rejected by him because she presumes to talk about Shakespeare, a subject her boyfriend regards as far above her intellectual level. As a result she drifts into the life of a part-time call girl and eventually also sleeps with Mark. In the novel it is Virginia who during this moment of intimacy discloses to Mark that Pete thinks him a fool. In the play Virginia has been eliminated completely, as though her presence as a catalyst and bone of contention had been an irrelevance, because the friendship of these adolescents was bound to come to an end in any case, simply through the gradual divergence of their own personalities and personal destinies.

The main structural difference between the radio and the stage version of *The Dwarfs* (apart from minor verbal adjustments and small cuts and additions) consists in that the radio play is very clearly structured around a series of long internal monologues by Len, which give it its firm and easily discernible pattern. In the stage version some of these monologues have been eliminated altogether or, in shortened versions, incorporated into scenes in which the other characters interject their questions or comments. Thus, for example, the account of the actual operation of the dwarfs ("The dwarfs are back on the job, keeping an eye on proceedings"), which occupies a central position in the radio play, has in the stage version been turned into Pete and Mark playing chess and being interrupted and annoyed by Len's much shortened description of the dwarfs. Another, equally central speech ("What are the dwarfs doing? They stumble in the gutters and produce their pocket watches. One with a face of chalk chucks the dregs of the daytime into a bin and seats himself on the lid ... etc.") is completely omitted, as is another beautiful and highly important monologue, in which Len complains about the dwarfs having gone on a picnic leaving him to sweep the yard, which, of course, perpares the way for the final speech, left standing in both versions, in which Len laments the final disappearance of the dwarfs. Therefore, in the stage version the dwarfs themselves have receded into the background. Pinter had to add abundant stage business to the script to make it actable on a stage divided into a number of simultaneous playing areas and provide transitions to enable the actors to take up new positions after the blackouts marking the end of scenes (and which, of course, are unnecessary in the much more swiftly moving medium of sound). This also shifts the emphasis away from the more static, monologing character (Len) to the more mobile antagonists, Mark and Pete. The heightened emphasis on internal monologue in the earlier radio version also highlights the link to the novel, which in turn shows clear signs of the influence of that master of the stream of consciousness, James Joyce, one of Pinter's literary idols and models. Pinter's decision to use his novel (which also contains considerable portions of internal monologue from Pete, omitted in the radio play) can thus be seen as due to his realization that radio is an ideal medium for this literary form. Monologues, internal or otherwise, work perfectly on radio but threaten to become boring or pretentious on the stage.

The Dwarfs was first broadcast on the BBC Third Programme on 2 December 1960, with Richard Pasco in the central part of Len. The production was directed by Barbara Bray (Donald McWhinnie, who hitherto directed Pinter's plays, had left the BBC precisely because Pinter had asked him to direct the stage premiere of *The Caretaker* and now had undertaken to direct the New York production of that play as well). In contrast to *A Night Out,* the audience reaction to *The Dwarfs* was exceptionally poor. Unlike Pinter's two previous radio plays, *The Dwarfs* was far more lyrical, lacked a clear-cut story line, and was (and is) it must be admitted, difficult to follow with its abrupt transitions between scenes, a fairly hazy time sequence, and hardly any indication of the scene of the action. In spite of this and, above all, because of its lyrical use of language, a heightened prose very closely akin to Pinter's early poems, *The Dwarfs* is a remarkable play and of particular importance for an understanding of the evolution of Pinter's themes and preoccupations. The identity crisis and the mental breakdown that Len suffers contain the germs of the subject matter of *The Birthday Party* as well as Aston's transformation in *The Caretaker* from a young man who talks too much into a brainwashed, taciturn creature whose once-teeming imagination has been swept barren by electroshock treatment. The sleek and facile Mark reappears in the characters of Mick in *The Caretaker* and Lenny in *The Homecoming,* while the sparring between Mark and Pete anticipates similar duels in *The Collection, The Basement,* and *Tea Party.*

The radio version of *The Dwarfs* is Pinter's most purely verbal play. Stemming as it does from the autobiographical novel of his earliest phase, in which he was also principally interested in becoming a poet, it also constitutes a link between his early poetry and his later dramatic use of language. The language of *The Dwarfs,* in Len's monologues, but also in Pete's account of his vision of the faces peeling off people in an underground train, is the exuberant free-associating, surrealist language used in that period by poets like Dylan Thomas. In his novel, from which he extracted the bulk of the play, Pinter was clearly striving to combine a realistic theme, the account of his boyhood friendships in East London, with a highly charged surrealistic element of lyricism and evocation of dream states. It is interesting to see how the dream element began to predominate in his earlier dramatic efforts before he achieved the perfect fusion between outward realism and the poetic metaphor arisng out of the realistic situation, which makes the audience wonder whether what they are seeing is real or meant to be taken for allegory or a dream in plays like *The Homecoming* or *Old Times.* In *The Dwarfs* this fusion already exists in a fairly simple state: Len's vision in *The Dwarfs* is realistic as it represents the symptoms of a nervous breakdown that is occurring in a perfectly real framework. What radio does, however, because of its ability to turn the spoken word into visual images is to bring the dreams vividly to life and make them more real than the realistic elements of the text.

The Dwarfs was, for some twenty years, the last of Pinter's works originally written with radio in mind. The immense success of *The Caretaker* had opened more immediately rewarding areas of activity to him. Yet the attractiveness of the radio medium remained as strong as ever for him, both as a writer and an actor.

In June 1962, less than a year after its first performance on television and a week before its opening on the stage of the Aldwych Theatre, *The Collection* was broadcast on the BBC's Third Programme in a radio version specially written by Pinter, with him in the part of Harry, Vivien Merchant as Stella, and Alan Bates as Bill, directed by Cedric Messina. For this version Pinter wrote two new scenes, introducing two new characters: a woman assistant of Stella's who asks Stella why she looks so worried and why her husband is not in the shop; and a taxi driver who talks at length to James, who has already spent several hours sitting in his taxi watching the door of Harry and Bill's house. The driver has a number of lengthy speeches describing (somewhat in the manner of Lenny's stories in *The Homecoming*) episodes of his nighttime adventures with customers. One in which he had to carry a woman who had fainted into her home where she was revived by her husband feeding her brandy olives, ends with the driver declaring, "I like olives," thus setting the stage for the subsequent discussion of olives between James and Bill, which ensues after Harry has been seen leaving the house and the taxi driver has broken out into fulsome thanks for a very big tip.

Another television play, *Night School,* first broadcast by Associated Rediffusion in July 1960 but considered by Pinter unworthy of publication, was, on persistent prodding by the BBC's radio drama department, brought back into circulation in a radio version prepared by the author himself and broadcast on 25 September 1966 (directed by Guy Vaesen, an old friend of Pinter's from his repertory days). Ironically, this is the only one of Pinter's plays that in the published editions of his works appears in the radio, rather than the television or stage, version. In adapting *Night School* for radio Pinter made no very essential amendments but improved the early text in a multitude of ways by small stylistic changes and cuts. *Night School* has become a popular radio text performed throughout the world, so that it can now be regarded as having its main existence in the radio medium. In technique *Night School* is close to *A Night Out;* thematically, it is a variation of a number of Pinter's favorite themes. Walter, a small-time crook, returns from prison to find that his two aunts (who mother him like a double version of Meg in *The Birthday Party*) have let his room to a tenant, a girl schoolteacher. Walter is keen to regain his territory, and the only way to achieve this is to return to his own bed as the girl's lover. To impress her he tells her tall tales about the tremendous jobs he had done; she in turn speaks of her highly intellectual occupation as a teacher. When suspicions arise in Walter's mind, however, about the girl's real occupation (he has found a photograph among her things that suggests she may be a nightclub hostess), he asks a friend of the family, a slightly more prosperous racketeer, Solto, to trace her real identity. Solto finds her, takes her out, and tells her that Walter is by no means the romantic criminal he pretended to be. The girl realizes in turn that her pretense of being a schoolteacher has been exploded and so she leaves her lodgings and is lost to Walter. Thus the theme of the battle for the room, as a symbol of security, is here combined with Pinter's favorite topic of fake memories and fictitious identities, as well as taking in the "pure woman/whore" dichotomy that pervades Pinter's work from his early novel (where Virginia is a schoolteacher but becomes a part-time call girl) to *The Homecoming*.

Pinter's mastery of all dramatic media (the stage, television, and the feature film as well as radio) allows him to work in any of these media when the idea that haunts him specifically suits one rather than the others. When, as often happened in the years after he had delivered his last radio play to the BBC's radio drama department, he was urged to write another original play for radio, he would invariably reply, of course he would want to write one, provided he had an idea that asked for radio treatment. And this, as it happened, was the case, after he had achieved another of his great stage successes with *Betrayal*. Out of the blue the BBC received a radio script, *Family Voices*.

Family Voices, written in 1980 and first broadcast by BBC Radio 3 on 22 January 1981, is quintessential Pinter. It contains echoes of his very first play, *The Room*—the leading character lives away from his family and is torn by longings for them while clearly fleeing from them, and one of the characters is actually called Riley; echoes also of *The Birthday Party*—the hero is a young man mothered by his landlady, with his family looking for him and being turned away at the door; echoes of *The Caretaker* in the form of a highly ambivalent father figure—"On his deathbed your father cursed you. He cursed me [the mother] too, to tell the truth. He cursed everyone in sight"; echoes also of *The Homecoming* in a mother figure seen split into an old woman (Mrs. Withers) and a young attractive one (Lady Withers) as well as an aggressively sexual schoolgirl incarnation (Jane Withers).

There are three voices in the play. One is that of a young man (at one point the mother speaks about his not yet being twenty-one) who has left home somewhere at the seaside (his mother reminisces about walks on the cliffs) for the big city. At first the exchange between this young man and his mother (the second voice) takes the form of letters that are probably never written and only exist in the mind of the speakers and certainly never reach their destination. The third voice, which twice makes an appearance toward the end of the play, is that of the father, who explicitly states that he is speaking from his grave. It can thus be safely assumed that the entire exchange between these three voices takes place in the mind of the principal character—the young man—who is imagining the letters he would want to write to his mother as well as the letters his mother would probably write to him, and the voice of his father—whom he presumes dead but who may well still be alive. As the play progresses, the letter convention is gradually dropped as the two—noncommunicating—voices of mother and son are more and more rapidly cross-cut.

The young man in whose mind the play takes place is very similar to Stanley in *The Birthday Party* also in that he is struggling to find himself as an integrated personality. In his very first "letter" he confesses:

At the moment I am dead drunk.
I had five pints in The Fishmongers Arms tonight, followed by three double scotches, and literally rolled home.

Only to withdraw that confession a few sentences later:

When I said I was drunk I was of course making a joke.
I bet you laughed.
Mother?
Did you get the joke? You know I never touch alcohol.

Only, a few sentences further on, to proclaim:

I get on very well with my landlady, Mrs. Withers. She tells me I am her solace. I have a drink with her at lunchtime and another one at teatime and then take her for a couple in the evening at The Fishmongers Arms.

The house in which the young man lives, like the one that Rose inhabits in *The Room,* seems mysteriously expandable. Apart from Mrs. Withers, who is in her seventies and cuddles the hero and tells him "You are my little pet," and Lady Withers and the schoolgirl Jane there is an old man in the house, called Benjamin Withers, who, while clearly mad, intimidates the hero with a cataract of language akin to that with which Mick in *The Caretaker* overwhelms Davies:

You know where you are? he said. You're in my room. It's not Euston station. Get me? It's a true oasis.

This is the only room in this house where you can pick up a caravanserai to all points West. Compris? Comprende? Get me? Are you prepared to follow me down the mountain? Look at me. My name's Withers. I'm there or thereabouts. Follow? Embargo on all duff terminology. With me? Embargo on all things redundant. All areas in that connection verboten. You're in a diseaseridden land, boxer. Keep your weight on all the left feet you can lay your hands on. Keep dancing. The old foxtrot is the classical response but that's not the response I'm talking about. Nor am I talking of the other response. Up the slaves. Get me? This is a place of creatures, up and down stairs. Creatures of the rhythmic splits, the sideswipes, the rums and roulettes, the macaroni tatters, the dumplings in jam mayonnaise, a catapulting ordure of gross and ramshackle shenanigans, openended paraphernalia. Follow me? ...

The other male inhabitant of the house is Riley, who speaks of himself as a policeman and takes a homosexually tinged interest in the young man's body when he intrudes on him as he is lying in his bath to tell him that he has just sent away the hero's mother and sister, who were inquiring about him:

He denied knowledge of me. No, he had not heard of me. No, there was no-one of that name resident ... I suggest, he said, that you both go back to where you come from, and stop bothering innocent, hardworking people with your slanders and your libels ... so piss off out of it before I call a copper.

The affinity of these two male characters (Withers and Riley) to Goldberg and McCann of *The Birthday Party* and their verbal terrorism is also very striking. Lady Withers has asked the hero to tea in a luxurious sitting room, much larger than one would have expected in what, at first, seemed a small suburban house with just one bathroom for all its inhabitants. During tea, the schoolgirl Jane sits with her feet in the hero's lap, with her toes moving almost hysterically, so that the bun he is eating "turned to solid rock." But when the hero offers to "help Jane with her homework" he is turned down by Lady Withers.

Everybody in the house is related, not only all the people called Withers, but Riley as well. He too is a relation of a sort:

What relation?
Is Lady Withers Jane's mother or sister?
If either is the case why isn't Jane called Lady Jane Withers?
Or perhaps she is. Or perhaps neither is the case? Or perhaps Mrs. Withers is actually the Honourable Mrs. Withers? But if that is the case what does that make Mr. Withers? And which Withers is he anyway? I mean what relation is he to the rest of the Witherses? And who is Riley?

The exile into a large family with an intricate web of aristocratic connections at times greatly pleases the hero:

Oh mother, I have found my home, my family. Little did I ever dream I could know such happiness.

But toward the end of the play when the (perhaps dead) father's voice has resounded through his mind, the young man is overcome by nostalgia for his lost family and home:

I'm coming back to you, mother, to hold you in my arms.
I am coming home.
I am coming also to clasp my father's shoulder ...

I am on my way back to you. I am about to make the journey back to you. What will you say to me?

The play concludes, however, with the father's voice saying:

I have so much to say to you. But I am quite dead. What I have to say to you will never be said.

If, in *The Homecoming,* the dead mother returned to the sons that had longed for her, in *Family Voices* the son's homecoming, it seems, will never take place.

In Pinter's unpublished novel *The Dwarfs* there is a passage, which does not appear in the radio play, in which Len is talking about a certain type of modern poet who climbs from word to word as though the words were stepping stones. "But tell me this," Len asks, "What do they do when they come to a line with no words in it at all? Can you answer that? What do they do when they come to a line with no words in it at all? Can you tell me that?"

On the written page, there is nothing poets can do when they come to a line that has no words at all in it. In *spoken* poetry they can remain silent and hold a pause; that pause can be filled up with the unspoken line, the line that has an import or a subtlety or an ambiguity that is beyond the power of words to be expressed. Radio is the ideal medium for spoken poetry, the ideal medium for the silence, the void between words, the impact of which depends on an exact sense of timing and proportioning, of flowing and broken rhythms. On the stage, or on the cinema or television screen, the silences can be made more pregnant and more meaningful by visual images. But it is only in radio that the silences can preserve their pristine purity, that they can direct attention to themselves *as silences* (while in a visual medium the images continue to speak or even to chatter when words cease); and in radio it is also possible to harness nonverbal sounds into a single stream of rhythmical utterance so that the ticking of a clock, steps approaching up a staircase, the excited expulsion of breath, can become elements in lines of poetry devoid of words. The radio play is the form of drama that comes closest to music in the basic structure of its composition, for here, as in music, everything ultimately depends on a sequence of sounds in a single dimension, that of time. In his work for the stage, the cinema, and television Harold Pinter has shown himself very much aware of these quasi-musical elements of dramatic structure. Only in radio, however, can this feeling for the musical articulation of a rhythmical flow of words and sounds and silences be displayed and made to yield its full effect in its purest form. Pinter is, undoubtedly, a master of highly structured language rhythms. That is why he has always been attracted to radio. And that is why his work for radio is of considerable importance in the context of the totality of his oeuvre.

A Note on the Texts

Only one of Pinter's radio texts appears in the generally accessible editions of his works: *Night School* in: Harold Pinter, *Tea Party and Other Plays* (London: Methuen, 1967). In the United States: *A Night Out; Night School, Revue Sketches* (New York: Grove Press, 1968).

The radio version of *A Slight Ache* is printed in a little magazine: *Tomorrow -4* (ed. by Ian Hamilton), Keble College, Oxford. The issue is undated, but as the fifth number is announced (contributions to reach the editor for it by 20 September 1960), the date of publication was pesumably spring or summer 1960.

All quotations from Pinter's work for radio in the preceding essay are taken from:
A Slight Ache, duplicated typescript, 28 pp., 1959, in BBC Play Library.
A Night Out, duplicated typescript, 33 pp., 1960, in BBC Play Library.
The Dwarfs, duplicated typescript, 22 pp., 1960, in BBC Play Library.
The Collection, duplicated typescript, 33 pp., 1962, in BBC Play Library.

The television script of *Night School* is extant in a typescript duplicated by Associated Rediffu-sion Ltd: act 1, 19 pp.; act 2, 21 pp.; act 3, 19 pp.; plus 3 unnumbered insert pp. On the titlepage there is the remark "stencilled 14/6/1960," "First Draft script."

The stage versions of *A Slight Ache* and *The Dwarfs,* as well as the television version of *A Night Out,* are contained in Harold Pinter, *A Slight Ache and Other Plays* (London: Methuen, 1961).
In the United States the stage versions of *A Slight Ache* and *The Dwarfs* are published in Harold Pinter, *Three Plays* (New York: Grove Press, 1962).
The television version of *A Night Out* is published in the United States in Harold Pinter, *A Night Out, Night School, Revue Sketches* (New York: Grove Press, 1968).
These texts also appear in the collected edition of Pinter's plays in Eyre Methuen's *Master Play-wrights Series* (published in the United States by Grove Press under the title of Pinter's *Complete Works*) as follows:
A Slight Ache (stage version) and *A Night Out* (television version) in Harold Pinter, *Plays: One* (1976);
The Dwarfs (stage version) and *The Collection* (radio version) in Harold Pinter, *Plays: Two* (1977).
The short play *Monologue* was published in an edition limited to 100 copies, signed by the author, (London: Covent Garden Press, 1973).
Family Voices was first published by Next Editions, London, in 1981. It is also contained in volume four of Pinter's *Complete Works,* published by Grove Press.

5

Tearing of Souls:
Harold Pinter's *A Slight Ache* on Radio and Stage

ALBERT WERTHEIM

Surely *A Slight Ache* is one of Harold Pinter's successfully disturbing plays. This early work was first heard as a radio broadcast on the BBC Third Programme for 29 July 1959 and was later staged at the Arts and subsequently the Criterion Theatre in London. The stage production at the Arts Theatre opened on 18 January 1961, nearly six months after the radio broadcast. Both broadcast and stage versions were produced by Donald McWhinnie, perhaps the most important and talented of England's radio producers. The translation of *A Slight Ache* from radio to stage, from invisibility to visibility, engenders significant changes in the texture, tone, and effect of the play.[1] These changes can illuminate the play, Pinter's dramatic talent, and the disparate possibilities of radio and theatre.

Both Pinter and McWhinnie were much aware of the changes wrought upon *A Slight Ache* as the play moved from radio to theatre and took on physical dimensions. A hitherto unnoticed radio interview with Pinter and McWhinnie nicely serves to bring out their feelings about the texture of *A Slight Ache* on stage as opposed to is texture on the air.

Shortly after Pinter's play had moved to the Criterion Theatre, Carl Wildman's BBC Network Three series "Talking of Theatre" presented a discussion that lasted slightly more than sixteen minutes in which Wildman, McWhinnie, and Pinter considered the possibilities of radio and stage production with particular reference to *A Slight Ache*. Recorded on 27 February 1961, the interview was then aired on the evening of March 7. Wildman's interest in conducting the interview emerged from the fact that Pinter was an actor and stage playwright who had written a radio play (the first of several as it turned out) and that McWhinnie was a noted radio producer turning his talents to a stage production of Pinter's play. The conversation among the three men crystallized important issues that help determine an understanding of *A Slight Ache* and of Pinter's aims as a dramatist.

Radio, of course, provides a realm in which the imagination of the audience is exploited in ways it cannot be when set designers have created a specific stage picture and when actors' forms provide embodiment for radio's disembodied voices. On radio, voice is primary, so in *A Slight Ache* the pivotal character of the Matchseller, who has no lines, becomes entirely the creation of the radio audience. And obviously Pinter and McWhinnie realized that as a strength. In reply to Wildman's question of whether *A Slight Ache* was written "specifically with the microphone in mind," the following interchange ensued:

Pinter: Oh yes, entirely, yes. This was an idea for radio which I had, which we spoke about ...

McWhinnie: So much so that it really seemed inconceivable in the last month or so, when we'd been producing *A Slight Ache* for the stage, it seemed inconceivable earlier that this play could ever be transferred on theatre. It made such clever use of radio techniques.

Wildman: Such as?

McWhinnie: Well, the fact that there are only two speaking characters, the third character never speaks and therefore is conjured up by the imagination of the audience, (Yes) prompted by the words of the other two characters, the long sort of soliloquies, self-communings, this kind of thing, and the fluid movement from scene to scene.

                    . . . .

Pinter: Again, I'm not sure, on the radio there's a kind of clarity, a purity, I find, of the image which comes over. On the stage, the tramp is there and the audience has him in the fore-front all the time and they're constantly switching their eye, I suppose, from one to the other, from the tramp to the man. On radio you just have the voice of the man and the woman, so there's a possibly more distinct, clearer image on the radio. (Pp. 3, 4)[2]

In the stage production the Matchseller was given form by an actor who stood with his back to the audience during the performance. Listening to the radio broadcast, the listener might well wonder whether the Matchseller, much discussed by Edward and Flora, was there at all or whether he might not in fact be their joint creation, a grotesque *folie à deux*—not altogether different from that of George and Martha in Albee's *Who's Afraid of Virginia Woolf?*[3]— onto which the couple might focus their hostilities and marital frustrations. On stage, with the figure of the Matchseller actually present, the possibility of the Matchseller's being entirely an imaginative figure is a less potent (though not impossible) one.

The question of the reality of the Matchseller is one on which *A Slight Ache* hinges, and in translating the play from one dramatic medium to another, McWhinnie and Pinter realized how the texture, tone, and impact of the play were altered:

Wildman: Now, how do you account for the success of its transference?
McWhinnie: We had to approach it afresh and not try to adapt it for the
              theatre, but to say what we think are its disadvantages from a
              theatrical point of view. Can we look at it in a different way and
              make them positive advantages.
Wildman: And did you ask the writer to adapt it in any way?
McWhinnie: We didn't, no, we came to it on the first day of rehearsal with, in
              fact, the radio script in front of us, (Yes) we said: Now, how can
              we possibly bring this into visual life ...
Pinter: We only had to make one alteration really. That was the point
              of climax in the play where the tramp, who doesn't speak, does
              make a positive action. On radio what I had to do was to
              emphasise his action, which was the turning-point of the play,
              the climax, to make him go through various motions, stand
              against the curtains, draw the curtains, take off his hat and do
              various things which were reported by the other man. (Mm) On
              the stage we found this was quite unnecessary and that a simple
              gesture, i.e., just standing, was quite enough.
McWhinnie: In fact, one of the things which it seemed vital to the radio pro-
              duction, which was that the third party should be silent and in-
              visible, became a great advantage to us because we introduced
              this real figure of a real old matchseller. (Yes) who doesn't
              speak but is there, and round whom everything revolves, and
              his presence, his actual visible presence becomes a tremendous-
              ly powerful and ....
Pinter: Yes. There's one thing I would say about that. On radio this
              play relied a great deal, I think, on its letting the imagination of
              the listener do a great deal of work, (Yes) in other words, what
              was this silent character—

                                          . . . .

              Yes, I think that while Donald's got a very strong point when he
              says that the tramp whom we can see on the stage, therefore we
              know that he is an old tramp, you know, and that closes the
              door somewhat—on the other hand, it doesn't, I think, ulti-
              mately because the audience unhappily still go through great
              tearings of their souls wondering who he is. (Pp. 3–4)

It is certainly revealing in this extended exchange how, without rewriting the
play for the stage, Pinter and McWhinnie discovered for themselves in the
course of production the changing possibilities for the tone of *A Slight Ache* as
the Matchseller changed from imagined to realized figure. For McWhinnie,
the Matchseller as portrayed by an actor becomes "a great advantage to us" as
a realized focus for Edward and Flora's concerns. It is illuminating, however,
that Pinter seems rather more skeptical about the stage production, seeming
to prefer the engagement of audience imagination that radio drama encourages yet arguing that the audience may nevertheless still "go through great
tearings of their souls" even when the Matchseller is an actual stage presence.

     It is revealing, too, that McWhinnie focuses his comments on the action or
perhaps plot of the play and on the Matchseller as the cynosure of that action,
"round whom everything revolves." Before McWhinnie can proceed far with

such an interpretation of the play, Pinter importantly, I think, cuts him off in mid-sentence and redirects the focus not on the action of the play but upon the listeners and audience. For Pinter here—and presumably elsewhere—the heart of the drama is not what happens on stage but what happens in the imaginations and souls of his listeners or theatre audience.

The rather obvious implication is that for Pinter his plays have no *message* that can be evoked by hermeneutical skill. When Carl Wildman suggests that there is a mystery surrounding Edward and Flora, and that that mystery somehow centers on the Matchseller, Pinter quickly picks up the comment, asserting:

Pinter: Yes quite. For me he's a figure, he's exactly what he's supposed to be, a matchseller, I don't regard him as an allegorical figure at all.
Wildman: Not a symbol?
Pinter: No, no. But I think his relation to the people is quite, I would think quite clear to myself. (P. 4)

In short, the Matchseller has meaning for Pinter but not the universalized meaning of a symbolic or allegorical figure. In other words, each member of the audience must, like Pinter himself, endow the Matchseller and the play's situation with personal, individual meaning. Pinter provides a dramatic and highly charged scenario to which audience, sharing in the creative process with the dramatist, gives personal meaning. It is perhaps for this reason that, whereas McWhinnie always refers to the Matchseller as matchseller, Pinter almost always calls the figure "an old tramp." The implication is that for Pinter the old man's occupation is less significant than the idea of a tramp, a transient figure of uncertain origins whose role in life is as unclear as his role in the lives of Edward and Flora or his role in the life of Pinter's drama. It is again evident that as McWhinnie once more attempts to invest the matchseller and the plot with objective meaning, Pinter abruptly cuts him off in mid-sentence to steer the conversation deftly away from such a discussion and back to the topic of radio versus playhouse:

McWhinnie: Yes, well they use him to crystallise their own, separate, private—
Pinter: Yes, yes, so possibly—I don't know which one can regard as more successful showing him. (*Laughter*) I still can't make up my mind, quite (No) you know, which is the better ... (P. 4)

One can only wonder whether the laughter recorded in the transcription indicates that McWhinnie and Wildman were aware of Pinter's tactic.

Although Wildman's brief interview with Pinter and McWhinnie concentrates on the strengths and weaknesses of having the Matchseller or tramp unseen or seen, the discussion leads one to consider other aspects of *A Slight Ache* that are advanced or hindered in a broadcast or stage production. Some of the particularities of *A Slight Ache* as radio drama have already been raised and addressed by Mary Jane Miller,[4] who notes particularly how the radio play directs the listeners to Pinter's nuances of language and linguistic tone, and to the sound of the wasp trapped in the marmalade.[5] She further points out that the physical changes the Matchseller undergoes, changes that may be only in the minds of Flora and Edward, "are perfectly credible in radio but very difficult to manage on stage."[6] Surely part of what Miller notices is that radio effectively brings the audience into close contact with the action and the players. They can see with the mind's eye what cannot be seen by the physical eye from the spectator section of the theatre: the wasp tangled in the sticky marmalade; the tangling vines of honeysuckle or convolvulus or japonica in the garden; the squashed wasp on Edward's plate; or the sweat that Edward claims is "pouring out"[7] of the Matchseller. At the same time the listener's inability to see enhances the fluidity of the play not merely in terms of the Matchseller's presence, as the Wildman interview brings out, or in terms of the changes from an old tramp to a youthful Barnabas, as Miller points out, but in terms of the very time and space of the play. Edward, who announces to Flora that he has "been engaged on the dimensionality and continuity of space ... and time ... for years" (p. 177), on radio, moves in a fluid space, a house containing rooms of unknown proportions and with unknown proximity to one another. He moves as well in fluid time, with scenes that fade in and fade out so that the listeners have little sense of what the passage of time has been. Time and space, then, in *A Slight Ache* are largely determined by the listener. The set, costumes, and lighting of a stage production would go a long way in fixing time and space for the audience though not necessarily entirely so.

Although language, speech rhythms, and verbal tone are highlighted on radio, the stage enables actors to create characters through physical gestures, so that Edward and Flora's physical proximity to the Matchseller or to one another as well as their more general body language must go a long way in shaping the texture and tone of a stage play. The way the Matchseller stands at the threshold of Edward's study, how his matches and tray are dropped, Edward's look as he calls the Matchseller "a bullock," Flora's physical stance or glance as she asks the Matchseller, "Do you care for goose?" are just a few of many moments in Pinter's play that, when seen, would take on special coloration in a way they would not when merely heard.

Wildman's radio interview with Pinter and McWhinnie raises the related issue of timing and interaction between players and spectators in the theatre, about which Pinter and McWhinnie seem to show differing preferences:

Pinter: I found a purity on radio. Working in radio myself, I felt that there's no audience, you're doing what you want to do cleanly and clearly.

Wildman: You mean without having to modify your performance for the audience?

Pinter: No, it doesn't affect your timing. Take for instance, speaking very technically, your timing, the exact timing you want. On the

> stage, of course, in performance the timing is dependent on the audience reaction, (Yes) which can destroy your timing or enhance it. It's a continual collaboration.

Wildman: Some people would say they would miss the contact that they can establish with the audience.

McWhinnie: I must say I find contact with the audience very satisfying.

Wildman: Yes, it can be stimulation it itself.

Pinter: It can be, perhaps I'm a little secretive. (P. 7)

Pinter's affection for radio, the interview reveals, was influenced in part by an airing of Samuel Beckett's brilliant radio play, *All That Fall* (3 January 1957), a broadcast, by the way, directed by Donald McWhinnie.

Pinter: I must say, about radio, I was fortunate enough to hear very recently *All That Fall* and I found in that all the best things in radio, and something which I think the stage finally must lack, and *All That Fall* allowed you to—as the listener—to go, to go way ahead, to make a voyage with, with the play in a kind of imaginative way, (Mm) but when you're looking at a theatre picture, whatever it is, I don't think you, you don't give that exactly the same—I'm not a theorist but it seems to me that there's a certain uniqueness about radio. (Mm) (P. 7)

The quality of imaginative voyage for the listener, who uses the drama as vehicle, that Pinter found in Beckett is surely a quality Pinter strove for and achieved in *A Slight Ache*.[8] It is, moreover, a concept that reinforces Pinter's emphasis upon the listeners or audience as opposed to text.

Finally, one must, in contemplating *A Slight Ache* on radio and on stage, consider the idea that Pinter has written a drama about seeing, about insight, and about vision.[9] From the very opening of the play, in which Edward and Flora concern themselves with whether the vines they see near the toolshed are honeysuckle, convolvulus, or japonica, the question of sight is raised. And with it, given the possible sexual ring and suggestiveness of words like *convolvulus, toolshed,* and *honeysuckle,* the question of insight arises; for, one wonders, do these characters see or fail to see the subtext of their conversation as well as the objective reality outside their window. The same matter of insight arises in the argument about whether wasps *bite, sting,* or *suck* and in Edward's repeatedly pointing to the Matchseller and naming him a *bullock.* The slight ache that provides the play's title is the aching pain that Edward suffers in his eyes, causing him to clench and blink. The ache is also one Edward seems to wish upon the wasp, which he attempts to blind with marmalade before killing him:

Ah yes, Tilt the pot. Tilt. Aah ... down here ... right down ... blinding him ... that's ... it. (P. 174)

Likewise, Flora comments on Edward's bloodshot eyes and then seems to force him to cry out in pain, "Aaah my eyes" (p. 178), as she accuses her husband of being frightened of the old man. Then, when the Matchseller has entered, Edward seems ready at least to blind him partially as he remarks, "Do forgive me peering but is that a glass eye you're wearing?" (p. 185). Flora by contrast exclaims ecstatically to the matchseller, "Your eyes, your eyes, your great big eyes" (p. 192). During his extended speech near the close of the play, Edward speaks of his changing vision of the Matchseller—"In fact every time I have seen you you have looked quite different to the time before. (*Pause*) Even now you look different. Very different" (p. 197)—and the pain in his eyes increases—"I've caught a cold. A germ. In my eyes. It was this morning. In my eyes. My eyes" (p. 198)—causing him to fall to the ground, where he remains until the play's conclusion. As one reads the text of *A Slight Ache*, one recognizes the possibilities Pinter suggests in writing a radio play about sight for a sightless audience.

On the radio, the degree of Edward's ache, the changing visage of the Matchseller, and the determination of whether or not the Matchseller is possessed of a glass eye are left to the mind's eye of the listener. On stage, the director must, of course, decide these things and to a large extent abrogate the ambiguity that exists in a radio broadcast. In either case, however, the audience must ask themselves at the conclusion of Pinter's enigmatic and profoundly disturbing play, "What have I just seen?" They must clarify for themselves the meaning of the actions, events, and language they have taken in and translate them into some vison of the play. For the radio audience, the first answer to the question must be, "Nothing," for indeed visually they have not seen anything; yet of course they may very well have seen the nature of the relationships among the characters and even have some insight about whether the Matchseller is seen physically or only mentally by Flora and Edward. Is *A Slight Ache* a Chinese box in which a radio audience mentally see characters they do not see physically, and these characters in turn mentally see a character they do not see physically? The question is a marvelously vexed one and one that goes to the heart of Pinter's dramaturgy. On stage, much of the Chinese-box effect is lost, but as Pinter astutely recognizes in the Wildman interview, "the audience unhappily still go through great tearings of their souls wondering who he is."

Carl Wildman's 1961 BBC interview with Harold Pinter and Donald McWhinnie provides a student of Pinter's work with both clarifications and new insights. It naturally underscores the reshaping of Pinter's dramatic material as *A Slight Ache* was translated from the air waves to the Arts and Criterion theatres, as it moved from the invisibility of radio to the visual reality of the stage. The interchange between the stage playwright who had written a radio drama and the radio director who was directing a play in a theatre raises broad and significant questions about the aesthetics and potential of both radio and stage dramaturgy. It raises as well narrow and significant questions about the role of Pinter's Matchseller within the construct of *A Slight Ache*. Finally, Pinter's comments in the interview, his reactions to Wildman and McWhinnie, and the way he cuts off their insights at critical junctures help the reader begin to see that, at an early stage in his playwriting career, Pinter had already determined to move the focus of his dramas away from the plot enacted on stage and toward the drama taking place within the brain and soul of each spectator.

Notes

1. Martin Esslin comments briefly on some of these changes in his *Pinter: A Study of his Plays* (London: Eyre Methuen, 1973), pp. 87–91.

2. *Talking of Theatre,* programme 31, BBC Network Three (7 March 1961), reproduction no. TLO 46571. The transcript of this program may be found in the Lilly Library of Indiana University, Bloomington. Quotations from the transcript are made with the kind permission of Donald McWhinnie, Harold Pinter, Carl Wildman, and the Trustees of the Lilly Library. Parentheses within quotations indicate responses by one or both of the other people present. Ellipses marks (...) within a quotation indicate a pause or a point at which a speech was cut off by someone else. Page numbers in parentheses at the close of quotations indicate page numbers in the transcript.

3. Other similarities with *Who's Afraid of Virginia Woolf?* have been noted in Steven H. Gale, *Butter's Going Up: A Critical Analysis of Harold Pinter's Work* (Durham, N.C.: Duke University Press, 1977), p. 76.

4. Mary Jane Miller, "Pinter as a Radio Dramatist," *Modern Drama* 17 (1974): 403–12.

5. Ibid., p. 405.

6. Ibid., p. 406.

7. Harold Pinter, *A Slight Ache* in *Complete Works: One* (New York: Grove Press, 1976), p. 186. Parentheses following quotations from the play contain page numbers in this edition.

8. This helps verify the relationship between Pinter and Beckett that Ruby Cohn saw early on. See Ruby Cohn, "The Absurdly Absurd: Avatars of Godot," *Comparative Literature Studies* 2 (1965): 233–40.

9. See Bernard F. Dukore, *Harold Pinter* (New York: Grove Press, 1982), p. 44, and Gale, *Butter's Going Up,* p. 79.

6

Toying with *The Dwarfs*:
The Textual Problems with
Pinter's "Corrections"

SCOTT GIANTVALLEY

On 2 December 1960 Harold Pinter's radio play *The Dwarfs* was first performed on the BBC Third Programme. It was published in 1961 in the Methuen edition of *A Slight Ache and Other Plays*, and Grove Press published the first U.S. edition in 1962 in *Three Plays*. The first stage performance took place on 18 September 1963 in London, In 1965 an acting version was published by Dramatists Play Service. *The Dwarfs* appeared "reprinted 1968 with corrections" in Methuen's *A Slight Ache and Other Plays*. Also in 1968, on January 28, it was performed on American television by the Public Broadcasting Laboratory in New York City.

Such is the history of this play of less than thirty pages, but it merely hints at the baroque intricacies of a textual study of this play, which I discovered when teaching it to my Theatre of the Absurd class at the University of Southern California. I was shocked when my students were unable to find in their texts a passage on which I was basing a key interpretation. To my surprise, this was not the only difference between my text and theirs, although there was no indication that their Grove Press edition was any different from mine. I sought a copy of their version in the library, but when I found a copy of the "first printing" from Grove (1962), I found another version altogether, neither mine nor theirs.

In researching the matter I found that Mary Jane Miller's article, "Pinter as a Radio Dramatist,"[1] had acknowledged and examined these three existing versions, as has Steven H. Gale in *Butter's Going Up: A Critical Analysis of Harold Pinter's Work*.[2] Miller's point, however, was simply that a work written originally for the radio could not take to the stage with full success, although Pinter had sought such success through revisions. Miller did not realize that the Grove edition to which she referred her readers no longer contained the version she described. Moreover, she deplored the second and third versions as equally destroying the point of the first version, when it is really the third that makes the truly radical and unsuccessful departure from the original. In concentrating on the differing demands of the two media, radio and stage, Miller fails to perceive that it is chiefly this final version's lack of consistency that determines its failure as a work of art. This lack of consistency I shall demonstrate by looking at the changes Pinter made and their effects on the presentation of character and character interaction and on the development of Pinter's patterns of imagery.

Before considering the changes themselves, we should be familiar with where the specific versions are published. For this discussion, I shall follow Miller's practice and "refer to the original radio play (in the Grove edition) as *Dwarfs I*, the first published stage version (Methuen, 1961) as *Dwarfs II* and the re-working (Methuen, 1968) as *Dwarfs III*."[3] Unfortunately, while her dates are correct, she does not appear to have observed that at the time her article was published (1974) Grove Press was no longer printing *Dwarfs I*. The first edition of *Three Plays*, in 1962, certainly used a script intended for radio (indicating sound effects but no stage directions), but by the "ninth printing" (before 1972), as the verso of the title-leaf calls it, Grove was keeping abreast of Methuen, replacing *Dwarfs I* with *Dwarfs II*, which added stage directions and made several changes in the dialogue. While the contents were changed considerably, however, neither cover nor title-leaf nor copyright information acknowledged this significant fact. By the "thirteenth printing" (before 1976), the text of *The Dwarfs* had been changed again, and Grove had replaced *Dwarfs II* with *Dwarfs III*, the version Methuen first printed in 1968. There was still no allusion made to the change, other than the addition of the cast list and production information of "a new version for the stage" (featuring John Hurt as Len), directly under the radio-performance cast list that had appeared in both *Dwarfs I* and *II*.[4]

Otherwise, each page of Grove's *Dwarfs III* is identical to the corresponding page in the 1968 Methuen version, except for an increase in the size of both print and page and the correction of three minor errors of spelling and punctuation from the 1968 Methuen. These three errors from Methuen's *Dwarfs III* are also present in Grove's *Dwarfs II*, which seems to have been set, as Methuen's *Dwarfs III* was, from Methuen's *Dwarfs II* rather than from Grove's *Dwarfs I*, in which the spelling and punctuation are correct. Apparently these three errors, carried over from Methuen's *Dwarfs II*, were not among the "corrections" that Methuen's *Dwarfs III* included in its text. We may wonder why Pinter (or his agents at Methuen) chose to describe the changes made in his text as "corrections" rather than as a new edition, a revision, or a new version; further, why Grove, which took at least four years to revise its text in accord with Methuen's 1968 version, did not include even Methuen's rather misleading acknowledgment of a difference in text when it changed versions.

We may also wonder why Grove originally stopped printing the otherwise unavailable radio script and printed *Dwarfs II*, duplicating what Methuen had provided. Steven Gale notes, in relation to Pinter's similarly revised play *The Caretaker*, that Grove claims merely to print what Methuen prints;[5] he also cites Grove spokesman Fred Jordan's claim that Grove was unaware of any changes; one wonders, however, at the considerable lag in time between Methuen's changes and Grove's. In response to my queries, Jordan agreed that it would have been proper to have included an introduction noting the change, or at least a statement to that effect affixed to the copyright information; he suggested that this may have been an oversight on the editor's part (but twice?). But apparently, he says, Pinter simply demanded that certain pages of his text be pulled and a new set printed in their place. Jordan wrote me that "the new version was printed at the insistence of Mr. Pinter who does not want the old version to be made available any more,"[6] a wish that certainly has been carried out successfully, even if his revisions have not. Apparently, Jordan and Grove Press accept the theory that whatever an author requests regarding his work (and his "re-workings," as Miller so aptly terms what Pinter has done with *The Dwarfs*) must be followed, editors and publishers yielding up their better judgments: "since Pinter signs his name to it, I suppose we shall have to grant him the right to have it appear the way he prefers it."

The changes, as Miller notes, were made for presentation on the stage, but interestingly, the "new version for the stage" that the 1963 cast list in *Dwarfs III* announces was actually published two years before the stage presentation. It corresponds not to *Dwarfs III*, as the heading suggests, but to *Dwarfs II*, as is apparent from the comments of 1963 reviewers, who refer not only to elements that appear in *Dwarfs II* and not in *Dwarfs I*,[7] but more significantly, to elements (that is, Len's many "interior monologues"[8]) characteristic of *Dwarfs II* but not *Dwarfs III*. Thus we discover that the 1963 stage version was apparently "new" only in the sense of never having been performed publicly, for it had already been published by Methuen in 1961—unless, indeed, it has itself never been published and actually corresponds to none of the versions that are accessible.

A survey of the complaints of various reviewers "that the play failed theatrically because of descriptive writing, abstractions, far-fetched imagery, and a lack of dramatic urgency"[9] might suggest that Pinter later revised the play in an attempt to counteract such criticisms, which he readily accepted, admitting to an interviewer after this stage production: "It does seem very confusing and obviously it can't be sucessful."[10] Nevertheless he did not refrain from trying to make it stageworthy, for, as Miller notes, "obviously, Pinter badly wanted *The Dwarfs* [which Pinter had originally conceived as a novel] to work as a stage play."[11] Miller demonstrates, however, that its failure as such is inevitable because of the transfer of the material to a medium for which it was not intended, agreeing with Simon Trussler that *The Dwarfs* is "the only one of Pinter's plays to date which does shrink when it is *seen*."[12] Trussler does not seem to realize that *The Drawfs* as seen onstage was quite a different work textually from *The Drawfs* as heard on the radio, or as read in the first Grove edition. Further, Miller's judgements of unsuitability for the stage are based on Pinter's "re-workings" of his original concept, especially the second, which not only does not appear to have been performed onstage under Pinter's aegis, but besides, stemming as it apparently does from Pinter's reaction to adverse criticism of the stage production and attempts to counteract that criticism, can hardly be regarded as such a completely conceived and unified work of art as *Dwarfs I*.

To see this one must look at the questions of how *Dwarfs III* is a different work from *Dwarfs I*, and whether it represents a unified work to the same extent as the original version. To learn the answers, I shall examine whether the revisions made for the final version are consistent with each other and with those parts of the text which remain, in order to achieve true artistic integrity.

Revision is not uncommon for Pinter, who, as a man very much of the theatre, has a strong interest in making his plays work onstage. Such major plays as *The Caretaker* (1960) and *The Birthday Party* (1959) have been revised, in 1965 and 1968 respectively, as the current Grove editions of these plays appropriately note. But a look at the revisions of *The Birthday Party*,[13] for example, which primarily involve deletions of a few lines here and there, reveals the lack of care on either Pinter's or Grove's part in making sure there are no lacunae or errors that have slipped through while doing such piecemeal changing. There are instances of two consecutive speeches from the same character, when intervening lines have been cut (see pp. 31 and 67); at another point occurs the following nonsensical exchange:

GOLDBERG: What's what? (McCANN does not answer.)
McCANN (turning to look at GOLDBERG, grimly): I'm not going up there again. (P. 73)

The meaningless stage direction after Goldberg's question is explained by the first version, in which Goldberg asks again, "What is what?" after McCann has not replied. In an earlier instance, McCann's exit and business offstage with the accompanying dialogue are deleted, but although McCann remains onstage and silent, Goldberg proceeds to inform him of the conversation he and Meg have just had in McCann's presence. While Pinter's deletions from this play do not affect the meaning in the drastic way that the revisions in *Dwarfs III* do, both share the trait of providing not as workable a playing script as the original version and show a piecemeal rather than thorough attitude toward revision.

But, just as the revision of *The Birthday Party* does not shift the meaning of the play and does not include anything that could not work onstage to provide a theatrical experience as satisfying as the original, so Pinter's first revision of the radio script—*Dwarfs II*—is not a major departure from the original. Primarily, *Dwarfs II* replaces the radio's emphasis on sound effects with the stage's emphasis on visuals—the physical presence of actors in front of an audience, requiring set descriptions, stage directions, and appropriate actions. For example, such actions as Pete's sniffing at the gherkins in disgust (p. 84), Len's trying the wine and then spitting it out (p. 92), and Len's finding an apple in Mark's fruit bowl and calling it "funny-looking" (p. 95) give visual representation to the images of distasteful and decaying food with which the dialogue of the play abounds. Rather than changing the emphasis, as Miller implies, the use of visual image serves to underline the verbal. In addition, words, lines, and speeches are added or cut, but the most extensive cut is a monologue about a page long in which Len describes the actions of his two friends when all three are together, a monologue clearly intended to be heard only in the absence of visual input.

Miller, in contrasting the versions, suggests that the radio version allows a listener to wonder about the concrete reality of Len's two friends, whether their struggle is really only "a symbolic projection of Len's own imagination, representing two unreconciled fragments of his own personality or perhaps the person he would like to be."[14] Is it true, as she suggests, that *The Dwarfs* "therefore cannot be redone adequately with vision on—or with a complex theatrical lighting plot—and imagination off"?[15] Is it necessarily true that through the portrayals of Pete and Mark, the direction, setting, and lighting, not to mention the words of the play itself, a similar effect cannot be achieved in suggesting the shadowy presence or nonpresence of the two friends and the vividness of Len's imagination, with Pete and Mark becoming "almost entirely projections of Len's consciousness"?[16] The shadowy, imaginary nature of a character has been used by Pinter elsewhere, in a play meant for the stage, *Old Times* (1971), in which Anna's arrival is first discussed by Deeley and Kate, making her very existence somewhat open to question; even her later physical presence onstage leaves questions in the viewer's mind as to her reality, as many critics of the stage version have noted. Would *Old Times* therefore make a successful radio play? Perhaps not, because the audience must be always aware of the presence of the third character, even when the other two are engaged in a long dialogue, often concerning that character. This is not to say, however, that *The Dwarfs* cannot work as well with the physical presence of actors as with only their voices.

Indeed, the "mysticism" of Len's speeches, which Miller terms "static," apparently *can* work in a visual medium, as demonstrated by the critically successful 1968 television production by the Public Broadcasting Laboratory, starring Jon Voight as Len. If on radio the actors "can, by their lengthening silence, simply fade from the listener's consciousness,"[17] the same fading can be achieved through lighting on the stage; Miller's further claim, "that the other two actors on stage must either react or not react to Len's soliloquies, so that the audience always know how they feel about what Len says,"[18] may be negated by the simple convention of theatrical blocking, which can place a character onstage so that his face cannot be seen and his reactions can thus remain unperceived by the audience. This is, in fact, a common device in

Pinter's work—characters who remain uninvolved in the dialogue, whose reactions remain enigmatic (see *Old Times*, *Betrayal*, *A Slight Ache*—this last originally a radio play but often performed onstage).

Yet it is not the mere physical presence of the actors on the stage that gives more concrete reality to Mark and Pete and takes emphasis away from Len's own consciousness. *Dwarfs II* adds to the dialogue of *Dwarfs I* information about Mark's and Pete's jobs, giving more of a notion of them as individuals apart from Len: Mark's profession as actor is made more explicit (p. 90); Pete is given a place in the work force of the city, from which he wishes to advance to "something deserving of the proper and active and voluntary application of my own powers" (p. 97). More radically, however, *Dwarfs III* takes the audience outside Len by having him share his obsession with the dwarfs no longer only with the audience, through internal monologues, but also with his friends. With this twist, the dwarfs gain a level of reality that the audience was not required to yield to them in the earlier versions, for in asking Mark and Pete, "Haven't you noticed?" (p. 94), Len makes clear his literal belief in them, even though Mark and Pete merely ignore him or urge him to "settle down" (p. 98). No longer can his visions of the dwarfs be perceived (as they can in *Dwarfs I* and *II*) as merely symbolic nightmares that Len is narrating to himself, embodying the fears and obsessions of his life and relationships, through vivid images culled from the events and impressions of his actual existence. In *Dwarfs III* reality has definitely eluded him.

The role of the dwarfs is simplified here and considerably diminished from the earlier versions, and, as Miller says, "the relationship of Mark and Pete with the competent, disparate, all-gorging dwarfs is less complex."[19] They become merely watchers of Mark and Pete whom Len has hired (p. 94); the sense of them as also oppressing Len is reduced from a long speech in both *Dwarfs I* (p. 96) and *II* (p. 98) to the following few lines:

They've left me to sweep the yard, to keep the place in order. It's a bloody liberty. They're supposed to be keeping you under observation. What do they think I am, a bloody charlady? I can't look after the place by myself, it's not possible. Piles and piles and piles of muck and leavings all over the place, spewed up spewed up, I'm not a skivvy, they don't pay me, I pay them. (P. 98)

This brief reference, while true to the spirit of the earlier versions, is puzzling in its current context, for this view of the dwarfs is not as sufficiently developed here as in the earlier versions to offset the more playful aspects of the dwarfs depicted in Len's speech immediately following (presented in the earlier versions in a soliloquy separated from this oppressive vision by at least a page of dialogue between Len and Mark). These deletions do not, however, as Miller contends, make "*Dwarfs III* a simpler, less static, and more explicit version for a theatre audience to understand"[20]; on the contrary, the briefer and more cryptic allusions to the dwarfs would tend to confuse an audience more than the earlier versions, despite reduction of the earlier versions' "static" qualities.

The images of Len's hallucinatory monologues are often echoes of the realistic events of his life, images or themes recognizable from his conversations with Mark and Pete; thus they act like recurring nightmares, in which his subconscious interprets the concerns of his conscious existence, through visions that chime "with his own immediate sense of reality," "as if Len is remoulding what his friends say in his own mind," as Trussler points out.[21] But in *Dwarfs III*, where Len presents these visions as real in his conversation with Mark and Pete, one is compelled to regard the dwarfs primarily as psychological manifestations of "mental illness"[22] rather than to concentrate on their imagistic or symbolic significance.

The substitution in *Dwarfs III* of dialogue for Len's four dwarfs monologues places us more on the outside of Len than on the inside, where we are placed by his monologues, which reveal things about Len of which Mark and Pete remain unaware, and which permit, as Miller states, "the auidence to perceive events through Len's senses, his memory and his hallucinations."[23] This "intense unrelieved concentration on the multiple levels of one man's consciousness," as Miller terms it, leads to a more satisfactory resolution than is provided in the latest version, where Len, having exposed his aberrations to his friends, emerges from his obsessions in isolation; no further remarks are exchanged among the three about the dwarfs that Len has told his friends about, or about the current condition of Len's mental health. In fact, his hospitalization is, according to Pete, for "kidney trouble. Not serious." In the original version, where Len's concern with the dwarfs is all interior, the obsessions are ultimately resolved in his own mind, and he is separated— appropriately and satisfactorily—from his two supposed friends, who are thus associated with the dwarfs, who stop bothering him at the same time that Mark and Pete break up their friendship.

Moreover, if a jarring note is struck when the theme of Mark and Pete's knowledge (even though apathetic) of Len's belief in the dwarfs fails to reappear, the final speech is even more disconcerting, when several themes appear, apparently in a final recapitulation but lacking the proper exposition and development earlier in the play. In *Dwarfs I* and *II* the final speech successfully resolves the dissonances the play has steadily set up; but in *Dwarfs III*, with most of the speech intact, so much relevant material has been deleted throughout the rest of the play that we no longer experience the same reverberations or even perceive the same meaning in it that the speech contains in *Dwarfs I* and *II*. In fact, there are elements in the speech that are unclear without the prior knowledge of the now-missing dwarfs monologues.

The final speech begins "They've stopped eating," but eating in *Dwarfs III* has been of minimal importance for the dwarfs in contrast to *Dwarfs I* and *II*. *Dwarfs III* makes no reference to the unusual foods they eat, like the porridge, which Len says is "like nothing I've ever tasted" (*Dwarfs I*, p. 99). In *Dwarfs III*, rather, the only time they are seen actually eating is when they "settle down for the night with a bun and a doughnut" (p. 98), a much milder and more childlike image than in *Dwarfs I* and *II*, which both include the following passage:

What about the rats I saved for you, that I plucked and hung out to dry, what about the rat steak I tried all ways to please you? They won't touch it, they don't see it. Where is it, they've hidden it, they're hiding it till the time I can no longer stand upright and I fall, they'll bring it out then, grimed then, green, varnished, rigid, and eat it as a victory dish. (p. 97).

In this image of the rat, associated with Len himself, "as a victory dish" for the dwarfs lies the key to the following lines from the final speech, which are identical in all three versions but which in *Dwarfs III* lack the important echo to the rat in the speech just quoted:

I'm left in the lurch. Not even a stale frankfurter, a slice of bacon rind, a leaf of cabbage, not even a mouldy piece of salami, like they used to sling me in the days when we told old tales by suntime. They sit, chock-full. But I smell a rat. They seem to be anticipating a rarer dish, a choicer spread.

The only other rat that appears in *Dwarfs III* is the rat corpse that Len describes in one monologue as being torn apart by Pete, whom Len's vision has transformed into a gull; the rat as a dish for the dwarfs, associated with Len but now signifying "a rarer dish" for which they are abandoning Len (perhaps the decaying friendship of Pete and Mark), is a developed image only in the earlier versions. In *Dwarfs III* there has been no previous dish suggested for the comparison implied by "rarer" and "choicer," so these phrases have lost the meaning they had in the first two versions, appearing merely like another non sequitur from someone insane.

Furthermore, in eliminating from the play most of the content of Len's four dwarfs monologues, Pinter also drops many verbal and imagistic echoes that relate the dwarfs to Pete and Mark, and to the sordid, decaying, rotting elements of Len's life and his relationship with his two friends. For example, the play's opening scene shows Len finding the stiff milk in Mark's apartment (*Dwarfs I*, p. 84); later he watches the dwarfs as "they all gobble the tinned milk" (*Dwarfs I*, p. 95); and in the final speech he sees "tin cans" as part of "the dwarfs' leavings," their rubble, which is finally cleared away. In *Dwarfs III* the tin cans at the end recall nothing earlier, since the milk that Len tries to pour in the beginning is in a bottle, and the connecting image of "tinned milk" has been deleted.

So, because we have experienced only a fraction of the original content of the four long dwarfs monologues, the final speech lacks the impact it has in *Dwarfs I* and *II*. We have not suffered along with Len, we have not heard described the degradations of the dwarfs' various activities to give us that sense of release which the final speech implies in depicting Len's emergence from the scraps of the dwarfs' leavings into a yard that is "clean" and "scrubbed," where "There is a lawn. There is a shrub. There is a flower." The identification of the dwarfs with the deteriorated relationship is still present, but the rich sense of catharsis and the simultaneous feeling of loneliness are lacking, because we have not really come to know the dwarfs in this new version of the play, which still bears their name. The dwarfs in the new version are incidential, not dominating presences, and deciphering in *Dwarfs III* their enigmatic role in Len's psyche requires a reader to go back to one of the earlier two versions for a more complete and meaningful imagistic context, with clearer reverberations through the rest of the text.

It is *Dwarfs I* or *Dwarfs II* that critics have focused upon, whether by intention or by lucky chance, for they are the versions that are the more complex and satisfying. *Dwarfs III*, though presumably Pinter's final word on the subject, is generally ignored, except by the rare critic like Miller or Gale,[24] who notes the weakening of the final revised version but whose page references to the different versions will be confusing since all three versions have been published by Grove (with pagination differing only minimally) and a reader cannot tell clearly which version is in hand without actually comparing texts. Most book-length studies, however, fail to note any distinction between the different versions and of course neglect to note that Grove has published three different ones under the same apparent edition. Even those who do realize that there is a stage version different from the radio script fail to specify which of the stage versions they are commenting on, apparently unaware that two exist. Unfortunately, those reading any of these critics may have difficulty reconciling the copy they have bought (especially if they have bought it within the past several years) with most of the critical commentary on it, since only the last, and least consistent, version is now in print.

It is disappointing that Pinter has not put the effort into *The Dwarfs* to give this fascinating text a full-scale revision that would maintain the internal consistency of the first version; he has been content, instead, with some piecemeal tinkering, which has served to distort rather than improve his original work. Yet even if one cannot always trust authors to trust their initial conceptions of work, one can at least hope that publishers will not do as Grove has done with regard to *The Dwarfs*, but will give appropriate bibliographic notice of what a volume actually contains.[25]

A version of this essay was delivered at the Society for Textual Studies Conference at the Graduate Center of the City University of New York, April 1981.

Notes

1. Mary Jane Miller, "Pinter as a Radio Dramatist," *Modern Drama* 17 (1974): 403–12.

2. Steven H. Gale, *Butter's Going Up: A Critical Analysis of Harold Pinter's Work* (Durham, N.C.: Duke University Press, 1977), pp. 263–65.

3. Miller, "Pinter as a Radio Dramatist," p. 407.

4. Harold Pinter, *Three Plays*, 13th printing (New York: Grove Press, 1962), p. 81.

5. Gale, *Butter's Going Up*, p. 258.

6. Letter from Fred Jordan of Grove Press, 13 May 1976, in response to my letter of 31 March 1976. Information on the printing history of *Three Plays,* as well as Pinter's correspondence with

the publishing company, would be difficult, if not impossible, to locate, Mr. Jordan informed me during a subsequent telephone conversation, since Grove had undergone several moves in the preceding few years.

7. For example, H. Thompson in the London *Times*, 19 September 1963, p. 16, writes that "Len ... owns his house but feels rootless," an allusion that occurs in *Dwarfs II* and *III* (p. 103) but not in *Dwarfs I*.

8. John Russell Taylor, "Half Pints of Pinter," *Plays and Players* 11 (November 1963): 38. Basil Boothroyd, in *Punch*, 25 September 1963, p. 467, refers to the dwarfs "singing hymns round the bonfire," an allusion that occurs in *Dwarfs II* (p. 100), not in *Dwarfs III*. Taylor, interestingly, in contrast to Miller, finds that *The Dwarfs* works quite well on stage, providing "a riveting experience in the theatre," even though "put on the stage more or less without textual changes." So he says, perhaps basing his comparison on the Methuen edition of the stage version (though not cited as such) already in print.

9. Herman T. Schroll, *Harold Pinter: A Study of His Reputation (1958–1969) and a Checklist* (Metuchen, N.J.: Scarecrow Press, 1971), p. 44.

10. Lawrence M. Bensky, "Harold Pinter: An Interview," in *Pinter: A Collection of Critical Essays*, ed. Arthur Ganz (Englewood Cliffs, N.J.: Prentice-Hall, 1972), p. 24.

11. Miller, "Pinter as a Radio Dramatist," p. 407.

12. Simon Trussler, *The Plays of Harold Pinter: An Assessment* (London: Victor Gollancz, 1973), p. 97. That this is not necessarily so was demonstrated by the Public Broadcasting Laboratory's performance on American television in 1968, to which critics and audiences reacted with interest. John McLaughlin wrote, "Pinter's theatricality is indisputable: intense and brilliant," in *America* 118 (10 February 1968): 193. According to Jack Gould of the *New York Times*, 29 January 1968, p. 63, Jon Voight "brought to the part of Len a poetic mysticism that sustained the work as a viewing experience." Audiences were becoming more accustomed to such interruptions of dramatic movement as long philosophical speeches, internal monologues, and the presentation of the visions of the mentally unstable, through the works of such playwrights as Edward Albee and Tom Stoppard. The times had merely to catch up with Pinter.

13. Harold Pinter, *The Birthday Party and The Room*, rev. ed. (New York: Grove Press, 1968), p. 73.

14. Miller, "Pinter as a Radio Dramatist," p. 408.

15. Ibid., p. 407.

16. Taylor, "A Room and Some Views in Harold Pinter," in *Pinter*, ed. Ganz, p. 114.

17. Miller, "Pinter as a Radio Dramatist," p. 409.

18. Ibid.

19. Ibid., p. 410.

20. Ibid., p. 412.

21. Trussler, *Plays of Pinter*, p. 98.

22. Martin Esslin, *Pinter: A Study of His Plays* (London: Methuen, 1973), p. 118.

23. Miller, "Pinter as a Radio Dramatist," p. 411.

24. Besides *Butter's Going Up*, see also Gale's *Harold Pinter: An Annotated Bibliography* (Boston: G. K. Hall, 1978), which notes the varied publication of the play though not which version is contained in a particular book.

25. In March 1984, Soho Repertory Theatre of New York City presented a production of *The Dwarfs* under the direction of Jerry Engelbach. Whether he knew of the earlier versions or not, the version performed was *Dwarfs III* (the only one available in scripts bought now). Despite Pinter's doubts about its viability onstage, the play succeeded quite well with its capacity audience on the day I saw it, giving a keen sense of the sexual tension among the three men and superbly conveying the brittleness of Len's sanity through Matthew Gottlieb's gripping performance. The compression of the references to the actual dwarfs, the major change *Dwarfs III* makes in the script, is still regrettable. Audience members may still wonder what the dwarfs had to do with the play.

7

Design and Discovery in Pinter's *The Lover*

AUSTIN E. QUIGLEY

Harold Pinter's *The Lover,* first performed on television in March 1963, was transferred to the London stage in September of the same year. The play has generated some critical disagreement,[1] but the attention it has received has been somewhat perfunctory, and not much in the way of persuasive discussion has been addressed to the play, to the critical problems it has generated, or to the light it might shed on Pinter's evolving techniques and concerns. This is unfortunate because the play has much to offer, both in its own right as a thought-provoking drama and in its capacity to render more accessible other puzzling Pinter plays.

One of the major reasons that the play has received little attention, however, is that it has seemed, to many, neither thought-provoking nor puzzling. The play deals with two primly dressed characters, Richard and Sarah, husband and wife, who enliven their afternoons by dressing more casually, taking new names, and playing the roles of lover and mistress—with each other. That final point is startling when first encountered in the play, but the issues of role-playing, divided selves, sexual inhibition, and sexual fantasy are all well worn in the modern theatre, and it is difficult to think of anything along these lines that will not look like simplistic Freud or warmed-over Genet. And it is, indeed, in these terms that much criticism has approached the play. But, in noting the play's conventionality, we should not overlook its originality, and in studying any Pinter play, we should be more than wary of confusing the simple issues it initially portrays with the much more complex implications it derives from them. Pinter may well begin where others have begun before him, but the point of arrival and the means of travel are what make his plays so distinctive and disturbing. The need for metaphors of movement and change is thrust upon us by plays whose movements and changes are often both subtle and savage. But to understand their impact, we must first explain a subtlety that seems often to rigidify or to disappear when we seek to pin it down.

Our critical vocabulary is part of the problem here. Such terms as *character, plot, scene, act, situation, costume,* and *set* are terms in a vocabulary of fixed forms by means of which we seek to explain a dramatic action that is in constant movement. The problem these terms present is not new, and neither is it insurmountable, if we keep in mind the strengths and limitations of any critical vocabulary. It is obviously possible to deal with motion and change in terms of a shift from one fixed state of affairs to another, with appropriate comparisons providing the basis for discussion of probable causes. But if, as is often the case with a Pinter play, the major focus of attention is *the process of change* itself, then we are liable to find ourselves somewhat at a loss. The initial and final states of affairs may not seem to merit the attention the play nevertheless seems to deserve. By focusing in inappropriate ways on the beginning and end of the play, we may miss much that passes in between and find ourselves ready, as have many critics of *The Lover,* to perceive only the conventionality of the play and overlook the originality, whose locus is much more widely dispersed.[2]

Strindberg, many years ago, lamented just such a problem in entrenched notions of the nature of character.[3] Both in the theatre and in the world beyond it, he felt, a tendency had developed to use the word *character* in the context of fixity and predictability. A *character* was someone who stood for and embodied some limited set of principles and traits. In the theatre, this reduced characters to types, with characteristic phrases, behavior, and costume. Outside the theatre, characters became stereotypes, people to be admired (if possible) for their principles, their firmness, their unyielding sameness. Anyone, in either sphere, who displayed a readiness to change, to behave unpredictably, was likely to be regarded as someone lacking character, someone who could not be relied upon. The confusion of descriptive and prescriptive uses of the term *character* exemplifies also a value confusion over the relative importance of fixity and change in human behavior—an issue at once at the heart of our critical vocabulary, of Pinter's work in general, and of *The Lover* in particular.

Richard and Sarah struggle, in *The Lover*, to locate and control the possibilities for, and the problems of, change in their relationship—change that is manifest first in variety and then in efforts to construct and control further variety. The stage set registers, in its central division, two major components of the couple's relationship and the difficulties of fusing them into a seamless whole. The stage is divided into *"two areas"* (p. 49),[4] with the living room stage right, and the bedroom, on a slightly different level, stage left. Separating and linking the two is a small hall and a short flight of stairs. The *"two areas"* of the stage provide a persistent visual manifestation of two aspects of Richard and Sarah's relationship: the public domain of a responsible husband-and-wife unit, and the private domain of two individuals with a passionate sexual bond. At the beginning of the play, Richard and Sarah move around the separate rooms and then contentedly meet in the living room; two-thirds of the way through the play, no longer content, they are separated in a brief tableau (*"they both stand quite still in the two rooms for a few moments"* [p. 73]); and at the end of the play, they are united once more in the living room (*"They are still, kneeling, she leaning over him"* [p. 84]). An inviting critical approach would thus be to establish the nature of their relationship at each of these key points, and also the nature of, and reasons for, the changes from one state of the relationship to another. The trouble is that it is very difficult to pin down the precise nature of the relationship at any of these times. The initial moment of husband-and-wife harmony includes an *"amiable"* (p. 49) discussion of an impending visit by the wife's lover; the subsequent moment of estrangement precedes a fulsome compliment by Richard to his wife (p. 75); and the final moment of renewed harmony includes a reiterated request for "change" from Richard (p. 84). But the key issue we must recognize from the outset is that our difficulty in deciding just where the couple has arrived at each point in the progression is a difficulty shared by the characters themselves.

An important instance of this uncertainty emerges when Richard and Sarah discuss the fact that each is involved in an ostensibly separate sexual relationship—Sarah with her lover, and Richard with a woman he describes as "a whore" (p. 55):

Sarah: I'm sorry your affair possesses so little dignity.
Richard: The dignity is in my marriage.
Sarah: Or sensibility.
Richard: The sensibility likewise. I wasn't looking for such attributes. I find
           them in you.
Sarah: Why did you look at all?
                          Slight pause.
Richard: What did you say?
Sarah: Why look ... elsewhere ... at all?
Richard: But my dear, you looked. Why shouldn't I look?
                          Pause.
Sarah: Who looked first?
Richard: You.
Sarah: I don't think that's true.
Richard: Who, then?
                  She looks at him with a slight smile.
                                                           (Pp. 57–58)

Habits of mind engendered by our critical vocabulary would lead us to assume that a brute historical fact is at issue here, and that only one of the two characters can be right about it. Either she looked first or he did; either she is lying or he is. But it is precisely this habit of mind that the play refuses to satisfy. It fails to provide us with the evidence necessary to decide the issue. We are forced to consider whether it is indeed possible that two participants in the same process could disagree about who began the process, and thus about the nature of the process itself.

The issue is a vital one because it not only raises the possibility that the two can have different notions of when the "looking elsewhere" game began, but also what exactly the game is that is being played from moment to moment.[5] When Sarah describes the relationship with her lover, it seems like *an extension* of her relationship with Richard (her lover is "terribly sweet," "very loving," "manly," with "a wonderful sense of humour" [p. 60]); but when Richard describes his relationship with his whore, it seems like a radical *contrast* to his relationship with Sarah ("Just a common or garden slut" [p. 55], "I wasn't looking for your double, was I? I wasn't looking for a woman I could respect, as you, whom I could admire and love, as I do you" [p. 57]). We are forced to consider whether it can be the case that though both are in some sense involved in the same games, these are not the same games for each of them. And if this is so, we might wonder who is in control of the games and of the changes they undergo.

There are certainly clear signs in the play's action that the two characters play the games differently. Richard, in his role as husband, is reluctant to betray his awareness that he also plays the lover in the afternoon. When Sarah accidentally wears, in the evening, the high-heeled shoes of her afternoon life, Richard reacts with puzzlement at their very existence. Sarah, on the other hand, mutters to herself that she has made a "mistake," and thus registers her awareness of both evening and afternoon roles.

Richard: What shoes are they?
Sarah: Mmnn?
Richard: Those shoes. They're unfamiliar. Very high-heeled, aren't they?
Sarah   (*muttering*): Mistake. Sorry.
Richard   (*not hearing*): Sorry? I beg your pardon?
Sarah: I'll ... take them off.
Richard: Not quite the most comfortable shoes for an evening at home, I would have thought.

(P. 54)

Likewise, when Richard, at a moment of crisis, talks about his hard day's work "sifting matters of high finance in the City" (p. 76), Sarah, again registering her awareness of what he and she actually did together in the afternoon, "*laughs*" (p. 76) somewhat derisively. In neither case, however, do these contrasting modes of behavior become themselves subjects for discussion. Only at one point does the basis of the relationship threaten to become a topic for explicit discussion. This occurs at the moment late in the play when Richard begins to behave in the evening as though it were the afternoon, bringing the bongo drum from the hall cupboard and asking Sarah what she and her lover do with it. Sarah "*with quiet anguish*" replies: "You've no right to question me. No right at all. It was our arrangement. No questions of this kind please. Don't, don't. It was our arrangement" (p. 81).

We thus confront two issues of major importance to the control of change in the play. On the one hand, some sort of arrangement has been made be-

tween the two characters about the kinds of questions, and the kinds of behavior, that are appropriate in their different roles. On the other hand, the
arrangement itself is not fully explicit, nor in final form. It allows, as the
action of the play demonstrates, variation, new interpretation, and creative
extension. The problem for the characters and for the audience is to discern
the significance of actions based on a not-fully-explicit social agreement—an
agreement that is acknowledged as normative rather than definitive in status.
It registers the history of a kind of harmony that regulates, but does not pre-
clude, future change. The agreement, which seems in good part tacit, offers a
place to start from, but not necessarily a place to remain at. And like most
other points on a journey, it was preceded by others. The questions: "what
exactly, at this moment, is the game being played here?" and "when did it
begin?" linger in our minds, but their status as appropriate questions is, by
this point, itself in question.

   As so often in Pinter's work, what seems at first bewildering on stage is less
so if we consider analogous situations offstage. We may be surprised to encounter on stage characters whose social relationships are not governed by
explicit rules, and whose lives are thus open to misinterpretation and not
clearly defined change, but such characters would surely not find themselves
out of place in the worlds that we ourselves live in. Pinter, ever ready to
counter stage traditions, does so fruitfully when the novelty reminds us of
overlooked features of our own daily lives. And once having focused our
attention upon them, Pinter proceeds to demonstrate implications of which
we should certainly become aware.

   Richard and Sarah interact in a series of shared games that are not fully
defined, nor completely separated. In the process of playing the games, they
bestow upon them degrees of definition and establish among them degrees of
separation. These guidelines emerge in action, are challenged in action, and
are affirmed or revised in action. Richard and Sarah enact rules, register pro-
hibitions, negotiate new agreements—all without recourse to explicit discussion, explicit rules, or exhaustive regulations. It is this process of affirmation,
extension, revision, and renewal that is dramatized in a play that takes
spheres of stability as domains to be created—domains to be rescued from,
but also established by, movement and change. The play moves neither from
nor toward a situation of unambiguous fixity, but offers, instead, movement
from one stability-instability mixture to another. This concern for change in
the action of the play requires us to look not for a preceding, succeeding, or
underlying unity that takes precedence over the changes, but for strands of
continuity among the changes that enable us, as they enable the characters, to
become intelligently engaged with the events on stage. But continuity, unlike
unity, does not imply overall consistency, and this presents problems for both
characters and audience.

   One of the more obvious strands of continuity is repeated reference to the
limits set upon respectable male-female sexual relationships by inherited social standards. Richard, in his afternoon role as Max, plays the part of a

park-keeper who rescues Sarah from the clutches of a crudely physical pursuer. As he does so, he remarks: "To treat a lovely young woman like you like that, it's unpardonable" (p. 66). Sarah comments on a similar restriction in a respectable man's behavior toward his wife: "You don't really think you could have what we have with your wife, do you?" (p. 70). These limitations on male-female relationships are linked, in the play, to the issue of when Richard and Sarah began the afternoon game of lover and mistress. Sarah, noting that she and Richard have been married ten years, points out: "I didn't take my lover ten years ago. Not quite. Not on the honeymoon" (p. 78). The honeymoon, a long-established social custom, offers, of course, the one occasion when these restrictions upon behavior toward respectable women and respectable wives are suspended—though it is expected that the young couple will take themselves off to some remote place to engage in these unrestricted activities. When they return to society after the honeymoon, they return to the restrictions and to the concerns Richard and Sarah voice about not upsetting one's neighbors and one's standing among them. Discussing the visits of her lover, Sarah remarks:

Sarah: He has a wonderful sense of humour.
Richard: Oh, jolly good. Makes you laugh, does he? Well, mind the neighbours don't hear you. The last thing we want is gossip.
                                    Pause.
Sarah: It's wonderful to live out here, so far away from the main road, so secluded.
Richard: Yes, I do agree.

                                                    (Pp. 60–61)

This strand in the action of the play suggests that Richard and Sarah are very conventional people who have internalized and organized their relationship in terms of established social values. But this incipient consistency must be set against other aspects of their afternoon behavior, which suggest that they are not conventional people at all, but people who are prepared to give their own individuality and complexity their due. The two contrasting views of Richard and Sarah would suggest, if this were a play in which consistency was a prerequisite for resolution, two alternative solutions to their problems. If they believe in those restricting social values, they should live by them and abandon the afternoon games. If they believe in their own individuality, they should ignore the neighbors, ignore the propriety restrictions on their sexual relationship, and fuse their afternoon roles with those of the morning and evening. But these consistency-imposing alternatives overlook two issues of central importance to the play: whether Richard and Sarah have the same attitudes toward inherited and individual standard, and whether a fusion of their divided lives into a fixed and unambiguous state might involve losses as well as gains.

An attempt to explore the first issue leads inexorably toward the second, for both issues involve fixity, change, and attempts to reconcile the two. If we look at the situation with which the play begins, we see immediately that it is a situation not of overall consistency, but of equilibrium between potentially opposing forces. Richard (in his office clothes) *"amiably"* (p. 49) asks Sarah (in her *"crisp, demure dress"* [p. 49]) whether her lover is coming today. Both characters smile contentedly at each other, and seem equally content when Richard returns in the evening. But we quickly see that the equilibrium is unstable. As already noted, Richard insists on behaving as though he has no knowledge of his afternoon role as lover. Sarah goes along with this aspect of their script, but it seems less central to her than to Richard. Furthermore, as also noted, Richard insists on the drastic difference between his relationship with Sarah and his relationship with his "whore" (p. 55). Sarah, who sees her afternoon relationship as an extension of her relationship with her husband, is startled by his sudden brutal characterization of the contrast he perceives between the women in his afternoon and evening relationships. Sarah, who had comfortably thought of her afternoon role as one of being a "mistress," is suddenly forced to cope with having it described as the role of a "whore" (pp. 55–57). Her interest in maintaining her two roles in *complementary* relationship collides with Richard's insistence upon establishing them as *contrasting*. In a world open always to change, concern for the either-or of consistency-inconsistency is replaced by concern for reconciling complementarity with contrast.

Once again, there is evidence in the play that this dynamic is a developing strand in the evolution of their relationship. Sarah's forgetfulness in keeping her costumes properly separated (p. 54 and p. 62) is matched by her repeated tendency to betray knowledge of their joint afternoon activities, and by her intermittent attempts *to adopt a nonrole stance* in dealing with Richard. Richard, however, insists from the outset upon the fiction of total separation of the roles and refuses to move into a nonrole stance when Sarah, at points of crisis, tries to force him to do so. With the name "Richard" restricted to one role and "Max" to another, Sarah is forced to resort fruitlessly to pronouns: "Listen. You mustn't worry about ... wives, husbands, things like that. It's silly. It's you, you now, here, here with me, here together, that's what it is, isn't it? You whisper to me, you take tea with me, you do that, don't you, that's what we are, that's us, love me" (pp. 71–72). This comment to Max is matched by a similar one to Richard when he wonders whether he is forgotten during Sarah's afternoons:

Sarah: How could I forget you?
Richard: Quite easily, I should think.
Sarah: But I'm in your house.
Richard: With another.
Sarah: But it's you I love.
Richard: I beg your pardon?
Sarah: But it's you I love.

(P. 54)

These efforts to make use of "you, me, us" vocabulary to establish nonrole contact is constantly thwarted by role-committed Richard and Max. Both Richard and Max do indeed "worry about wives, husbands, things like that"; they worry about the integrity of, and appropriate relationships among, contrasting roles. And as we follow this strand through the play, we find ourselves locating in complementarity and contrast a continuing source of instability in the relationship, one that not only offers insight into the forces of change, but also into the need for, and nature of, the stabilizing games.

It is Richard, it seems, who most strongly registers the influence of established social roles and social values. It is he who insists most emphatically upon the value of the conventional marriage roles and upon respecting their integrity. One might then move, more hastily than one should, to the conclusion that it is Richard for whom these elaborate games are needed. As husband, he cannot shake off the restrictions that established public images place upon the sexual relationships he contracts with his wife. Only when freed from that role and given a contrasting one can he engage in more adventurous sexual behavior. Sarah, it seems, is much more flexible. She is always more than and other than any role she is playing and is ready to adapt roles to meet her needs, rather than adapt herself to meet the needs of contrasting, preexisting roles.[6] For Richard, the reverse is true, and Sarah, it seems, goes along with his intrarole perspective to enable him to exercise a various, if fragmented, individuality that can satisfy her various, but not discontinuous, needs. When Sarah worries about the potential losses if they abandon these games (p. 78), she is registering a fear of what she will then be unable to share with Richard, a fear of what he will no longer be able to countenance in himself.

It is difficult to overlook in Sarah that plasticity as a source of power which so often gives Pinter's female characters superiority over their male counterparts. But when we look more closely at the power of female plasticity and the weakness of male rigidity, we find that the dichotomy is rarely so clear and the benefits and liabilities not so neatly distributed. The power of female plasticity frequently offers little more than a situational superiority that is not without its subsequent costs. This is true for Rose in *The Room,* for Stella in *The Collection,* for Ruth in *The Homecoming,* for Beth in *Landscape,* and for Kate in *Old Times*. It is also true in *The Lover,* as Pinter works on and works out the benefits and liabilities of differing kinds of flexibility and inflexibility in social relationships. And it is certainly not the case that value is all on one side, nor is it the simplistic case that men are solely inflexible and women solely flexible. Rather, it is the case that the two sexes exhibit differing kinds of, and differing mixtures of, flexibility and inflexibility, and these vary by individual as well as by sex. The games played by Richard and Sarah are needed, we discover, just as much to deal with Sarah's flexibility as to deal with Richard's rigidity.

In *The Lover* it is clear that Richard recognizes, and lives by, an incompatibility between the roles of established middle-class husband and licentious lover. But these are not just indications of his own sexual inhibitions; rather, they manifest a recognition that different kinds of value are grounded in each role, and that to fuse the two is not to gain the benefits of both but to lose one or the other. The role of the public, dignified, and admired wife is one in which he locates value, and in which he wishes Sarah to locate value.

Richard: Yes, I find you very beautiful. I have great pride in being seen with you. When we're out to dinner, or at the theatre ... Or at the Hunt Ball ... Great pride, to walk with you as my wife on my arm. To see you smile, laugh, walk, talk, bend, be still. To hear your command of contemporary phraseology, your delicate use of the very latest idiomatic expression, so subtly employed ... And to know you are my wife. It's a source of a profound satisfaction to me.   (P. 75)

Richard, in his formal evening clothes, in his pinstripe suit, and in his bowler hat, knows that there are values worth preserving in the relationships that go with them. What is at issue for Richard is not a matter of choosing the best role of those which society has made available but of finding the best way of enjoying the benefits of their differences. We can thus offer a positive, as well as a negative, estimate of his role-restricted, fragmented behavior, and see that Sarah's incipient plasticity could indeed provide losses as well as gains. It is just those losses which are warded off by Richard's insistence upon the contrastive nature of the games and roles assigned to afternoon and evening.

We should also note that, just as Richard's seeming inflexibility has to be regarded in the light of his accompanying mode of flexibility (via fragmentation), so also Sarah's mode of flexibility has to be regarded in the light of an implicit inflexibility. Sarah's predisposition toward a continuity across roles sets potential limits on their relationship, upon the variety it can circumscribe and contain. Paradoxically, she then becomes as vulnerable to the charge of inflexibility as Richard. She can readily adapt to seeing herself in the complementary roles of wife and mistress, both being women of "grace, elegance, wit, imagination" (p. 70), but she is startled and disturbed by the thought that Richard/Max might conceive of her in the contrasting role of a whore:

Richard: But I haven't got a mistress. I'm very well acquainted with a whore, but I haven't got a mistress. There's a world of difference.
Sarah: A whore?
Richard (*taking an olive*): Yes. Just a common or garden slut. Not worth talking about. Handy between trains, nothing more.
Sarah: You don't travel by train. You travel by car.
Richard: Quite. A quick cup of cocoa while they're checking the oil and water.
                                     Pause.
Sarah: Sounds utterly sterile.
Richard: No.
                                     Pause.
                                      . . . .

Sarah: Is she witty?
Richard (*laughing*): These terms just don't apply. You can't sensibly in-
            quire whether a whore is witty. It's of no significance whether she is
            or she isn't. She's simply a whore, a functionary who either pleases
            or displeases.
Sarah: And she pleases you?
Richard: Today she is pleasing.
            Tomorrow ...? One can't say.
            He moves towards the bedroom door taking off his jacket.
Sarah: I must say I find your attitude to women rather alarming.
                                                            (Pp. 55–57)

Sarah's final rejoinder, focusing on "women," and thus on a continuity
among the various roles they play, runs into conflict with Richard's insistence
that he wasn't looking for continuity, but for discontinuity. He was not interested in grace, elegance, dignity, or sensibility in his other relationship: "I
wasn't looking for such attributes. I find them in you" (p. 57). If Richard's
interest in variety can cut him off from certain kinds of continuity, Sarah's
interest in continuity can cut her off from certain kinds of variety. Both,
however, register, in their actions, concern for the value of both continuity
and variety in their relationship. And to recognize that important fact is to
locate the point of transition from our first question, of whether Richard and
Sarah have the same attitudes toward inherited and individual standards (they
do not), to our second question of whether a fusion of their fragmented lives
into a fixed and unambiguous state might involve losses as well as gains.

We have already begun to answer the second question by noting how
Richard's attitudes, behavior, and comments indicate the to some degree independent value of contrasting modes of male-female relationships. There
are things he can enjoy with a whore that depend upon the contrast with a
wife. But that is by no means the most important of the senses in which there
would be losses as well as gains if these autonomous and contrasting domains
were to become complementary or be merged with each other. When we
look more closely at the action of the play, we discover that these opposing
domains are valuable not just for what their independent structures allow,
but also for the ways in which their contrasting values can be made to interact.
This occurs in two ways in the play, one in the context of violation, the other
in the context of balance.

The more obvious form of interaction is the one that contributes a stimulating sense of violation and desecration to the risqué afternoon relationship.
Again and again, such phrases as "I'm waiting for my husband" (p. 65),
"Now look, I'm sorry. I'm married" (p. 66), "To treat a lovely young woman
like you like that" (p. 66), and "I'm a married woman. You can't treat me like
this" (p. 67) come up in the afternoon games. The evening role is partially
integrated, as other, into the afternoon role, and this process is given a visual
manifestation in the location for the afternoon affair. The couple meets reg-
ularly in the formal and elegant living room of the house, and one of their
games culminates in an elaborate visual pun that underlines the importance of

the location. Max crawls *"under the table"* (p. 67) at center stage to run his hands up Sarah's leg and pull her down beneath it. The *"under the table"* metaphor, reinforced by the lowering of blinds and the living-room decor, enhances the afternoon's element of the risqué in a game that includes and exceeds elements of the marital relationship, which itself includes and exceeds elements of the lover-mistress relationship. Richard, as husband, asks Sarah about her lover; she, as wife, asks him about his mistress-whore. He, as lover, plays with the notion of being married; she, as mistress, does likewise. And when we recognize the interaction between the various roles, we finally find ourselves in a position to come to terms with the nature of variety in this relationship, its importance to both characters, the importance it, in turn, bestows upon continuity and change for both characters, and the reason why the word "balance" is so pivotal in the adjustments the characters make to their lives and to their relationship.

When things start going wrong with the initial arrangement that the play dramatizes, both characters resort quickly to a concern for balance. This issue comes up obliquely with Richard, explicitly with Sarah, indirectly with Max, visually in the stage set, and, for our purposes, the most important of all, repeatedly in the couple's mode of interaction. It is only by recognizing the role of balance and balancing in the play that we can gain appropriate access to a play that seeks to reconcile complementarity with contrast, and fixity with change. At the beginning of the play Richard asks *"amiably"* (p. 49) about Sarah's lover, but when he begins to feel less amiable about the lover, the word "balance" intrudes immediately.

Richard: Oh, by the way ... I rather wanted to ask you something.
Sarah: What?
Richard: Does it ever occur to you that while you're spending the afternoon
           being unfaithful to me I'm sitting at a desk going through balance
           sheets and graphs?
Sarah: What a funny question.
Richard: No, I'm curious.
Sarah: You've never asked me that before.
Richard: I've always wanted to know.
                      Slight Pause.

                                                  (P. 53)

The conversation tails off as Sarah ponders her answer, and we will return later to the significance of her subsequent response. For the moment, we simply note that Richard raises the same issue again, half a dozen sentences later, and in the context of assuring himself that he is "not completely forgotten" (p. 54) in the afternoons. The concern for balance at the office is also a concern for balance in the relative status of Sarah's husband and lover.

Sarah, likewise concerned that things seem to be going wrong, has recourse to the same issue. Fearing that Richard is needlessly getting jealous of the afternoon lover, she seeks to stabilize and maintain both aspects of their relationship by declaring her balanced interest in both.

Sarah: .... you're happy, aren't you? You're not in any way jealous?
Richard: No.
Sarah: Good. Because I think things are beautifully balanced, Richard.
(P. 61)

Max and Sarah, in their afternoon games, register the importance of balance in their relationship by the modes of interaction they exhibit and the topics they discuss. They balance the powers and responsibilities in their relationship by alternately playing the roles of pursuer and pursued, and when their afternoon games move to their physical consummation, it is in the context of balancing marital commitment and individual freedom, female reluctance and male urgency, female passion and male loyalty, physical entrapment and psychological freedom, moral concern and emotional excitement— all encountered, enacted, and balanced in a game that reaches its climax under a table designedly located at center stage, at the point where the two balanced halves of the stage-set meet.

As the stage-set consistently reminds us, male-female relationships exist both in bed and out, and what Richard and Sarah constantly seek is the kind of balance among the several components of their relationship that will make two different (but not fixed) people repeatedly happy. The word "balance" is vital to both of them, for it is the basis for both harmony *and variety* in their relationship. If it were only harmony that were at issue, the play would lose its most vital element of significance and originality. The action of the play would be directed toward the choosing of a single mode of consistency. But balance, for Richard and Sarah, is not just a means of stabilizing their relationship, it is also a means of changing it in initially unforeseen, but nevertheless controllable, ways. Their relationship is not the single negotiated balance of compromised differences; it is an ongoing process of distributing and balancing differences, and thereby making maximum use of, rather then eliminating, the differences that divide and unite them.

This point is crucial, for it provides us with the necessary means of engaging our understanding with a play that, instead of focusing upon fixed and enduring states of affairs, explores characters in the process of ongoing, but not random, change. Richard and Sarah seem to have achieved, at the outset, a fruitful balance between their complex and contrasting needs and desires. The afternoon-evening division between husband-wife and lover-mistress offers them both, at this point, excitement and contentment. Yet when Richard begins to worry about the length and frequency of the lover's visits, about the husband's consequently diminished value, and about the sameness of a pattern of behavior that has been in place for a while, it is clear that change is needed. We should note that although Sarah, too, is interested in preserving balance, she does not immediately resist change. For her, as for Richard, any current balance may be the basis for balanced extension, revision, and change. When Richard asks whether she thinks of her husband "going through balance sheets" (p. 53) at the office while she is with her lover, she finds this "a funny question" (p. 53) and points out that he has never asked her that before. But after two pauses, she responds by trying to fit the new question and subsequent discussion of it into their joint script. Her pauses, hesitations, and vaguenesses register the breaking of new ground.

> *Slight Pause*
>
> Sarah: Well, of course it occurs to me.
> Richard: Oh, it does?
> Sarah: Mmnn.
>
> *Slight Pause*
>
> Richard: What's your attitude to that, then?
> Sarah: It makes it all the more piquant.
> Richard: Does it really?
> Sarah: Of course.
> Richard: You mean while you're with him ... you actually have a picture of me, sitting at my desk going through balance sheets?
> Sarah: Only at ... certain times.
> Richard: Of course.
> Sarah: Not all the time.
> Richard: Well, naturally.
> Sarah: At particular moments.
> Richard: Mmnn. But, in fact, I'm not completely forgotten?
> Sarah: Not by any means.
> Richard: That's rather touching, I must admit.
>
> *Pause.*
>
> (Pp. 53–54)

This new issue makes possible a shift in the existing balance in the relationship by changing the way the two characters evaluate each other's roles, by changing the degree of explicitness with which they discuss them, and by thus bringing about the possibility of new roles. And any such change can, of course, be both threatening and appealing. Sarah, having sought to neutralize any threat by giving both of Richard's roles their due, has responded to the first issue, but she soon goes on to respond to the second by exploring the new possibilities offered her. If Richard now wishes to discuss her afternoons in more detail, she will respond by discussing his afternoons in more detail. *Together*, they will find out where this might lead.

> Richard: So you had a picture of me this afternoon, did you, sitting in my office?
> Sarah: I did, yes. It wasn't a terribly convincing one, though.
> Richard: Oh, why not?
> Sarah: Because I knew you weren't there. I knew you were with your mistress.
>
> *Pause.*
>
> (Pp. 54–55)

Discussion of Richard's mistress or whore then ensues, with startling results—for Sarah when she discovers how Richard views his afternoon relationship, and for Richard when he discovers how Sarah deals with two, newly explicit, bits of information: (a) that he is not at the office in the afternoon, and (b) that he is with a whore, not, as Sarah assumed in raising the issue, with a mistress.

What we must recognize here is the way in which Richard signals his desire for a change in the balance of the relationship (by beginning to talk more about Sarah's afternoons), and how Sarah willingly follows his lead and responds by beginning to talk of his afternoons; then we note how Richard, with new terrain available, begins to use it to promote further, not fully specified change. Sarah, initially willing to follow his lead, is puzzled and hurt by the novelty she confronts but keeps trying to find her appropriate new role in some new balance. To recognize the nature of, and to understand the importance of, this mode of interaction is to begin to understand the ways in which change is generated and controlled in the play. And we can begin to characterize the continuity of this interaction if we note the key line Richard uses to defend himself when Sarah objects to being regarded, in the afternoon, as a whore. He points out that she has been absolutely frank with him about her lover, and that "I must follow your example" (p. 56).

Like so many phrases in the play, this one, too, accumulates significance as its application ripples through the play. The notion of following an example is fundamental to the way in which the two characters balance their relationship, and, in balancing it, change it, and themselves. Richard's (and Max's) introduction of novelty to the relationship is by no means unusual, and Sarah's responses register both a willingness to consider what new balances will offer and a reluctance to lose what old balances have enabled. The major threads of continuity that run through the games are those guiding mutual interaction on the basis of example, reciprocal response, balance, new example, reciprocal response, new balance, and so on. The anxiety that change might involve more loss than gain is weighed against a hope that the reverse might be true, and against a fear that lengthy lack of change may undermine the value of a preceding balance. When Sarah fears that Max's new game will be more destructive than constructive, she slams the table (that visual emblem of balance in the play) and begs him to stop. But even as she does so, she acknowledges that his general mode of behavior, as distinct from its current manifestation, is something of which she fully approves.

> *She slams the table.*
>
> Sarah: Stop it! What's the matter with you? What's happened to you? (*Quietly.*) Please, please, stop it. What are you doing, playing a game?
> Max: A game? I don't play games.
> Sarah: Don't you? You do. Oh, you do. You do. Usually I like them.
>
> (P. 71)

Sarah likes new games and responds willingly to them. He offers a change, she seeks a new role within it, in the process developing the game further, to which he responds, and to which she responds, *until they work out together a new balance by following and developing each other's example.*

If we have, at times, been baffled by a play that offers states of affairs whose nature is not fully understood by either character, whose continuation involves tacit acceptance of, but incomplete knowledge of, game rules, whose origin is roughly but not precisely definable, and whose prime instigator is not easily located, we would do well to ponder the implications of interaction on the basis of example and extrapolation. If we wonder how Richard and Sarah could disagree over who initiated the "looking elsewhere" game that forms the basis of the play's initial balance, we might well note, in general, the process by which the action of the play proceeds, and, in particular, the process by which the final balance of the play comes about. Who, we might ask, starts and controls the new game that imports bongo drum and "whispering time" (p. 83) from the afternoon into the evening?

Richard, we should note, has been registering the need for change throughout the play. In his concern to preserve differences as a resource for the relationship, he has increasingly insisted on *contrast* between afternoon and evening roles. He has sought to resist the possibility of fusion, and the elimination of stimulating difference that Sarah's interest in *complementarity* offers. Sarah's mixing of costumes, her increased and extended encounters with her lover, and her inability thus to carry out her "wifely duties" (p. 76) have all contributed to Richard's determination to insist upon what he regards as valued differences. The sudden characterization of Sarah as a whore is a tactical move in this direction, as are the several indications of jealousy, and of responsibility to spouses and children, and the concern for boniness versus plumpness in women. But we would be wrong to see these solely as tactical or solely as part of a preconceived design to bring about some fully thought through new balance. They are partly gestures in new directions and partly responses to Sarah's failures to maintain what is for him an appropriate balance. Her actions are likewise reactions to his actions. And what happens when the old balance is upset is that all sorts of previously balanced conflicting forces become unbalanced and, therefore, sources of concern.

The issues raised by both characters are, thus, never solely tactical. Richard's interests in a wife, a mistress, and a whore are both tactical and substantive, as are his needs for a slim woman and for "enormous women. Like bullocks with udders. Vast great uddered bullocks" (p. 72). So also are his concerns for fidelity and infidelity, for sexual variety and sexual decorum, for individual freedom and marital and public responsibility. Sarah's resistance to change, her concern for continuity, and her willingness to change are likewise tactical and substantive. Thus, at a point of acute anger, she projects one alternative game that might redistribute her conflicting concerns—she announces that there are other lovers she entertains whom neither Richard nor Max knows. Her reactions to the suggestive milkman suffice to put this in doubt as an already existing game, but it offers a threat for the future. Once out of balance, the characters' conflicting needs and desires change from sources of mutually balanced benefit to forces that threaten the very existence of the relationship—an observation that goes a long way toward establishing the role of game-playing in their lives. We have no direct access to the origin of these games, however, and the most we can do is extrapolate from the way in which games emerge from interaction during the play. A new balance is clearly needed to harness these dangerous forces once more, and a new balance emerges from action and interaction, from example and response, from replication and extension of new initiatives on either side.

It is thus very difficult to establish who begins any new game, and this is exhibited in the emergence of a new game at the end of the play. Richard, we might wish to argue, initiates the change that brings about the new balance, but it is in response to Sarah's behavior in terms of the old one. Richard calls his wife, for the first time, "adulteress" (p. 80), brings the bongo drum from the hall cupboard in the evening, starts to imitate (follow the example of) Sarah's and her lover's behavior in the afternoons ("How does he use it?", "What do you do with it?" [p. 81]), and moves into the afternoon script of entrapment in the park-keeper's hut. Sarah, in anguish, fearing loss of what the old balance enabled, resists desperately for a while, but confronted by Richard's insistence, *she follows his example, moves into the afternoon game, but begins to extend and revise it as she does so.* In a key formulation for the process of interaction of the play, she responds to his instigation of change by taking it over and making it her own: "I'll explain," she says, and checking his reactions, begins to enunciate the new script and assign appropriate costumes for them both. And as she does so, she crawls under the table, following his earlier example, and extending it, in the process of instituting, in this central location, a new and necessary balance:

Sarah: I'm trapped.
        Pause.
    What will my husband say?
        Pause.
    He expects me. He's waiting. I can't get out. I'm trapped. You've no right to treat a married woman like this. Have you? Think, think, think of what you're doing.
    She looks at him, bends and begins to crawl under the table towards him. She emerges from under the table and kneels at his feet, looking up. Her hand goes up his leg. He is looking down at her.
    You're very forward. You really are. Oh, you really are. But my husband will understand. My husband does understand. Come here. Come down here. I'll explain. After all, think of my marriage. He adores me. Come here and I'll whisper to you. I'll whisper it. It's whispering time. Isn't it?
    She takes his hands. He sinks to his knees, with her. They are kneeling together, close. She strokes his face.
    It's a very late tea. Isn't it? But I think I like it. Aren't you sweet? I've never seen you before after sunset. My husband's at a late-night conference. Yes, you look different. Why are you wearing this strange suit, and this tie? You usually wear something else, don't you? Take off your jacket. Mmmnn? Would you like me to

> change? Would you like me to change my clothes? I'll change for
> you, darling. Shall I? Would you like that?
> > *Silence. She is very close to him.*
> Richard: Yes.
> > *Pause.*
> Change.
> > *Pause.*
> Change.
> > *Pause.*
> Change your clothes.
> > *Pause.*
> You lovely whore.
> > *They are still, kneeling,*
> > *she leaning over him.*

(Pp. 83–84)

Richard, we might wish to say, signals the need for change and initiates it, but
Sarah guides it and gives it its script, its costume, and its relationship to previous games. This game, like the others, evolves from their joint action and
interaction; it is, in part, a product of design and, in part, the result of discovery. The characters' contrasting interest and needs, their contrasting attitudes
toward continuity and change, and their contrasting physical, psychological,
and emotional histories generate and regenerate periods of fixity and periods
of change—two elements that themselves manifest contrasting needs that require balanced representation in the relationship.

It is thus impossible to establish definitively whose game the new game is,
who began it, or even exactly what it is and when it began. This lack of exact
information does not, however, prevent the games from functioning successfully. These notions of exactness derive from a critical vocabulary designed to
deal with fixed states of affairs, temporarily interrupted perhaps, but subsequently restored in some new definitive form. They anticipate a kind of fixity
and a kind of explicitness that are not to be found in a Pinter play. Richard
and Sarah's concluding relationship emerges by a process of interaction from
their earlier relationship. The concluding relationship, like the earlier relationship, is one of the temporarily balanced, but not clearly enunciated,
forces, deriving from the ongoing needs and desires of two people who
mutually, but incompletely and inconclusively, define each other. They move
from one working balance to another, discovering, in the process, more about
what they might be and what they might become.

As the couple's interaction repeatedly indicates, and as the final scene
confirms, the characters are neither wholly fixed nor wholly free. Neither
their point of departure nor their point of arrival is a matter of free choice or
explicit calculation. They begin from where their last negotiated balance left
them, and they end up where new modes of interaction lead. Sarah cannot
establish a fully continuous nonrole relationship no matter how insistent her
use of pronouns. Richard cannot have one woman who is simultaneously
fat and thin. His twice-repeated appeal for generalized change narrows to a

request for a change of clothes. The phrase "lovely whore" announces a new emotional balance that must exist without extreme physical correlates, a balance that must temporarily accommodate both characters' needs for complementarity and contrast. Physical, psychological, emotional, and social constraints remain integral parts of a relationship that takes constraints, differences, and difficulties and balances and rebalances them against needs, desires, wishes, and fantasies. Richard and Sarah are neither fixed nor random in their behavior. As Strindberg's reformed notion of character would suggest, they are ever in the process of coming into being[7]—not freely, but via the context and constraints of their own pasts. They exhibit not fixity and unity as characters, but differing degrees and differing kinds of flexibility and continuity. Though each has a history, neither registers a desire to be defined solely by it, or to cling tenaciously to it. Their lives and actions, up to any point of balance, offer a place to start from, rather than a final destination. The same can be said of any new balance achieved between them. For Richard and Sarah, change and variety are every bit as important as fixity and conformity. But, as their whole mode of interaction repeatedly exemplifies, they would not wish to choose only one in preference to the other. Rather, they would seek, as they have sought, an appropriate balance, for a little while, before reaching toward another.

To recognize the importance of change in *The Lover,* and the consequences it has for modes of fixity, kinds of explicitness, complexity of motivation, and modes of character interaction is to locate a necessary context for coming to terms with the puzzling nature of so many Pinter plays. Again and again we will find ourselves in difficulty if we prematurely attribute fixed motivation to characters who are exploring themselves as they explore the possibilities that situations make available to them. It we attribute to them clearer goals, more rigid selfhood, and more detailed understanding than their words and actions display, we are in danger of imposing upon them, and upon the plays, generic expectations that are at best inappropriate and, at worst, seriously misleading. But we would also be wrong to conclude that, if Pinter's plays offer such fluidity, they are thus beyond interpretation and comprehension. Nothing could be further from the truth. As the preceding discussion of *The Lover* indicates, modes of interpretation focusing on continuities and changes provide enlightening access to the plays. Novelty of generic structure offers us not incomprehension, but new forms of comprehension, new grounds for new kinds of access to knowledge of ourselves, and of our worlds.

In his subsequent work, Pinter goes on to explore further implications of his earlier work. Like the characters in *The Lover,* he uses earlier points of balance as points of departure, bases for subsequent extrapolation and exploration. When we encounter in his later work a more explicit concern for time and for memory than is visible in his earlier work, we would do well to keep in mind the concern for change, for exploration, and for discovery in relationships that characterizes his early work. The issues of fixity and change on the one hand, and of time and memory on the other, are intimately related and mutually explanatory. *The Lover,* like so many Pinter plays, exemplifies the processes by which characters and relationships may grow and decline. We see enacted before us not just the illustration of preexisting fixity, but the modes of interaction by means of which change is pursued and controlled in relationships and by means of which new balances emerge from old ones. In this play the balance is sought as a basis for mutual satisfaction. Elsewhere, it is often imposed as part of, or as a result of, a battle for control. In either case, we must look for continuity rather than unity in characters whose lives are on the move, and we must note carefully the degrees of design and discovery in their motivations and achievements; only in this context will we find appropriate modes of access to the processes by which the characters encounter and control stability and change in themselves, in their relationships, and in the worlds that surround them.

Notes

1. Steven H. Gale provides a useful summary of criticism addressed to the play in *Butter's Going Up: A Critical Analysis of Harold Pinter's Work* (Durham, N.C.: Duke University Press, 1977), pp. 135–36. His study of the play is also valuable, for it notes the importance of links between questions, balance, and change in the play.

2. In an illuminating essay on Pinter's work, Thomas F. Van Laan draws attention to the dangers critics face when they read too much of a conventional kind into the hints the plays offer of a narrative sequence. He suggests that we quickly slide from legitimate inferences to unpersuasive inventions when we seek to align Pinter's plays with more conventional plays. In critical practice, this amounts to filling in narrative gaps that are meant to be experienced as gaps. Van Laan underestimates, to some extent, the degree to which audience understanding in general, and literary interpretation in particular, involve the making of connections between, and the locating of thematic patterns among, distinct textural elements. But his two main points—that we can overread plays by inventing rather than inferring connections, and that to do so with a Pinter play is to eradicate one of its distinctive and important features—seem to me entirely right. The critic's task is to achieve the appropriate generic balance between inferential connection and functional discontinuity. See Thomas F. Van Laan, *"The Dumb Waiter:* Pinter's Play with the Audience," *Modern Drama* 24 (December 1981): 494–502.

3. In his Preface to *Miss Julie,* August Strindberg argues for "multiplicity of motives," and thus for "characterless" characters. The term "character," he notes, "became the middle-class term for an automaton, one whose nature had become fixed or who had adapted himself to a particular role in life. In fact a person who had ceased to grow was called a character, while one continuing to develop ... was called characterless, in a derogatory sense, of course, because he was so hard to catch, classify, and keep track of. [Onstage] a character came to signify a man fixed and finished: one who invariably appeared either drunk or jocular or melancholy, and characterization required nothing more than a physical defect such as a club-foot, a wooden leg, a red nose; or the fellow might be made to repeat some such phrase as: 'That's capital!' or: 'Barkis is willin'!'... Because they are modern characters, living in a period of transition more feverishly hysterical than its predecessors at least, I have drawn my figures vacillating, disintegrated, a blend of old and new." From Strindberg, Preface to *Miss Julie,* in *Six Plays of Strindberg,* trans. Elizabeth Sprigge (New York: Doubleday, 1955), pp. 64–65.

4. All page references are to Harold Pinter's *The Lover,* in *"The Collection" and "The Lover"* (London: Methuen, 1966).

5. Throughout, I use the word "game," as the play does, to designate a means of organizing reality, not a means of avoiding it.

6. This aspect of her behavior is exemplified in the scene with the milkman in which Sarah, dressed in her "mistress" costume, rejects the milkman's suggestive remarks and behaves as if she were wearing her demure, wifely dress.

7. Walter Kerr draws attention to the importance of this feature of the play, but unfortunately, he seeks to interpret it in terms of Jean-Paul Sartre's theories of existentialism. The notion that existence precedes essence can confuse the very issues it is meant to clarify. Frank Lentricchia suggests some of the problems with Sartre's approach in his *After the New Criticism* (Chicago: University of Chicago Press, 1980), pp. 44–53. Kerr, too quick to move away from the details of the play to those of the theory, fails to make the most of his own perceptions. See Walter Kerr, *Harold Pinter* (New York: Columbia University Press, 1968), pp. 31–32.

8

Intended Audience Response, *The Homecoming,* and the "Ironic Mode of Identification"

CHRISTOPHER C. HUDGINS

Harold Pinter's *The Homecoming* has elicited some surprisingly negative critical responses. One critic feels so "soiled" by the play that he calls it "pornographic," adding that "to suspend disbelief in this play is to call a temporary halt to one's humanity." Another concludes that Pinter's irony in this play leads to "vile and irresponsible art." At the same time, many critics have praised *The Homecoming* as a brilliant play, and it remains the most popular work in the canon. In his recent book, Steven Gale calls it Pinter's "most representative, his best, and his most important drama."[1] Such bizzarely different critical responses to *The Homecoming* reflect the range of responses in a typical audience. We have not really grappled with this problem of audience response in dramatic criticism, but several reader-response theorists provide viable frameworks for the beginnings of such analysis.

The theories grouped under this broad heading vary greatly, on the one extreme emphasizing an almost complete subjectivity of reader response and on the other the control the work exerts over the reader as a "class." Those in the attractive middle ground emphasize the interdependence of the reader's subjective response and the work itself. All of the reader-response theorists, however, reject the New Critics' "affective fallacy," and many reject the "intentionally fallacy" as well.[2]

I find two theories of reader response particularly valuable for understanding contemporary theater in general and Pinter's work in particular. In "The Writer's Audience Is Always a Fiction," Walter J. Ong argues that the effective writer always imagines the particular audience for which he or she is writing. He maintains that the artist includes "implicit signals" in the work to let the audience know what role to play; the audience, in turn, must attempt to make itself correspond to the role that the author dictates for it. I understand such "implicit signals" to serve as indexes of intended response. Ong's first example of such an index is Hemingway's use of the definite article or demonstrative pronoun "that," which Ong argues casts the reader "in the role of a close companion of the writer," one who shares a great deal of his knowledge or memories. That is, "*the* man" as opposed to "*a* man" assumes, or forces, a degree of shared experience that, in Hemingway's hands, encourages "high self-esteem" in the reader.[3] Pinter, as we shall see, fictionalizes for himself a different audience; at least at first, his characters are always "*a* man" or "*a* woman," unknown, distant, and not in the least encouraging of high self-esteem in members of the audience.

In "Literary History as a Challenge to Literary Theory," Hans Robert Jauss clarifies the effect of this dynamic. He suggests that much of modern literature refuses to make direct moral statements; such refusal both "distances" the reader or audience and forces the audience to question its perception by presenting it "with an opaque reality which can no longer be understood from the previous horizons of expectations."[4] For example, the reader of Gustave Flaubert's *Madame Bovary* is forced "into an alienating insecurity" and "in the face of a still meaningless reality, must himself find the question which will enable him to discover the perception of the world and the interpersonal problem to which the work's answer is directed" (pp. 35, 37). In effect, playing the role the author dictates for it, the audience must create meaning in response to subtle indicators in the text.

Calling for a "receptional aesthetic" in "Levels of Identification of Hero and Audience," Jauss suggests that aesthetic distance and identification are not mutually exclusive. In other words, "alienating insecurity" in the face of a work going beyond the contemporary audience's horizons of expectations, as in *Madame Bovary*, or *The Homecoming,* does not prohibit identification. Jauss suggests that "it is precisely in such (emotional) identification, and not in detached aesthetic reflectiveness, that the transformation of aesthetic experience into ... communicative action is accomplished."[5] Identification with a character in a work distanced by its violation of convention or by its refusal of direct thematic statement depends on the willingness of the spectator to broaden the basis of his or her identification; this requires a difficult recognition of the similarity of his or her own life to the lives of the apparently strange characters he or she observes on stage. For the work to "make sense" the audience must infer some basis of comparison, some similarity between itself and the characters it observes. Because such works are ambiguous, subtle, and complex, however, the spectator *can* refuse identification and thereby neutralize the work ethically (p. 289).

Jauss's fifth mode of identification, "ironic identification with the hero," most aptly describes the response Pinter's works intend. The artist uses this mode to undermine the purely aesthetic, reflective response of the audience, on the one hand, and to prevent mere pleasurable identification on the other. Such a procedure *can* result in an emotional communication of an idea in violation of the norm. Jauss writes, "by 'ironic identification' we mean a level of aesthetic reception upon which an identification that the reader would otherwise have expected is denied him in order to jolt him out of his undisturbed attentiveness to the aesthetic object and to direct his awakened reflection toward the conditions of illusion and the possibilities of interpretation; this can lead to a situation where the aesthetic disposition as such, by means of its negation,... is called into question." Thus the ironic mode of identification can achieve "the liberation ... of the receptive consciousness" through what might be described as a shock effect dependent on the violation of convention or expectations (p. 313). The aesthetic distance can finally lead to a norm-breaking emotional identification even with characters who at first glance seem grotesque. The technique depends on a "positivization of the negative," through which the audience should recognize that the portrayal of a seemingly atypical character as a negative figure shows the ridiculousness of what is actually the ruling norm from the artist's perspective (p. 313). The unintended response to works dependent on the ironic mode of identification is horror, boredom, or indifference. The "disturbed reader or observer ... regard(s) his denied identification as an enjoyable scandal," and his laughter "degenerates into mere derision" that avoids both recognition and the possibility of communication (pp. 316, 313). In effect, Jauss here describes the extremes of audience response to a Pinter play.

From Jauss's perspective, then, a work that provides no direct statement of a theme or a moral norm *can* produce a change in morality, or attitude, or philosophy *because* of its refusal to give the audience anything pleasant to identify with. Jauss notes that such an intended response initially depends on the spectator's ability to "lift himself out of the immediacy of identification onto a level of critical reflection concerning what is presented" (pp. 310–11). I term this combination of responses an *intellectual identification,* dependent first on thoughtful and then on emotional responses to *indexes* in the text. For Jauss, the audience, the "acting subject must first become a spectator, listener, viewer, or reader in order to achieve that attitude of disinterested approval which enables him to reify the object of aesthetic awareness and so allows him to identify himself with what is being presented, or with the hero" (p. 286). Such identification, in turn, produces a "negative thematic statement": it frees the audience to respond positively to a negative example newly recognized as typical or normative. The opposite of such an intended response simply allows the spectator to deride the figures on stage.

I am suggesting that Pinter "fictionalizes" for himself audiences willing to struggle to recognize themselves in his plays, in his "negative examples," and to condemn much of their own behavior as they do so. This response involves both an intellectual or creative response to indexes in the play and an emotional, potentially painful identification that allows that intellectual response to go beyond the "purely aesthetic," to communicate an idea in violation of the norm—broadly, that we are like the characters on the stage and should struggle, creatively, to change both our perspective and our behavior. Clearly, many elements of such a response are subjective, dependent on what the audience brings to the play, but there are broad limits of authorial intent that we can determine and that help us understand the play more fully. As Jauss notes, the question of subjectivity of different readers can only be asked after understanding which "transsubjective horizon of understanding determines the impact of the text" ("Challenge," p. 13).[6]

Pinter has made several revealing statements about his attitudes toward audience response. In an interview with Mel Gussow he notes that "What is required is an act of concentration and (audiences) so rarely seem disposed to give it."[7] Purely intellectual responses, however, are not adequate from Pinter's perspective because they refuse emotional identification or even recognition; by calling everything a symbol, he says, "it is easy to put up a pretty efficient smoke screen, on the part of the critics or the audience, against recognition, against an active and willing participation ... a character become symbol, can be talked about but need not be lived with."[8] To "live with" a Pinter character requires both a careful, intellectual questioning and a subsequent recognition of self in that character. The unitended response to Pinter's negative examples embodies a continuing distancing of that character or an "easy jollification" at the character's expense:

where the comic and the tragic (for want of a better word) are closely interwoven, certain members of an audience will always give emphasis to the comic as opposed to the other, for by so doing they rationalize the other out of existence.... Where ... this indiscriminate mirth is found, I feel it represents a cheerful patronage of the character on the part of the merrymakers, and thus participation is avoided. This laughter is in fact a mode of precaution, a smoke screen, a refusal to accept what is happening as recognizable (which I think it is).[9]

Pinter attempts to produce such recognition at first with a series of indexes that often function as distancing devices, "making the familiar strange," as Brecht would have it, and thus forcing the audience to question the "opaque" reality he presents. In a 1968 interview, Pinter commented that "A theatrical offering should impose a focus on what the audience must give attention to—the 'close-up' on stage is achieved by word and (dramatic) action."[10] These focal points must finally be seen as part of the larger whole. In reply to a letter deploring Pinter's failure to include a moral standpoint in his work, Pinter wrote: "I do not sit in a cozy didactic corner in *one* room speaking through a loudspeaker. My pre-occupation is not a cozy corner. It is the house."[11] The comment suggests that the audience must synthesize these focal points, often in retrospect. As Pinter says in the Gussow interview, he does not believe that the playwright can teach anything directly because of the arrogance involved in such a stance.[12] What the audience learns from a Pinter play, then, depends on the audience's creative inferences gleaned from the focal indexes of intended response; the distanced, intellectual attention the plays require should gradually lead to the emotional identification Pinter's vision of participation implies.

Several of Pinter's comments point to this specific intent in *The Homecoming*. In a *Saturday Review* article, Henry Hewes quotes Pinter as saying that this family is not evil, but slightly desperate. "At the end of the play," Pinter adds, "Ruth is in possession of a certain kind of freedom. She can do what she wants, and it is not at all certain that she will go off to Greek St. [and become a whore]."[13] By implication, Ruth's limited freedom results from her perfectly justified revolt against her desperate family's attempts to control her. As Pinter comments, the violence in his work "is really only an expression of the question of dominance and subservience," which is a response to a constant "threat." In turn, that threat "has got to do with this question of being in the uppermost position or attempting to be .... It's a very common, everyday thing."[14] Thus the characters on Pinter's stage, from his perspective, reflect behavior with which members of the audience should be able to identify on various levels, illuminating their own reality as they do so.

The intended audience recognition that such dominance-subservience relationships are "common," even within a "loving" family, entails a marked departure from "normative" perspectives. Pinter "fictionalizes" for himself an audience that should also recognize the source or motivation for such behavior, an even more difficult and disturbing task. His comments and the canon itself reveal that he sees such motivation as based in the refusal to be known or to know oneself and the refusal to deal with the reality of death. The famous line that language is "a strategem to cover nakedness" necessitated by the "fear of disclosing the poverty within the self" points toward one element of that intended recognition.[15] The earlier, less subtle works in the canon also reveal the fear of knowing the self in all its complexity and the fear of death as central motivating factors for this type of behavior. In both the early poems and in *The Dwarfs*, a play based on his early unpublished novel, Pinter further suggests that such a recognition of negative examples and motivations can produce a positive result. Though more subtly presented and richly varied, Pinter's broad themes remain similar in the mature work. Our understanding of the earlier work, then, helps us understand the dynamic of intended response, of the "intellectual identification," the latter works require.

In *The Dwarfs*, Len argues that we substitute simplistic identities based on possession, on dominance, or subservience, because we fear to confront the complexity of ourselves, including our more unsavory sides. Though Len finally fails in his attempt to deal with his multisided identity, his many "reflections," Pinter's poems suggest that such confrontation is healthy, while refusal of confrontation is "killing," producing a sterility or "a poverty" of the self; much of the poetry also emphasizes that our refusal to see fully our reality or ourselves is based in a fear of death. "You in the Night" (1952), for example, suggests that the reader should strive for the courage to confront that fear and that such confrontation can produce a limited but passionate freedom.[16] The poem directly addresses the reader and asks him or her to confront even the painful portions of experience fully. The "you" in the title emphasizes that Pinter intends his audience, in its own "night," to identify with other "trapped" characters. He tells his reader that he or she "should hear/The thunder and the walking air," "shall bear/Where mastering weathers are." The images suggest that much of human experience is painful. However, the awareness that "honoured hope/Shall fail upon the slate," itself "Break(s) the winter down/That clamours at your feet." Though "enamouring altars," or religious escapes, are tempting, the poet nevertheless urges "you'll tread the tightrope." By implication, even the absurdist freedom and passion for the present that the awareness of death, of ultimate hopelessness, can produce should not be looked upon as certain or as saving; the poem suggests that the reader must be aware of temptations toward exaltation as well as toward despair, and must attempt to walk the tightrope between the two, conscious of both but yielding to neither. Broadly, this is the positive response Pinter intends his audience to create when confronted with the more subtle mature work.

"The Error of Alarm" (1956; *Poems,* p. 15), reveals much about the less obvious authorial intent in *The Homecoming*. It beings, " *A woman speaks*"; thinking about intercourse, she has felt a "pulse in the dark" that she could not stop and that results in "The error of alarm." These are subtle reactions; she cannot summon a witness to the "bargain," the implicit agreement between herself and her lover or husband. Describing the basis of such a bargain, though, she says, "If my thigh approve him/I am the sum of his dread." She understands that the male fears that she controls him if she gets more pleasure from the experience than he does. She recognizes that any such feminine threat produces an aggressive, controlling response on the man's part. Summarizing her lover's idea of a good "bargain," she suggests that he wants the woman to "cajole" him, to coax him with false words, to flatter him, and he wants her mouth to "allay him," to put fears to rest. Only then will she be "his proper bride." The woman yields to his desire. As a result, she "die(s) the dear ritual/And he is my bier." This is a metaphorical suicide, growing out of the fear of confronting experience fully. The "error" or "fault of alarm" lies in the woman's yielding despite her recognition of the "killing" masculine conception of her identity as merely that through which to solidify his own. She should not be "alarmed" at this situation between the sexes, submitting to his control out of her own fear, but should confront it, and should refuse to "die." Pinter's labeling this woman's behavior erroneous suggests that he intends his audience to recognize that Ruth's refusal of the same "error" in *The Homecoming* embodies a courageous revolt.

Armed with both authorial comment and clearer, less subtle thematic statements from the earlier work, we can more easily recognize the process through which indexes to intended response in *The Homecoming* first cast the audience in the role of attentive questioners; those indexes gradually point to an intellectual and emotional recognition of the aggressive nature of love and the sources and results of such aggression. One of the most important of these indexes is Pinter's brilliant, if atypical, use of exposition. As Pinter comments, "The explicit form which is so often taken in twentieth-century drama is ... cheating. The playwright assumes that we have a great deal of information about all his characters, who explain themselves to the audience.... When the curtain goes up on one of my plays, you are faced with a situation, a particular situation, two people sitting in a room, which hasn't happened before, and is just happening at this moment, and we know no more about them than I know about you, sitting at this table."[17]

Despite Pinter's refusal to "cheat" by revealing character in an artificial way, the first scenes in *The Homecoming* do serve as exposition for the family dynamic. While his rejection of traditional exposition embodies an uncompromising realism on one level, its effect is to make us question the characters' seemingly strange behavior. Pinter's realism entails a subtly patterned mimesis; the audience's initial bewilderment is meant to force it to pay close attention to that patterning, which should produce an understanding that all of these characters are playing the power-control game Peter Hall calls "taking the piss." The cockney phrase describes the mockery Hall understands as central to the play; a character is uncertain of whether or not he is being mocked and consequently must "take the piss." The family plays the game in pursuit of a coolness, a lack of vulnerability, which is their only defense other than mounting their own offense, a tactic often too dangerous.[18] In the first scene, for example, Lenny's mocking banter with Sam as he comes in, tired from driving his "limo," is typical. Sam's only retort is to remain calm, to pretend not to see the mockery.[19] The exchange should serve as an index of intended response, should prepare the audience to recognize the same attempt to keep cool, to deny the mocker the satisfaction of an openly hostile reply, that characterizes Teddy's response to the family's more intensely hostile mockery of his profession and of his relationship with Ruth. This first scene allows us to understand and to recognize as not uncommon the more horrifying game that Teddy and the family play later in the work.

When Ruth and Teddy enter, we have no idea who they are, no conventional exposition. The second scene nonetheless provides indexes of intended response that allow us to understand the nature of Ruth and Teddy's relationship. For example, soon after their entrance, Ruth replies to Teddy's supposedly concerned question that she *is* a little tired. Within two pages of dialogue, she has denied that she is tired and then decided to take a walk (pp. 21–23). The inconsistency, in conjunction with repetition, focuses our attention on a pattern of power-control behavior similar to that we have just observed in the first scene, but more subtly manifested. Here Pinter depicts a husband's condescending attempt to control his wife, to tell her what's good for her, even when to go to bed. Ruth puts up with this until it becomes unbearable, at which point she revolts, with calm forcefulness. Teddy is unable to dissuade her and, like a miserable child, goes to the window, watching, chewing his knuckles. Significantly, Ruth assures him that she *is* coming back. Though comic, the line suggests the dissatisfactory nature of the relationship and reflects the subtle control and aggression that make it so.

The scene establishes the pattern of Ruth's action throughout the play and mirrors a depressingly familiar relationship that the audience should gradually be able to recognize.

Pinter's failure to provide traditional exposition also focuses the questioning audience's attention on Teddy's attitude toward the house. Immediately following the blackout after Max's line, "I remember my father," Teddy suddenly appears at the threshold with Ruth and suitcases. The blackout emphasizes Max's line, which serves as an index of intended response to the following scene, almost as a label. Tossing the key in his hand, Teddy says, "Well, the key worked. *Pause.* They haven't changed the lock" (pp. 19–20). Our lack of knowledge forces us to ask why he left in the first place, where he has been, and, more important, why he has come back. Prefaced by Max's line, Teddy's attitude toward the house emerges as characterized by a deep nostalgia, a yearning for a return of the stability and security of an imagined childhood peace. Like Mark in *The Dwarfs*, who wishes to define himself, his identity, in terms of his room, Teddy wants to have faith that that key opens the door into a refuge, a place safe from disorienting threats. Other factors clearly motivate his return, too; a desire to flaunt his success and his wife before his family is certainly one of these. But Teddy's homecoming, his search for security, like Max's nostalgic memory, simply does not work, for even this early in the play, everything has clearly changed. Lenny has moved downstairs from his childhood bedroom, and his friends frequently invade Teddy's empty room; Teddy's leave-taking itself has changed the house.

Similarly, the lack of traditional exposition focuses our attention on another central question—or distances the ensuing action: why does the family attack Teddy so violently? Lenny's long speech mockingly praising Teddy's success in America includes further indexes of intended response. That Ruth is upstairs with Joey during this speech makes it doubly ironic. In the first place, the family does resent just the success that Lenny tells Teddy they admire. Teddy's pathetic refusal to respond to Lenny's questions about belief in God has previously characterized that success as completely sterile (pp. 51–52). Nonetheless, the family resents Teddy's superior, condescending attitude; they also resent Teddy's having left the home in the first place, for his departure questions the validity of their own ego defenses. In response to this threat, Lenny paints a picture of that secure family life Teddy has missed. This nostalgic picture focuses our attention by its inconsistency with what we have observed. "We live a closer life," he says, and suggests that all are happy with their occupations and pastimes, even that Max's cooking is excellent. He adds, "we do make up a unit, Teddy, and you're an integral part of it." And so, concludes Lenny, we expect a "bit of grace,... a bit of generosity of mind, a bit of liberality of spirit, to reassure us" when you do come back. He implies that they have not gotten it (pp. 64–65).

"Reassure" is a strange word in this context and as such serves as an index of intended response—"a reassurance of what?" should be the question the audience asks itself. The "answer" intended is that the family simply wants some reassurance that its security, which Teddy had questioned by leaving, is based on firm ground, some admission that he has missed them, that he has been wrong to leave. Instead, Teddy sneaks into the house in the middle of the night, completely unexpected, and behaves with cool distance and superiority. Like so many other Pinter invaders, he threatens a false security. Thus, the family, in order to protect its own vision of such security, to "*reassure*" itself, must "get" Teddy, primarily through attacking his "new" wife. They are almost as surprised as we when she purposefully appears to yield to the attack. The basic situation, the prosperous son returning to his less successful kin, is indeed a common, recognizable, everyday occurrence, distanced by exaggeration. And gradually the audience should be able to identify with such characters.

Pinter's depiction of his characters in *The Homecoming* as fluid, shifting personalities embodies another index of intended response. As the process of ironic identification continues, we should both recognize that all of us have many "reflections," as Len suggests in *The Dwarfs,* and question the motivation for these particular characters' sudden shifts or changes. Teddy, at first, is apparently a warm, loving, concerned, and somewhat childish husband; during the course of the play, he is revealed as vengeful, elitist, condescending, and impotent. Lenny appears first as a bitterly angry young man; other reflections of his personality include the bright, vital questioner, the pimp who sees himself as the violent oppressor of women, the weak and insecure sexual aggressor, the affectionate son and family member, and the businessman, attempting to be hard-nosed and failing. Max shifts back and forth between the aggressive and dissatisfied old man, the warm father, the hostile father, and the kindly grandfather. Finally, Ruth is the cold somewhat unsympathetic wife, the aggressive, sexual woman, the warm domestic wife, the sexually compliant female, apparently yielding herself up to male visions of dominance, the loving, comforting mother, and the competent businesswoman. Reductions of Ruth's roles to mother-wife-whore are far too simplistic.

Such rapidly shifting patterns of behavior do not make sense, at first, to most members of an audience. The consequent "opaqueness" of the reality with which they are presented forces a questioning of the interpretive possibilities of the play. And for the questioning audience, Pinter almost always points to specific motivation for such shifts. Ruth's shifts from one role to another, for example, are usually prompted by masculine aggression. Both Lenny's and Teddy's attempts to dominate her early in the play prompt a revolt, as do similar attempts later on. In like manner, the men's sudden shifts frequently represent responses to attempts at domination or control, or to actions that deflate their egos. Max's apparently baffling shift at the beginning of act 2 is typical. Describing an idyllic past with Jessie and the boys, Max almost glows with pleasure; Ruth interrupts and asks him about his association with the group of butchers that he had hoped would provide more luxuries for Jessie. He replies that they "turned out to be a bunch of criminals like everyone else," goes on to complain about the cigar he has previously praised, and ends with a vicious attack on Sam (pp. 45–48).

In context, the incident serves as an index to intended response, a "jolting" questioning that should produce a recognition of the relationship between shifting identity, aggression, and the insecurity that causes it. In the previous scene, Max has accepted Ruth as his daughter-in-law, and Teddy as his son, because they have produced grandchildren. Here he nostalgically reminisces about his past to solidify his identity, to boast of his own prowess as reflected in his ability to care for a wife and family. Ruth's question reminds Max of his failure at such endeavors, which in turn amplifies his insecurity, producing his alternate vision of the generations as "one cast iron bunch of crap after another." In effect, Ruth's comment destroys his momentary vision of potency and security. Max's renewed insecurity necessitates the aggressive behavior, the attack on Sam. Both the nostalgic memory and the aggressive attack represent escapist attempts to avoid any confrontation with that insecurity.

Such escapes take various forms in *The Homecoming*. The struggle to possess Ruth, the lying, bragging memories, the visions of religion ridiculed by Lenny's banter, all emerge as attempts to solidify the self, to gain security. Several indicators of intended response to such a dynamic of escapist behavior reside in Teddy's long speech about maintaining intellectual equilibrium (pp. 61–62). The statement's tone of desperate seriousness focuses our attention; it is provoked by Ruth's encounters with Lenny on the dance floor and Joey on the couch, her revolt from Teddy's identity-defining or self-defining control or possession. Mocking Teddy's intellectuality, Ruth asks if he has sent his family any of his critical works. Teddy replies defensively that his family "wouldn't understand my works" because its members cannot achieve "intellectual equilibrium." The sudden blackout at the conclusion of this speech, its content, and its rhythm are all indexes to intended response. At first Teddy's language is forceful, as without hesitation he begins to describe his concept of intellectual equilibrium. At his most cogent, he suggests that living correctly necessitates allying or balancing distance and involvement with one's environment, operating "on" things *and* operating "in" things. But Teddy cannot balance the two; he always tries to operate *on* things; he desperately struggles to maintain objectivity as he utters this speech. Teddy *first* says "It's a question of how far you can operate on things and not in things"; almost as if correcting himself, he then adds that it is necessary to balance the two. And then, in increasingly jerky, fragmented statements, he returns to the speech's primary emphasis, his need to operate objectively, to remain uninvolved. Here it is Ruth's betrayal that Teddy cannot deal with emotionally. "You're just objects," says Teddy, "that I observe." Ironically, his final line subtextually damns his own actions: "You won't get me being ... I won't be lost in it."

On one level, this line is simply a statement that Teddy begins in one way and concludes in another. He decides on the more formal "I won't be lost in

it" rather than "*You* won't get me being lost in it" (my italics), subtly emphasizing that his family has not effected his condition. But "You won't get me
being ..." also puns on "being" as an existential word, subtextually suggesting that Teddy will never be caught "living." His refusal of subjectivity, of
involvement, destroys any possibility of life. The shift to "I won't be lost in
it," humorously, or at least ironically, followed by the blackout, suggests that
it is just this attempt at an escapist objectivity that destroys Teddy, that makes
him more lost than the at least vital, active people he tries to regard as objects. Pinter depicts Teddy as a negative example, but intends a recognition,
an identification, and a positive response. As audience members, we have
perhaps been watching these characters as objects, or, more broadly, been
guilty of assuming this perspective outside the theater, refusing subjective,
emotional involvement as an escape from our reality. Teddy briefly advocates
a more healthful balance between objectivity and subjectivity, but ironically
cannot achieve it and is even unaware of his failure. The audience is intended
to identify with or recognize such failure, which necessitates both a refusal of
escapist, objective "certainty" and a willingness to change.

The most pervasive index to such an intended positive response to negative
examples involves references to killing, aging, and death throughout the play.
The attitudes of children toward their parents' death and aging is central here.
In the Pinter canon, those attitudes entail both a paradoxical glorying in the
process of parental aging as confirming the child's own youth and potency and
a refusal to accept it fully, a horror of it, simply because the parents' death
reminds the child of his or her own mortality. Conversely, the parent both
glories in his or her children as an escape from death's implications, and resents and hates their youthfulness as his or her own death approaches. Both
attitudes are frequently leavened with a genuine love.[20]

Lenny's aggressive responses to Max's old-mannish puttering about in the
first scene, in contrast to his apparently caring behavior toward the old man in
later scenes, first points us in this direction. More specifically, several of
Max's lines focus our attention on parental attitudes toward children in the
context of death. He says that to prove his respect for his father, he "learned
to carve a carcass at his knee. I commemorated his name in blood. I gave
birth to three grown men! All on my own bat!" (p. 40). The context of these
lines, Max's memory of his father's dying words, suggests that Max hated and
feared his father partially because of an insecurity rooted in the fear of
death.[21] That fear leads to aggressive, "killing" behavior, the carving of car-
casses. The line "I commemorated his name in blood" refers to this butchery;
at the same time, the line refers to Max's siring three children. Such com-
memoration is for himself as well, an attempt to escape confrontation with
death. This subtextual pattern informs our response to Max's sudden welcom-
ing of Ruth and Teddy when he discovers that Teddy has also sired three
children (p. 43). As Teddy leaves, with Sam's unmourned "corpse" on the
floor, Max suggests that Teddy take the children a picture of their grandfather
(p. 79). Again, Max's concern with children is contextualized by the presence

of that body.

Similar connections abound. As Lenny begins his attempt to control Ruth, he matter-of-factly tells her a story detailing his deciding not to kill a woman who approached him sexually only because of the bother of disposing of the corpse. Lenny attempts to dominate Ruth through this implicit threat, and the story itself emphasizes that such attempts are "killing" (p. 31). Joey's and Lenny's story about the "birds" takes place in the rubble of a bombed site (p. 67), and Joey threatens to kill anyone who repeats that Teddy "gets the gravy from Ruth." Repeatedly, sexual possessiveness and aggressive attempts to control others are revealed as rooted in the fear of death. Such fear, such insecurity, prompts these characters to destroy others, to possess them, in attempts to avoid or momentarily defeat their own fear of mortality. Recognition of this pattern in the lives of Pinter's characters on the aesthetic or intellectual level can serve as the first step toward the audience member's intended emotional recognition of similar patterns in his or her own life.

Early in the play Lenny's obsessive concern with that annoying tick more subtly points toward this same response. Lenny complains to Teddy that he has not been able to sleep, that some sort of tick has been disturbing him. In response to Teddy's suggestion that it is probably a clock, Lenny says that he had better stifle it (p. 25). Again focusing our attention on that clock, on first meeting Ruth, Lenny asks her advice on the problem but comments that he is not convinced that it is the clock that disturbs him at all: "I mean there are lots of things which tick in the night, don't you find that?" (p. 28). He then goes for the glass of water that Ruth has already refused. Lenny's tick is clearly related to the fear of death, both through its associations with the clock and with the "death tick" of folklore Pinter refers to more specifically in *The Dwarfs*. His first solution is to stifle the tick, to kill it by suffocation. In his attempts to do so, he begins to "stifle" Ruth, forcing on her "refreshment" that she does not desire. In effect, this early scene, in a distanced, intellectual fashion, clarifies the play's action and points toward the more emotional concluding scenes.

Part of the difficulty of responding to these scenes results from Ruth's strange farewell to Teddy. By the end of the play, Ruth has clearly indicated her decision to remain with the family. The group has made its proposal to Teddy, who briefly objects but continues his escapist behavior by himself informing Ruth of the family's offer (pp. 75–67). He is once again playing the game of "taking the piss" by pretending not to be disturbed—"I don't mind," he tells her. But he still offers her the alternative he'd prefer: "Or you can come home with me" (p. 76). Lenny responds to this threat of losing Ruth by immediately offering her a flat of her own and their bargaining ensues, with Ruth clearly dominating the negotiations. But Teddy makes the final condition of the arrangement clear by pointing out to Ruth, with absolute calm, that she will "Keep everyone company." He is still struggling desperately to "operate on things," striving not to let the family see that they have gotten to him on an emotional level. At this point the appalled Sam blurts out his confession about MacGregor and Jessie in a pathetic attempt to stop the deal and collapses. We respond with some degree of startled emotion in the audience, but the family is nonplussed. Max denies the truth, humorously, of what Sam has said, and Teddy simply complains about the inconvenience of Sam's not being able to drive him to the airport. After Teddy matter-of-factly takes his leave of everyone except Ruth, he approaches the front door. But when Ruth calls out to him, "Eddie," he turns and she says, "Don't become a stranger" (p. 80). With no comment, he leaves.

This farewell is intensely ironic. Ruth's calling her husband "Eddie" for the first time in the play perhaps suggests simply that she is using an intimate nickname, but the flip "Don't become a stranger" in this context is even more terribly inappropriate. Thus distanced, the line suggests an implicit criticism of Teddy's failure to react in a more "balanced," more emotional fashion, as he perhaps has in the past, in his "Eddie" incarnation. His attempts to remain uninvolved, unemotional, and in control have cost him his relationship with Ruth. In effect, he has already become a stranger. At the same time, Ruth is now behaving much like the rest of the family; the line rubs in her own power here, the forcefulness of her decision or victory, and her refusal to allow Teddy the last "word" by his silence, his refusal to even tell her goodbye. Ironically, she has come home, not Teddy, who has become isolated, without comfort, like so many other Pinter "intruders" banished from his fellows by his own fearful, defensive responses—in a word, a stranger.

The last scene provides a final index to intended response, reemphasizing the fruitlessness and sterility of such behavior. With Sam's "body" still on the floor, Max begins to worry that Ruth has played a trick on the family, that she will use them. He falls to his knees, begins to sob, stops sobbing, and crawls around Sam's body to Ruth, who is calmly sitting in his chair, stroking Joey's head. "I'm not an old man," Max asserts; "Do you hear me?" He raises his face and *yells* "Kiss me." The tableau is held for a moment, and the curtain falls (p. 82).

This is a powerful scene, intellectually *and* emotionally, if we have allowed the indexes in the play to broaden the basis of our identification. By this point, we should both recognize and sympathize with most of these characters. Max's denial of his age in immediate juxtaposition with his shouted command emphasizes that Max's attempts at sexual aggression and control embody an attempted denial of death. Though understandable and intensely moving, Max's behavior is a negative example. Like all the other characters, Max ignores Sam's "death." His crawling around the body to reach Ruth reinforces his avoidance. Such a need to avoid the implications of others' deaths springs from our desperate fear of our own mortality; but such failure of confrontation, or repression, in Pinter's world, results in aggression, which, in turn, leads to the pathetic isolation mirrored in this final scene. Sexual aggression, indeed all attempts at control, forcefully emerge as rooted in the fear of death, a profound insecurity that necessitates violent and isolating ego defenses. We should be able, ironically, to identify with such behavior and potentially to free ourselves from at least some of it.[22]

We can, of course, refuse such an emotional response, avoid any kind of positive response dependent on identification. Such refusal characterizes many of the negative critical responses to the play. Pinter, though, intends a balanced, intellectual identification, which should grow out of careful, questioning, attention to all of the characters in this play and to the subtextual elements that surround them. The critical condemnation that Pinter's works contain no moral statement and are cold and emotionless results from a failure on the part of the audience to play the role Pinter dictates for it, to concentrate fully, to recognize and live with these characters. That requires a broadening of the basis of identification, often painful, which produces a sympathy for these characters, many of whom are very much like ourselves; nonetheless, responding creatively, or positively, to the ironic identification that the play calls for necessitates a revolt from the negative examples we see in the mirror of that Pinter stage. It is a pair of old themes that we are asked to create from these negative examples: *memento mori* and Know Thyself. That both ideas lead to fuller, better lives is consistent with a grand tradition, especially if we learn the lesson through identification with negative examples.

Notes

1. Simon Trussler, *The Plays of Harold Pinter: An Assessment* (London: Victor Gallancz Ltd., 1973), pp. 125, 134; Bert O. States, "Pinter's *Homecoming*: The Shock of Nonrecognition," *Hudson Review* 21 (1968): 476–86; repr. *Pinter: A Collection of Critical Essays*, ed. Authur Ganz (Englewood Cliffs, N. J. Prentice-Hall, 1972), pp. 147, 159; Steven H. Gale, *Butter's Going Up: A Critical Analysis of Harold Pinter's Work* (Durham, N. C.: Duke University Press, 1977), p. 136.

2. Steven Mailloux, "Reader-Response Criticism," *Genre* 10 (1977): 413–32, provides a valuable, concise introduction to the range and complexity of reader-response criticism.

3. Walter J. Ong, "The Writer's Audience Is Always a Fiction," *PMLA* 90 (1975): 9–21; Ong's starting point in this essay is the manner in which writers, as opposed to various raconteurs within the oral tradition, interact with their audiences. He notes that drama is the first genre to be controlled by writing; thus, despite the fact that performer and audience communicate or interrelate more directly than novelist and reader, the basic points of Ong's position transfer to the theatrical audience in relation to the playwright; admittedly, the transfer is complicated by the fact that the director, cast, staging, etc. must serve as intermediaries for the playwright's "indexing" of intended response.

4. Hans Robert Jauss, "Literary History as a Challenge to Literary Theory," trans. Elizabeth Benzinger, *New Literary History* 2 (1970–71): 37. Further references to this article will be indicated parenthetically.

5. Hans Robert Jauss, "Levels of Identification of Hero and Audience," trans. Benjamin and Helga Bennett, *New Literary History* 5 (1973–74): 284–85. Further references to this article will be indicated parenthetically.

6. A wide variety of writers have commented on this process from a less theoretical point of view. For example, John Arden, in "What's Theatre For?" *Performance* 1 (1972): 10–11, writes that to deal with a malfunction in a spacecraft the land crew first tries to reproduce it in a mock-up, "the idea being that once the fault in the model had been correctly reproduced, the way to

repair it could also be found.... But if the astronauts weren't listening, or if their radio wasn't working, then clearly nothing could be done to improve their situation." He understands this as an analogy for the "negative" thematic statement. Paul Tillich, in "Existentialism and Psychotherapy," in *Psychoanalysis and Existential Philosophy,* ed. Hendrik M. Ruitenbeek (New York: Dutton, 1962), p. 6, sums up this idea nicely: "There is no existentialist description of the negativities of the human predicament without an underlying image of what man ought to be. The cutting power of existentialist novels, painting, even philosophical analysis of man's predicament is rooted in the implicit contrast between the negativities they show and the positives they silently presuppose." Even if we reject the often misunderstood label of "existentialism," Tillich's description of the positive implicit in the negative portrayal aptly describes the effect Pinter's works intend.

7. Mel Gussow, "A Conversation (Pause) with Harold Pinter," *New York Times Magazine,* 5 December 1971, p. 135. Clearly we must be cautious when using authorial comment in this manner to contextualize or support a particular vision of intent or of indexes of intended response in the play. However, just as obviously as Pinter's famous comment that he writes about the "weasel under the cocktail table" was meant as a joke, which he later lambasted critics for taking seriously, the comments here are clearly serious—and I think accurate and consistent with the plays themselves and their effect.

8. Harold Pinter, "Writing for Myself," *Twentieth Century,* February 1961, p. 174.

9. Harold Pinter, *Sunday Times* (London), 14 August 1960; cited in Martin Esslin, *The Peopled Wound: The Work of Harold Pinter* (Garden City, N.Y.: Doubleday, 1970), p. 45.

10. Judith Crist, "A Mystery: Pinter on Pinter," *Look* 32 (24 Dec. 1968): 77.

11. Esslin, *The Peopled Wound,* pp. 246–47.

12. Gussow, "A Conversation," p. 135.

13. Henry Hewes, "Probing Pinter's Play," *Saturday Review,* 8 April 1967, p. 58.

14. Lawrence M. Bensky, "Harold Pinter: An Interview," in *Writers at Work: The Paris Review Interviews, Third Series,* ed. George Plimpton (New York: Viking, 1967); repr. *Theater at Work,* ed. Charles Marowitz and Simon Trussler (London: Methuen, 1967), pp. 105–6; repr. *Pinter: A Collection,* ed. Ganz, pp. 19–33.

15. Pinter, "Writing for the Theatre," *Evergreen* 8 (1964): 82; repr. *The New British Drama,* ed. Henry Popkin (New York: Grove Press, 1964); originally a speech to the National Student Drama Festival at Bristol, published as "Pinter Between the Lines," *Sunday Times Magazine* (London), 4 March 1962, p. 25.

16. Pinter, *Poems* (London: Enitharmon, 1968), p. 9; further references to this edition will be indicated parenthetically. For a fuller development of this argument, see my article "Dance to a Cut-Throat Temper: Harold Pinter's Poetry as an Index to Intended Audience Response," *Comparative Drama* 12 (1978): 214–32.

17. Harold Pinter, in an interview with John Sherwood, BBC European Service, in the series "The Rising Generation," 3 March 1960 (duplicated manuscript); cited in Esslin, *The Peopled Wound,* p. 31.

18. Peter Hall, "A Director's Approach," an interview with Irving Wardle in *A Casebook on Harold Pinter's "The Homecoming,"* ed. John Lahr (New York: Grove Press, 1971), p. 14.

19. Harold Pinter, *The Homecoming* (New York: Grove Press, 1965), pp. 11–14; further reference to this edition will be indicated parenthetically.

20. *Tea Party* and *The Pumpkin Eater* are particularly relevant here.

21. In "An Actor's Approach: An Interview with Paul Rogers," conducted by John Lahr in his *Casebook* on *The Homecoming,* p. 152, Paul Rogers comments that Pinter emphasized in rehearsal that Max hated his father when Rogers mistook that hatred for sentimentality in this speech. The hatred clearly emerges in several performances I have seen, as well as in The American Film Theatre's version of the play.

22. Despite typical critical reliance on Freud and Jung, the theories of Alfred Adler, R. D. Laing, and Norman O. Brown more clearly elucidate Pinter's works. These theorists delineate the shifting nature of identity as normative, the predominance of isolating control relationships in our lives, and the possibility of achieving a type of freedom through self-knowledge and confronta-

tion. They also suggest that the source of aggressive behavior lies in insecurity of various sorts. Brown and Laing, in particular, clarify the relationship of such insecurity to the fear of death. Adler's conception of the will to power, Laing's more radical vision of the "divided self," and Brown's dictum that the root of insecurity lies in the individual's failure to acknowledge death accurately frame or contextualize Pinter's world, and several of their theories are implicitly present in my description of that world. See, for example, Alfred Adler, *Understanding Human Nature,* trans. Walter Beran Woolfe (Garden City, N. Y.: Garden City Publishing, 1927); R. D. Laing, *The Divided Self: A Study of Sanity and Madness* (London: Tavistock, 1960); Norman O. Brown, *Life Against Death: The Psychoanalytic Meaning of History* (Middleton, Conn.: Wesleyan University Press, 1959).

9

Pinter's *Silence:* Experience without Character

A. R. BRAUNMULLER

The important thing for the remembering author is not what he experienced, but the weaving of his memory, the Penelope work of recollection. Or should one call it, rather, a Penelope work of forgetting?

—*Walter Benjamin*

Acts and relations repeated in time have filled Harold Pinter's plays almost from the first. The construction is perhaps most familiar in *The Homecoming:* triads of brothers (and sons) have circled around single equivocal female figures through several generations. One generation's acts repeat an earlier generation's, and the future appears to hold the present situation, for Teddy will return to an American home very like the English one that spawned him and drew him back. Memory bears the traces of these acts. More and more frequently, the characters use memory to define themselves and their situations; they attempt to shape their static and human environment through memory. For example, *The Dumb Waiter*'s two gunmen endlessly quiz their remembered pasts and hope to define the present as one more element in a known series; in *The Birthday Party,* memory enshrines comically Edenic childhoods and, more terrifyingly, permits an individual's gradual effacement when other characters seize his memories as their own. Pinter's later work has shown that acts and relations repeated in time cannot be separated from memory; as the stage action becomes more and more muted, remembered action constitutes plot (*Old Times*) and the characters' self-consciousness, their "character" (*Old Times* and *No Man's Land*), and finally the ground of their relations with one another (in both plays). His latest full-length play, *Betrayal,* moves memory's complexity into the relation between audience and drama. Our own experience of the play now includes the uncertainties, the half-glimpsed knowledges, the abundant, confusing facts once represented in, and restricted to, the characters.[1]

Landscape and *Silence,* two short and superficially uncharacteristic plays written between *The Homecoming* and *Old Times,* mark Pinter's most overt experiments with the ideas and issues that appear somewhat obliquely in the better-known plays before and after.[2] While the two plays share many features distinguishing them from Pinter's other work, *Silence* offers a greater linguistic range and more varied types of speech and memory than its partner. *Landscape* does, however, corroborate a number of points I wish to make. In both plays, for example, one may see Pinter quite clearly paying homage to European drama of the immediately prewar and postwar periods: *Silence*'s naked set ("Three areas"), the monologic and disjunctive speeches, the sparse and undramatic dialogues or encounters all have a familiar feel, but not in Pinter's oeuvre. Rüdiger Imhof, for example, finds that "Rumsey [in *Silence*] bears a close affinity to ... Winnie in [Samuel Beckett's] *Happy Days*."[3] Some of Beth's memory-fantasies in *Silence*'s sister-play, *Landscape*, might be distorted recollections of Winnie and Willie in their sandscape. Beckett's Mrs. Rooney, too, has difficulties with other people that anticipate Rumsey's and Ellen's: "I estrange them all. They come towards me, uninvited, bygones bygones, full of kindness, anxious to help ...."[4] At the end of *All That Fall*, Mrs. Rooney's husband desperately tries to tell a story and angrily illuminates a pun that undergirds many a Pinterian moment: "I can vouch for it, I tell you! Do you want my relation or don't you?" (p. 76).

The sharply reduced concern for even a technical realism, most prominent in *Silence,* permits Pinter a wide verbal latitude. He now typifies experience through the style conveying that experience; an individual character's "style" yields to a "style" of a given category of experience. *Silence*'s dialogues (all three) are terse, unfigurative, unanecdotal, but the monologues vary from the "normal" (and highly complex) Pinterian level,

I'm at my last gasp with this unendurable racket. I kicked open the door and stood before them. Someone called me Grandad and told me to button it. It's they should button it.[5]

to quite unexpectedly evocative, sometimes figurative levels,

Pleasant alone and watch the folding light. My animals are quiet. My heart never bangs. I read in the evenings. There is no-one to tell me what is expected or not expected of me. There is nothing required of me.   (P. 35)

In these plays, Pinter finally seems to have defeated the crossword-puzzle response he so detests. Even the most dedicated snapper up of unconsidered trifles can only struggle to weave a coherent and chronological pattern among characters and events so tenuously connected and so fragmentarily relayed.

Like the set, the dramatis personae receive a very naked introduction. Chronology alone matters: "a girl in her twenties"; "a man of forty"; "a man in his middle thirties." Their ages matter a great deal, because time and hence memory are important from the outset. The first two speeches are in the present tense (as if told), and since the actors are manifestly not performing the actions recounted, we accept the present tense as "historical," even though the audience appears the only available listener. Given this initiation, we discover that much of the text appears to be retrospective narrative (memory); the tenses shift from present to past and back, but each speaker recounts experiences as if from some distant, chronologically future, viewpoint. A "memory style" has developed to convey these experiences. Here are three examples, drawn from each character's first speech:

I walk with my girl who wears a grey blouse when she walks and grey shoes and walks with me readily wearing her clothes considered for me. Her grey clothes.   (P. 33)

There are two. One who is with me sometimes, and another. He listens to me. I tell him what I know. We walk by the dogs. Sometimes the wind is so high he does not hear me. I lead him to a tree, clasp closely to him and whisper to him, wind going, dogs stop, and he hears me.   (Pp. 33–34)

Caught a bus to the town. Crowds. Lights round the market, rain and stinking. Showed her the bumping lights. Took her down around the dumps. Black roads and girders. She clutching me. This way the way I bring you. Pubs throw the doors smack into the night. Cars barking and the lights. She with me, clutching.   (P. 34)

Though it is not impossible that the two men to whom Ellen refers are in fact the other two speakers and that they similarly refer to her, the language bleaches the speaker out of the experience. Even experiences that might have only recently occurred, indeed, even relations that might still be continuing, receive a detached, slightly overvivid presentation.

At the other extreme from the memory-style is the language of events present to the audience: the three short dialogues that punctuate the play. Here, of course, there can be no question of narration and, likewise no question of the events' presentness. Yet, each of these dialogues "fits" into the haphazard and fragmented account the characters seem to have given of past experiences. Like some conversations in *Old Times*, these three dialogues appear to be historical conversations reenacted so as to make two present times simultaneous. They deny their ostensible nature in another way. Not only do they seem repeated and reenacted, they are wholly negative—dialogues of nonexchange, dialogues in which the speakers fail to enter into a relation. In the first, Ellen refuses to go for a walk with Bates and then rebuffs his attempts to find some alternative entertainment. Pinter's speakers might be Didi and Gogo or Hamm and Clov:

Do you want to go anywhere else?
Yes.
Where?
I don't know.   (P. 38)

The second "conversation," between Ellen and Rumsey, looks more promising when she admires some (invisible) "shelves" and his printing job: "It's beautiful." Yet, subsequent conversational openings—her childhood mem-

ories, her cooking, his music— all fail to produce more than the announcement of their existence, and the exchange finally dies:

It's very dark outside.
It's high up.
Does it get darker the higher you get?
No. (P. 42)

The last dialogue repeats Ellen's intransigent refusal to "find a young man";
she and Rumsey trade a few futile (perhaps very familiar) repetitions of the
pattern—find a young man ... no—and the conversation ends, as negative
and uncommunicative as it began.

Somewhere between the "memory style" and the terse negativism of the
conversations lies another category of speeches. These speeches seem to re-
count experiences in which the speakers are considerably older than their
physical appearances (and Pinter's instructions) suggest. The clearest example from Rumsey's speeches has already been partly quoted: he claims "I've
lost nothing" and then goes on to describe his rural tranquillity, his freedom
from ill health (or from emotional excitement)—"My heart never bangs"—
and concludes, "There is nothing required of me." Bates remembers being
called "Grandad" and later remembers (or retells) a "stupid conversation"
with his landlady. She asks a series of questions:

Where do you come from? What do you do with yourself? What kind of life
have you had? You seem fit. A bit grumpy. You can smile, surely, at something? Surely you have smiled, at a thing in your life? At something? Has
there been no pleasantness in your life? No kind of loveliness in your life?
Are you nothing but a childish old man, suffocating himself? (P. 43)

Ellen also speaks of herself as someone considerably older than a person "in
her twenties" when she recalls her "drinking companion ... a friendly
woman, quite elderly" who asks her "about my early life ... about the sexual
part of my youth." Ellen continues, "I'm old, I tell her, my youth was somewhere else, anyway I don't remember" (p. 36). The speech ends with Ellen's
reaction to the sexy talk and remembered youth: "But I'm still quite pretty
really, quite nice eyes, nice skin" (p. 37).

These speeches and a few other fragments that seem to cohere with them
are quite extraordinary. Given their narrative form (as if told to the audience,
or to *an* audience), they necessarily sound like memories, but with few exceptions they are memories that none of the characters could realistically have ...
or have had. A rationalizing audience will attempt some complex jugglings;
one possible conclusion is that each speaker has a "future memory," that is,
each treats some fantasied future experience as if it were already a memory.[6]
These future memories and the speeches in the "memory style" share re-
miniscential verbal signs, but the future memories have a stylistic level very

near the Pinterian norm from which the memory style so often departs. These two types of speeches enclose almost all of the experiences that the characters have had, perhaps are having, and imagine they will have ... or will have had. It is a tantalizing and wonderful situation: the three characters experience their lives in so fragmented, so detached, so qualified a fashion as to transform those experiences, even apparently contemporary ones, into memories. In the memory style, of course, we detect certain compensatory shadings, hope's roseate hue—and self-deception's. Moreover, as the stylistic level approaches Pinter's usual dramatic dialect, the speeches move into a fantasied or imaginary future of loss, and that future is itself treated as remembered.

If we reject the rationalistic but chimerical temptation to construct "timetables" (and hence plots), we can see Pinter's more profound purposes in these stylistic differentiations and the use of memory. *Silence* investigates the nature of experience by showing us three characters for whom events and circumstances are vastly more significant than the human perceiver. From a welter of perceptions, the characters strive to create selves, but even their interactions (the dialogues) lack conflict and hence fail to provide definition.

Rumsey and Ellen quite explicitly recognize their failure to find a relation with their surroundings. Rumsey muses,

Sometimes I see people. They walk towards me, no, not so, walk in my direction, but never reaching me, turning left, or disappearing, and then reappearing, to disappear into the wood.

So many ways to lose sight of them, then to recapture sight of them. They are sharp at first sight ... then smudged ... then lost ... then glimpsed again ... then gone.   (P. 40)

The more distant, the sharper—just as the "remembered" experiences are; people do not approach "me," they only "walk in my direction." Ellen, too, has trouble perceiving people:

After my work each day I walk back through people but I don't notice them. I'm not in a dream or anything of that sort. On the contrary. I'm quite wide awake to the world around me. But not to the people. There must be something in them to notice, to pay attention to, something of interest in them. In fact I know there is. I'm certain of it. But I pass through them noticing nothing.   (P. 46)

For Bates, such experience is even more constricted:

I walk in my mind. But can't get out of the walls, into a wind. Meadows are walled, and lakes. The sky's a wall.   (Pp. 39–40)

Once I had a little girl. I took it for walks. I held it by its hand. It looked up at me and said, I see something in a tree, a shape, a shadow. It is leaning down. It is looking at us.   (P. 40)

The natural world becomes the indifferent, jostling, confined cityscape he seems once to have offered Ellen; the little girl declines to "it," a thing no more human nor comforting nor known than "something in a tree, a shape, a shadow."

Whatever the date or the status of the characters' memories, each is depersonalized; each lacks a central consciousness. Though many memories have a very sharp focus, the central perceiver (the speaker who conveys them) is very faint. The physical surroundings or the curiously dehumanized human environment almost annihilate the perception to which they might be referred. Rumsey acts:

I shall walk down to my horse and see how my horse is. He'll come towards me.

Perhaps he doesn't need me. My visit, my care, will be like any other visit, any other care. I can't believe it.   (P. 39)

Though Rumsey claims he "can't believe" the horse's indifference, his anxiety makes clear that he does believe it. Like the people who are "smudged ... then lost" for Ellen, the horse only comes "towards" Rumsey; it never arrives. Hence the repetitive "my horse," as he tries to draw the animal's existence into relation with his own. Often, the characters must check their existence against an outer one. Rumsey reports:

She walks from the door to the window to see the way she has come, to confirm that the house which grew nearer is the same one she stands in, that the path and the bushes are the same, that the gate is the same.   (P. 34)

And Bates describes the city as a mechanical, agentless environment:

Caught a bus to the town. Crowds. Lights round the market, rain and stinking.   (P. 34)

The point is not the external world's indifference, or that of other people, but each character's failure to be present to that world and to those people. Even the future memories concentrate on others' points of view—the "young people" making noise, the landlady questioning, the elderly drinking companion's talk of sex.

This condition—the characters' failure to center their experiences on themselves, the sense that those experiences exist prior to and outside of their perceivers—is not some version of *anomie*. Rather, the whirling time-senses, the fragmented and the elaborated memories, all attempt to come back to the perceiver; the characters make futile but energetic attempts to relate themselves. Each attempts to constitute a "character" out of memories, or experience, or both. That each of the dialogues represents an unavailing search for relation also means that no speaker can find a reciprocal definition with another, even if the dialogues do recall actual conversations. Similarly, each of the elaborate memory-style speeches returns to what the experience meant about, not *for*, the speaker. We must reverse the direction of our interpretation and move from character to experience rather than repeat their failure to move in the opposite direction. Their world is fragmented because they are themselves not merely fragmented consciousness, but equally fragments of their world. Earlier, I used a fairly typical locution in describing the characters as perceivers, but of course they are not. More accurately, they might be described as transmitters: they are the voices of events and circumstances, of a centrifugal force unshaped by a perceiving consciousness. As the play runs down into ever more broken remnants of the original fragmentary speeches, we recognize the characters' failure to make themselves, to be their own authors, to re-present themselves to an audience and to themselves.

Somewhat paradoxically, *Silence*'s characters attempt to treat their experiences in ways resembling the actor's manifestation of his script. In the terms Jacques Derrida outlines when discussing "The Theorem and the Theatre" (*Of Grammatology*), these characters are not present in their own person. Derrida argues that Jean Jacques Rousseau believed that "the identity of the representer and the represented may be accomplished ... by the effacement of the representer and the personal presence of the represented...."[7] Pursuing the thought, the critic eventually finds a Rousseauean "elusion"—"the fact that representation does not suddenly encroach upon presence; it inhabits it as the very condition of its experience, of desire, and of enjoyment..." (p. 312). For reasons that I will explore in a moment, Pinter's characters cast their experience into memory, a form which almost guarantees that it should remain re-presented. The characters cannot accommodate event and experience of event simultaneously. Pinter's aesthetic (or philosophic) vision gives event priority—at least in *Silence*—and the characters are condemned to haunt memory as they seek experience.

Silence lacks the coercive speech acts so common elsewhere in Pinter's plays. Here no tales seek to persuade another of the speaker's indifference or invulnerability, of his physical or sexual power. Indeed, conflict does not drive the play forward in time: the intersections of speech and actors (the three dialogues) prove to be neither violent nor energizing. Silences fall after the dialogues, but not before; the actors drift into contact, propelled by their own speeches' inner development. No doubt the dialogues appear to enact— in the audience's present—conversations and acts that have already been absorbed into the individual character's speeches, their re-presented pasts, their spoken memories. In the theatre, as we hear these present recreations of dialogues that may have occurred before (or even after) the characters' present, we face re-representation. The characters stage their intersections for themselves. And nothing happens; no action issues from dialogue. Whatever action might follow dialogue has already occurred and has already failed to satisfy the characters' demands for identity and confirmation.

The play's treatment of speech and time arises from the characters' extraordinary, unitary project: to maintain-in-being. Quoting Bishop Berkeley, Beckett writes:

Esse est percipi.
All extraneous perception suppressed, animal, human, divine, self-perception maintains in being.
Search of non-being in flight from extraneous perception breaking down in inescapability of self-perception.

. . . .

It will not be clear until the end of film that pursuing perceiver is not extraneous, but self.[8]

For Pinter, self-perception requires constant effort, and that effort must be memory. His characters might well rewrite Descartes: *reminisor ergo sum,* or (in the theatre) *reminiscor et narro ergo sum.* Maintaining-in-being finds its most satisfying verbal form in memory (past narrative) because only there do all the linguistic signs declare occurrence rather than hope or desire. Only the past indicative or historical present will do. Subjunctive or optative forms leave the self to chance. Yet this project inevitably leads the characters to stage themselves to themselves: they make even their futures into represented memories.

Dialogue offers (as Beckett's theatre demonstrates) the illusion of sharing the burden. Two can maintain-in-being better than one. *Silence* has only failed dialogues, dialogues that have been absorbed into memory even before they are restaged for our benefit and to the characters' despair. The burden cannot be shared, nor can it be supported individually. After their initial representation (pp. 33–37) and development (pp. 39–41), the relations-recollections begin to decline and intermingle without contact (pp. 43–44) and then decay rapidly (pp. 45–46) into the concluding interwoven fragments (pp. 46–52). Dialogue and the direction *Silence* mark off each stage but the last, which is preceded by a solo from Ellen, also followed by *Silence.* The final tour-de-force offers the audience a mosaic of chance con-/dis-junctions. Here, at the end, dialogue's utter impossibility appears most clearly: the characters can neither represent themselves to each other nor to themselves. They have even lost their ability to rerepresent themselves-in-dialogue. Ellen and her "elderly friend," Rumsey and his horse, Bates and the "bastards in the other room"—even remembered dialogue-relation—can no longer help the characters to maintain their integral and distinct consciousnesses.

Silence has the formal appearance of a dramatic, even a graphic, sketch.

Using this stripped medium, Pinter breaks through his earlier interest, his characters' power struggles, and finds a plain vision of the weakness or failure that nurtured those struggles. His next two full-length plays, *Old Times* and *No Man's Land,* mingle these discoveries with some of the old self-confident aggression, but in both plays the characters employ memory as a flexible medium of self-definition even though that self-definition appears within the conflict of domination and submission. As early in his career as *The Dumb Waiter,* Pinter showed his characters attempting to domesticate the inexplicable through fantasy: the two gunmen respond to the dumb waiter's increasingly bizarre and insistent demands by "naturalizing" their basement—against all evidence—into a former restaurant kitchen. In *Silence,* reality's constitution has shifted wholly to threatening or inexplicable circumstance (the shapes in the trees, or the darkness higher up). Unable to confront their environment directly, as the gunmen tried to do, *Silence*'s characters resort to memory—real or pretended, it makes no difference—as a means to experience their environment.

As a consequence of their natures and, perhaps, as a consequence of their world's nature (at least as Pinter conceives it), the characters "stage" or "represent" their experiences through memory. At the beginning of this essay, I quoted from Benjamin's "The Image of Proust"; he later observes, "an experienced event is finite—at any rate, confined to one sphere of experience; a remembered event is infinite, because it is only a key to everything that happened before it and after it."[9] *Silence*'s characters grasp for this key because they hope to prevent circumstances from changing "on their own." Very occasionally, they are ruminations on the fundamental weaknesses (or, more neutrally, perceptions and preconditions of existence) that force all the memories. Ellen and Rumsey alternately think of freedom, a freedom from anxiety and requirement:

Ellen

When I run ... when I run ... when I run ... over the grass ...
Rumsey
She floats ... under me. Floating ... under me.
Ellen
I turn. I turn. I wheel. I glide. I wheel. In stunning light. The horizon moves from the sun. I am crushed by the light.   (P. 40)

Bates's speech is more closely linked to his consciousness:

Funny. Sometimes I press my hand on my forehead, calmingly, feel all the dust drain out, let it go, feel the grit slip away. Funny moment. That calm moment.   (P. 41)

All three seek a recreative power in memory: it releases them from the moment's demands, and it permits, or seems to permit, the mind to discover relation and control. For these characters, no finite experienced event exists, only the infinite remembered experience. In the remembering, the experience expands and blots out its human containers/contents. They fragment, and as they lose memory's tenuous control, they fall silent.

Notes

1. On memory in Pinter's later plays, see (among others): John Russell Taylor, *Harold Pinter, Writers and Their Work*, 212 (Harlow, England: Longmans, 1969); Steven H. Gale, *Butter's Going Up: A Critical Analysis of Harold Pinter's Work* (Durham, N.C.: Duke University Press, 1977); my essay "Harold Pinter: The Metamorphosis of Memory," in *Essays on Contemporary British Drama*, ed. Hedwig Bock and Albert Wertheim (Hamburg: Hueber; New York: Adler, 1981).

2. *Landscape* was first broadcast on 25 April 1968; *Landscape* and *Silence* were first staged on 2 July 1969, and both plays were first published in 1969.

3. Rüdiger Imhof, "Pinter's *Silence:* The Impossibility of Communication," *Modern Drama* 17, (December 1974): 455.

4. Samuel Beckett, *All That Fall*, in *Krapp's Last Tape and Other Dramatic Pieces* (New York: Grove Press, 1960), p. 53; subsequent references to this volume will be incorporated parenthetically into the text.

5. Harold Pinter, *Landscape and Silence* (New York: Grove Press, 1970), p. 35; subsequent references to this volume will be incorporated parenthetically into the text.

6. For multiple time schemes in Pinter's *Night,* including "the limitless future that is also an eternal present when they [the characters] will remember the time when they remembered remembering," see Thomas P. Adler's suggestive "Pinter's *Night:* A Stroll Down Memory Lane," *Modern Drama* 17, no. 4 (December 1974): 646.

7. Jacques Derrida, *Of Grammatology,* trans. G. C. Spivak (Baltimore: Johns Hopkins University Press, 1976), p. 305; subsequent references to this volume will be incorporated parenthetically into the text.

8. Samuel Beckett, *Film* (original project), in *Cascando and Other Short Dramatic Pieces* (New York: Grove Press, 1970), p. 75.

9. Walter Benjamin, "The Image of Proust," in *Illuminations,* ed. Hannah Arendt, trans. Harry Zohn (New York: Schocken Books, 1969), p. 202.

10
Pinter/Proust/Pinter

THOMAS P. ADLER

In his "Introduction" to *The Proust Screenplay* (completed in 1973 and published in 1977, but still unproduced), Harold Pinter comments that "The subject [of the work] was Time"; he then alludes briefly to the Marcel of *Le Temps retrouvé* (*Time Rediscovered*), the seventh and concluding volume of Marcel Proust's *À la recherche du temps perdu* or *In Search of Lost Time*—a more accurate rendering of the original title than the traditional *Remembrance of Things Past*[1]—as someone for whom the "memory of the experience [of childhood], is more real, more acute, than the experience itself."[2] Since these two motifs—time and memory—have been among the dramatist's chief concerns, especially from the period of *Landscape* and *Silence* (1968–69) on, Pinter, who earlier had written several successful screen adaptations, would understandably be drawn to Proust, and it is not surprising to hear him call the time devoted to adapting Proust's massive novel "the best working year of my life" (p. x). My intention here is not to undertake on elaborate comparison-contrast of the screenplay and its source, pointing out what has been retained and what excised, what, if anything, has been gained and what, almost certainly, lost; as Pinter admits, he and his collaborators—film director Joseph Losey and BBC radio script editor Barbara Bray—"knew [they] could in no sense rival the work. But could [they] be true to it?" (p. x). Rather, I intend something at once more modest and yet, I trust, more pertinent for students of Pinter by asking: What relationship exists, in structure and ideas, between *The Proust Screenplay* and Pinter's recent dramas? In my endeavor to suggest at least the outlines of a response, I will travel three "ways": (1) provide an overview of Proust's theory of memory; (2) outline a Pinter "theory" of memory culled from several of the later plays; and (3) analyze the text of the filmscript in relation to a few of the plays to see what light it casts on them and they on it, asking what is Proustian about it and what Pinteresque.

i

To accomplish the first aim—that is, to define Proust's view of memory—we need to look at basically two main sources: his letter of December 1913 to René Blum, and chapter 3 of *Time Rediscovered* entitled "An Afternoon Party at the House of the Princesse de Guermantes." In the former, Proust distinguishes what he calls "involuntary memory" from voluntary memory, expressing his preference, at least insofar as his own novel is concerned, for the first over the second.[3] Whereas voluntary memory, vitiated with prejudice, sentimentality, and bias, is equated with "intellectual and visual memory [that] give us only inexact facsimiles of the past, which no more resemble it than pictures by bad painters resemble the spring,"[4] involuntary memory, pure and clean and *not* controlled by an act of the will, allows us to see as in a revelation the past reality in a way that we did not perceive it even when we lived it. As Proust writes in his letter to Blum, involuntary memory causes him not simply to recall but to refind and relive "a part of my life, which I had forgotten and which, all of a sudden, I rediscover while eating a bit of *madeleine* which I dip in some tea, a taste which enchants me before I have identified and recognized it as one that I had formerly known every morning; immediately my whole life at that period is revived and, as I say in the book, like the Japanese game in which little pieces of paper dipped in a bowl of water become people, flowers, etc., all the people and gardens of that period of my life arise out of a cup of tea" (p. 213). The result of this "chance" encounter with an object that "stimulates" the involuntary memory is, as Howard Moss comments, that "we actually grasp the past as the present, as if time had literally stopped. ... *then* becomes *now* in reality, not symbolically."[5]

In the lengthy concluding chapter of his multivolume novel, Proust philosophizes about time, memory, reality, and art. The great fact of existence is mutability, and so he views time as an essentially destructive force. Physically, we live and move and "occupy a place in the dimension of Time," but, as Proust says, our "place in Time ... is perpetually being augmented"[6] because of the "continuous" nature of existence. Yet mutability and mortality are countered by memory, which, spiritually, is the locus where we have our being. For if time is flux, memory that conquers and "suppresses" the action of time is "fixity" (pp. 224, 259). From one perspective it remains true, of course, that even memory is subject to time, since the mind is weakened by being joined to the body and so memory dims and fades. But as this occurs, so, too, does the fear of death diminish, since Proust acknowledges that because of time's action in continually supplanting what has come before he has already died many times over. Yet memory, since it holds in its grasp "fragments of existence withdrawn from Time" (p. 136), resists change. In fact, to live in the realm of memory fully alert and at work becomes the only means of perceiving reality, since, for Proust, reality is "purely mental" (p. 166); memory might be called the supreme reality, for "really everything is in the mind" rather than "in the object" perceived by the senses (p. 164). Each of us, therefore, conquers time by carrying all of our past within us: nothing is ever really lost or ceases to exist, because "threads" from all the "different planes" of time are woven together into a rich "web" so that all things exist at one and the same time within us simultaneously (p. 258). Thus as Wallace Fowlie remarks, "our 'real' life is not chronological."[7] It falls to art, then, fed by the involuntary memory, to defeat time by capturing and conveying the "realities that were outside Time" (p. 179). As Moss remarks, "The enbalmer of original enchantments, [memory] is the only human faculty that can outwit the advance of chronological time. Art, the enbalmer of memory, is the only human vocation in which the time regained by memory can be permanently fixed" (p. 18). Moss further comments: "reality itself is merely the outer shell of a suprareality that is hidden from us. Albertine's body, the steeples, and the trees are apprehended by Marcel's senses. But they are all outer envelopes enclosing vital cryptograms to which he does not have the code" (p. 95). Only art that depends on memory as its handmaiden can unlock the "spiritual equivalent" or "meaning" of sense impressions; perceive the suprareality; discover the "extra-temporal" self—"the timeless man within" him that Proust understands to be the only "true life"—that ordinarily remains hidden; and, finally, provide others "with the means of reading what lay inside themselves" (pp. 133, 169, 140, 260).

Pinter, too, within his creative works, conveys his ideas on these same topics of time, memory, reality, and art. For Pinter, as for Proust, physical time holds less consequence than mental time. In *Silence* (1969), for example, Pinter pictures three characters each mentally frozen in a different dimension of time, signified linguistically by the tense of the verbs they choose: Rumsey exists in a perpetual present (his first and last utterances start with "I walk"[8]); Bates resides in an eternal past ("Caught a bus" [pp. 34, 52] begins his first and final sentences); and Ellen, as the point that completes the triangle, lives in a reality that accommodates the demands of the two men, as well as finally in an interior reality of future recall that encompasses both Rumsey's eternal present and Bates's unending past ("Certainly. I can remember," she says at the end [p. 52]). Time for all of them is a ceaseless repetition, a kind of hell from which there is no exit.[9] In *Landscape* (1968)—the play performed as a companion piece—Pinter views the retreat from time into memory as a way of placating, even of denying, time. Beth, fearing the process of change and refusing to accept the inevitable diminishment ("Of course, when I'm older I won't be the same as I am, I won't be what I am, my skirts, my long legs, I'll be older, I won't be the same" [p. 24]), consciously chooses to live totally in a memory time of a more romantic past of physical attractiveness and fecundity, when a child never conceived was still a possibility. For her, the past is the only present. Beth's description of the sand on the beach that "kept on slipping, mixing the contours" (p. 20) of the human forms that lay on it, might be a metaphor for the way that memory fluctuates, in the same way that Kate's reflection in *Old Times* (1971) about the appeal of the sea residing in our inability to "say where it begins or ends"[10] could also characterize the nature of memory. In that mesmerizing drama, in fact, we discover Pinter's fullest definition of the workings of memory, and the truth that memory may provide a more intense reality than sensory data. Memory—in the person of Anna who is already present in the room though unacknowledged—exists as something dim that can be brought into focus. Whether we welcome the past by inviting it in, or whether we attempt to annihilate the past by forgetting it, our memory of it is for Pinter, as it was for Proust, the central reality of our lives. As Anna says: "There are some things one remembers even though they may never have happened. There are things I remember which may never have happened but as I recall them so they take place" (pp. 31–32). The past receives whatever reality it possesses by being remembered in the present; and even if something never occurred in actuality, thinking can make it so. Once thought, the idea or event exists. Memory, in the extreme, is creation, in the sense of making something out of nothing—a more radical notion than that held by Proust. Furthermore, memory is relative—the character doing the remembering can alter or modify the past at will; and, since this is so, everything is at least potentially true for someone remembering. So, paradoxically, memory is also absolute—more real than reality, more present than the present, truer than the truth. In "Night" (1969), for instance, the revue sketch published along with *Lanscape* and *Silence,* the Man acknowledges this by assenting totally to the memory world of his wife, expunging from his personality and his past whatever is necessary to accord with the Woman's mental reality.[11]

In Pinter, the connection between memory and art becomes explicit in *No Man's Land* (1975). In that work, the analogue for memory is a dream, of which Hirst inquires: "Did it exist? It's gone. It never existed. It remains."[12] When memory, the most fertile of man's faculties, ceases to function as an active, creative power with the onset of death, then man resides permanently "in no man's land. Which never moves, which never changes, which never grows older, but which remains forever, icy and silent" (p. 95). Death—life devoid of memory or limited to one unalterable memory without any possibility of ever reinvigorating any other moment from the past—is equivalent in its fixity to a work of art, which is a form permanently frozen.[13] Within the play itself, the artifact is the photograph that freezes life and stops time—immortalizing life as it was at the moment—but that can also serve as a spur to memory, helping to evoke the past. As Hirst remarks about the photos in his album, "I had my world. I have it. ... We're talking of my youth, which can never leave me" (p. 45). But the photograph can only catch a static past moment rather than unleash the living past that the involuntary memory does for Proust. Art for Pinter is much less dynamic and organic than it was for Proust; the photograph can, at best, "remind you ... of what you once were" (p. 79), but not reveal who you now are. It does not, in short, plumb the suprareality. Ideologically, then, Pinter diverges most sharply from Proust in two respects: (1) memory for his characters is almost exclusively voluntary rather than involuntary; and (2) no evidence exists for art's ability to capture and convey the spiritual dimension. In *Old Times,* Anna—whom Arthur Ganz terms "the past incarnate"[14]—is summoned up by Kate and Deeley to participate in a battle for control fought most openly in the singing matches; at three decisive points in the play, action from the past is literally reenacted as if it were the present (pp. 43–46, 59–60, 62–63). In *No Man's Land* the work of art—the photograph—rather than be created from what is remembered, as is the case with art in Proust, is used instead as a spur *to* memory in order to escape the reality of time passing, to calm one from the fear of death. Memory is in no sense the initiator of art, however, and the artifact primarily freezes the sensory data rather than conveys a spiritual dimension.

ii

Our natural inclination is to feel that the cinema, unrestricted spatially and temporally and fully able to visualize thought, would be the most ideally suited of all artistic media for accomplishing the Proustian play of mind and memory. Indeed, in a 1935 essay that first appeared in *Trend* magazine, Paul Goodman argued that Proust's novel is essentially "cinematic in technique," linking "the Proustian free-association with the dissolving flow of cinema, the Proustian *idée fixe* with the focusing of the camera, the Proustian revelation with the unexpected juxtaposition of the cutting-room, and the passivity of the Proustian narrator with the photographic quality of the newsreel."[15] Yet Proust himself, within the final chapter of *In Search of Lost Time*—which John Updike has termed "this most luxuriously verbal of prose fictions"[16]— denies that this is so. Arguing against those critics who "regard the novel as a sort of procession of things upon the motion picture screen," Proust insists that "nothing is further from what we have really perceived than the vision that the cinematography presents" (p. 142), perhaps a natural position to hold if one considers the cinema an outgrowth and further extension of photography, and thus an art of the real that captures only the surface of things. The novel, on the other hand, built up in a manner analogous to constructing a cathedral, conjoins for Proust immediate sensations and memories. In other words, Proust believes that the cinema can simulate only "intellectual and visual" (or voluntary) memory that captures the immediate sensory data, whereas the novel can be the medium for imitating the involuntary memory and imagination. As he writes, "what we call reality is a certain connection between these immediate sensations and the memories which envelop us simultaneously with them—a connection that is suppressed in a simple cinematographic vision, which just because it professes to confine itself to the truth in fact departs widely from it—a unique connection which the writer has to rediscover in order to link forever in his phrase the two sets of phenomena which reality joins together" (p. 147). We might turn briefly, then, to Pinter's *Proust Screenplay* to see if this assessment of the cinema's limitations is borne out in fact. What we will discover, I suggest, is that Pinter *can* convey cinematographically the manner in which Proustian involuntary memory functions, but he does this only very late in the film script. In his "Introduction" to the printed version, Pinter indicates that he is structuring the work on two simultaneous movements. "The architecture of the film," he writes, "should be based on two main and contrasting principles: one, a movement, chiefly narrative, toward disillusion, and the other, more intermittent, toward revelation, rising to where time that was lost is found, and fixed forever in art" (p. ix). Pinter more successfully achieves the first than the second of these. The movement "toward disillusion" is reflected in three ways: (1) through visualizing the way that physical beauty is destroyed by the ravages of time; (2) through showing the breakdown of the aristocratic class and its diminishing value system; and (3) through dramatizing the inevitable jealousy in personal relationships.

Along with seeing the characters age physically over the forty or so years covered by the film, we best perceive the emphasis on time's destructive power in shots near the beginning and end that draw attention to the "grotesquely made up, grotesquely old faces," the "limping crooked men, half-paralyzed women, bodies trembling, faces caked with makeup.... the eyes tiny behind pouches of flesh" (pp. 4, 171) that Marcel sees at the Prince de Guermantes's party, as well as in the aging and eventual death of his beloved grandmother and the (reported) death of Swann. Sporadically, we are shown the philistines of an "atrophied" aristocracy and upper bourgeoisie on the brink of world catastrophe, afflicted by snobbism, boredom, and emptiness but desperately trying to maintain a facade—not unlike the class and circumstances later pictured by Jean Renoir in *The Rules of the Game*. Finally, almost every relationship is either tinged with or absolutely destroyed by sexual jealousy of one form or another. Pinter has, in essence, made these ordinarily triangular configurations with their obsessive jealousy central to his film script—even its pervasive subject—as they are, too, in many, if not most, of his plays. (There is, at the same time, much less emphasis on the problem of verifiability than in his works for the stage.) Among other such relationships here, we find the jealousy of Marcel's father over the boy's close attachment to the mother; Marcel's jealousy of Andrée and the friend of Mlle. Vinteuil over their relationship with Albertine; Swann's jealousy over Odette's friendship with Mme. Verdurin; Saint-Loup's jealousy over Rachel's acquaintance with the dancer.

The countermovement "toward revelation" is felt mainly in the gentle nudging Marcel receives from others, especially de Norpois and Saint-Loup, about setting out on his vocation as a writer. By the end of the film script, Marcel has come ot accept the fact of his own aging and mortality (he corrects himself and admits to being "An old man" [p. 172] when he invites Gilberte to dine with him), as well as to understand that, "pre-occupied ... with other matters," he has "wasted [his] life" (p. 164) by deflecting himself for so long from his vocation. When Gilberte introduces him to her young daughter, Mlle. de Saint-Loup, who unites Swann's way with Guermantes's way, she is like an apparition, a turning back of the clock to help him recapture the "childhood he remember[s] almost nothing of" (p. 163). She is an inspiration, his Muse; but more than that, as Fowlie says, she "will personify the literary work to come" (p. 251). When, in the voiceover that ends the screenplay, Marcel announces, "It was time to begin" (p. 177), what he heralds in is his newfound commitment to his art, which in Proust takes the place of and transcends the society he demolishes. Yet we do not apprehend from reading the screenplay, as we do from Proust's novel, the sense that the work we have just finished is the book that Marcel has written. At best, despite the past tense that he chooses over the present, it is something that he *will* write.

Dispensing with the "Overture" to *Swann's Way,* which echoes artistically many of the ideas formulated theoretically in the letter to Blum, Pinter adopts what seems, at first glance anyway, a much less chronological sequence than Proust had for his narrative, by framing the *Screenplay* with the party at the Prince de Guermantes's; the year of the party (1921), when Marcel is forty-one, becomes the "now" or the "present" in the viewer's frame of reference, and everything inbetween becomes a flashback—although, as my schematic diagram suggests, the past material within the frame is presented in a basically chronological fashion; such a charting of the central episodes in the movie's flow helps us see that the film script is actually less confusing than Enoch Brater suggests when he writes that "the frequent changes are by no means immediately clear. The confusion each time a cut is made is important: it forces us to re-orient ourselves in relation to a past recorded on a reel furiously on the run." In short, the past is not as "fractured, unstable, and ultimately hazy"[17] as Brater describes it for the characters in *The Proust Screenplay* as it is for those in Pinter's own dramas for the stage and television. Pinter focuses—again as my diagram shows—on fourteen periods in Marcel's life (from 1888, when Marcel is eight, on). There are certain points, however, at which a few shots, or even several shots, interrupt the linear progress to give us flashes of images from the past alive by chance in Marcel's mind. For example, in the midst of a segment occurring in 1898 when he is nineteen, he sees mentally, as we do in shots on the screen, events from 1893 and from earlier in 1898 of, respectively, the Duchesse at the wedding in the Combray church and of her at the opera. If it is usual for Pinter to play with chronology in such film scripts as *The Pumpkin Eater* (1964) and *Accident* (1967), it is not unheard of for Pinter to violate normal time sequence or linear chronology in his drama either; one notable instance occurs in the television play *The Basement* (1967), which dramatizes a triangular relationship taking place in the present and the past, or perhaps in the present and the future, since some of the scenes seem as though they might be Godard-like flashforwards in the musings of one of the characters.

The montage sequence that opens *The Proust Screenplay,* built up from thirty-four separate shots—only six of which picture events from the 1921 party—reflects cinematically Proust's notion that in our memory all things exist simultaneously in an eternal present, "encapsulating," as Brater says, "Proustian duration" (p. 122). It is here that we first see the yellow screen, actually a piece of yellow wall from Vermeer's *View of Delft* (a painting that

THE CHRONOLOGICAL STRUCTURE OF PINTER'S *PROUST SCREENPLAY:*

(Frame) 1921: Marcel at 41;
Party at the
Prince de
Guermantes's

(A) 1888: Marcel at 8; *hears garden bell* at Combray; Father "submits"

(B) 1898: Marcel at 19

(C) 1893: Marcel at 13; walks the Guermantes's Way; sees the Duchesse

(D) 1901: Marcel at 21; with Albertine

(E) 1893: Marcel at 13; goes Swann's Way; sees Gilberte·

(F) 1879–80: Swann and Odette

(G) 1895: Marcel at 15; sees Mlle. Vinteuil and "friend"; *sees steeples*

(H) 1897: Marcel at 17; sees Odette

(I) 1898: Marcel at 18; goes to Balbec with Grandmother;
*looks at sea from window with towel rack in foreground;
sees trees on way to Hudimesnil*

(J) 1899: Marcel at 19; Grandmother dies

(K) 1900: Marcel at 20; talks with the dying Swann about
Vermeer's "View of Delft"—*yellow wall*

(L) 1910: Marcel at 21

(M) 1917: Marcel at 37;
sanatorium. Also (Q)

(N) 1902: Marcel at 22; *hears Vinteuil sonata;*
Albertine dies

(O) 1903: Marcel at 23; *looks at balcony
window from gondola in Venice*

(P) 1915: Marcel at 35

(Frame) 1921: Marcel at 41; party;
*trips over uneven stones
as in Venice*; sees Mlle.
de Saint-Loup

Marcel tells Swann is "the most beautiful ... in the world" [p. 89]), thereby
immortalizing Proust's own love for it.[18] In this opening sequence Pinter
shows us as well the trees from the railway carriage; the sea from a window
with a towel rack in the foreground; a window in Venice seen from a gondola;
the dining room at Balbec; the sanatorium, with Marcel "motionless as an
owl" (p. 5); Marcel in Balbec, "bending over his boots, grief-stricken" (p. 5);
the three church steeples; and the garden gate at Combray. We also hear the
sounds of the garden gate bell and the "little phrase" from Vinteuil's sonata
that will act as catalysts to involuntary memory. Later, we will see the point at
which each of these images first entered Marcel's life and became permanently impressed upon his memory. But not until near the end of the filmplay,
however, when Marcel on the way to the Guermantes's party "trips over uneven paving stones" (p. 165), do we see the capability of the cinema for recreating the activity of the involuntary memory: As Marcel "puts his foot
back on the lower paving stone," Pinter cuts to a "Very dim quick flash of
Venice," followed by a cut to "Marcel's face," and—four shots later—to
"Blue mosaics in Saint Mark's Church" (p. 166). This concretizes for the
viewer Proust's theorizing and establishes that perhaps Proust's strictures
against the cinematic form were not totally warranted. Now we understand,
in retrospect, the full relationship between the "waiter inadvertently knock-
[ing] a spoon against a plate" (p. 3) and the "sound of a garden gate bell";
and between "Marcel wip[ing] his lips with a stiff napkin, which crackles"
(p. 4) and a towel as it is hung up to dry. So, by the end of the movie—if it is ever
filmed—the audience *will* experience memory in two of its most important
Proustian guises: as a network of relationships where each thing is somehow
connected with every other thing; and as an involuntary response to some
glorious chance occurrence, through which the past becomes the present and
time lost is found—and the journey in search of the true self within can begin.

As we have seen, *Old Times,* the drama Pinter wrote immediately before
setting to work on his *Proust Screenplay,* contains the fullest statement of his
own philosophy of time and memory and reality, and the one he penned
immediately after, *No Man's Land,* of his views on art. I think it is even
possible that his most recent full-length play, *Betrayal* (1978), evidences his
immersion in Proust. Not that it concerns memory, which it does in only the
most cursory fashion; indeed, the lack of any significant memory structure in
Betrayal may help account for its peculiar flatness and blandness.[19] But
perhaps *Betrayal* reflects the obsession with the past and even the flashback
structure that one finds in the *Screenplay. Betrayal,* which begins in 1977 and
then proceeds (mostly) backward in time several years to show how a triangular relationship (with both heterosexual and latent homosexual permutations)
came to be what it is, is virtually all past. We might even judge that there is
too much past, too much exposition of things ordinarily left enigmatic and
ambiguous and mysterious in Pinter, and not enough present. Rather than
begin and go forward as it could have, it begins and goes backward, but only
in "fact" and seldom in memory. It is that interplay of present reality and past

memory, or, more specifically, of the present reality *as* enlarged by involuntary memories of the past and of this past viewed in the uncompromising light of the present, that occupies and inspires Proust, and that adumbrates the later Pinter when he is at his best, as in *Old Times*—a title virtually interchangeable with *Time Lost* and *Rediscovered*.[20]

Notes

1. In his review of Terence Kilmartin's new translation of Proust, V. S. Pritchett comments: "the English title 'Remembrance of Things Past' evokes a drifting into the twilight of recollection; the French '*À la Recherche du Temps Perdu*' is intellectual—it defines the search for an exact recovery of what has been obscured by the memory of memory, and is a scientific expedition, an analysis of evidence, started off by involuntary memory" ("Proust," *New Yorker*, 12 October 1981, p. 191).

2. Harold Pinter, *The Proust Screenplay* (New York: Grove Press, 1977), p. x. Further references appear within parentheses in the text.

3. Proust gently chides Bergson for not "mak[ing] this distinction." For a brief discussion of Bergson and Proust, see chapter 1 of Margaret Church's *Time and Reality: Studies in Contemporary Fiction* (Chapel Hill: University of North Carolina Press, 1963). Shortly before her death, Professor Church, one of my collegues at Purdue, provided some helpful suggestions on the Proust sections of this paper.

4. Mina Curtiss, trans., *Letters of Marcel Proust* (London: Chatto and Windus, 1950), p. 213. Further references appear within parentheses in the text.

5. Howard Moss, *The Magic Lantern of Marcel Proust* (New York: Macmillan, 1962), pp. 94–95. Further references appear within parentheses in the text.

6. Marcel Proust, *The Past Recaptured* (New York: Vintage Books, 1971), pp. 270, 272. Further references appear within parentheses in the text.

7. Wallace Fowlie, *A Reading of Proust* (Chicago: University of Chicago Press, 1975), p. 96. Further references appear within parentheses in the text.

8. Harold Pinter, *Landscape and Silence* (New York: Grove Press, 1970), pp. 33, 52. Further references appear within parentheses in the text.

9. As Rüdiger Imhof comments: "They experience time as a never-ending series of repetitions. Time, for them, is extended to almost eternal dimensions, and everything appears to have happened long ago" ("Pinter's *Silence:* The Impossibility of Communication", *Modern Drama* 17, no. 4 [December 1974]: 458).

10. Harold Pinter, *Old Times* (New York: Grove Press, 1971), p. 59. Further references appear within parentheses in the text.

11. For a fuller discussion of this sketch, see my "Pinter's *Night:* A Stroll Down Memory Lane," *Modern Drama* 17, no. 4 (December 1974): 461–65.

12. Harold Pinter, *No Man's Land* (London: Eyre Methuen, 1974), p. 46. Further references appear within paretheses in the text.

13. For a fuller discussion, see my "From Flux to Fixity: Art and Death in Pinter's *No Man's Land*," *Arizona Quarterly* 35, no. 3 (Autumn 1979): 197–204.

14. Arthur Ganz, "Mixing Memory and Desire: Pinter's Vision in *Landscape, Silence*, and *Old Times*," in *Pinter: A Collection of Critical Essays*, ed. Arthur Ganz (Englewood-Cliffs, N.J.: Prentice-Hall, 1972), p. 171.

15. Paul Goodman, "The Proustian Camera Eye," in *American Film Criticism: From the Beginnings to "Citizen Kane*," ed. Stanley Kauffmann and Bruce Henstell (New York: Liveright, 1972), pp. 313–14.

16. John Updike, "Pinter's Unproduced Proust Printed," *New Yorker*, 20 February 1978, p. 133.

17. Enoch Brater, "Time and Memory in Pinter's Proust Screenplay," *Comparative Drama* 13, no. 2 (Summer 1979): 123, 125. Further references appear within parentheses in the text.

18. Andre Maurois, *The World of Marcel Proust,* trans. Moura Budberg (New York: Harper and Row, 1960), p. 278.

19. Brater, on the contrary, writes admiringly—in a second article—of *Betrayal's* "cinematic structure" as an advance that allows for a more objective point of view on the past: "No longer is the past recaptured, recycled, and reinterpreted through memory. Instead, it is invented for us and staged as documentary evidence which we are then obliged to 'judge' for ourselves" ("Cinematic Fidelity and Pinter's *Betrayal,*" *Modern Drama* 24, no. 4 [December 1981]: 508).

20. Since this essay was completed, two other articles have appeared that supplement it in useful ways. Mark Graham's "The Proust Screenplay: *Temps perdu* for Harold Pinter?" *Literature/Film Quarterly* 10, no. 1 (1982): 38–52, is a partial shot-analysis of the film script, focusing on the cinematic means by which Pinter conveys Proust's fusion of objective reality and subjective perception, of present and past, through memory. David Davidson's "Pinter in No Man's Land: *The Proust Screenplay,*" *Comparative Literature* 34, no. 2 (Spring 1982): 157–70, finds the film script feeble on practically all counts—other than in its use of point-of-view shots— in comparison with the novel, arguing that Pinter has failed to create an innovative filmic language comparable in richness and eloquence to Proust's literary language. The most laudatory assessment of Pinter's film script remains Stanley Kauffmann's early review, in which he judged it "incomparably the best screen adaptation ever made of a great work and ... in itself a work of genius.... a re-composition in another art" that "rises ... to the level of his best theater work" (*The New Republic,* 24–31 December 1977, p. 22).

11

The French Lieutenant's Woman: Screenplay and Adaptation

ENOCH BRATER

Pinter's accomplishment as a major voice in contemporary theater has tended to overshadow the career he has pursued almost simultaneously, that of professional screenwriter for the British film industry. So highly regarded has Pinter's work been in this medium that when, soon after completing the novel, John Fowles began to consider a movie version of *The French Lieutenant's Woman,* his thoughts immediately turned to the playwright as the man for the job. But the match was not to be—at least not yet. Pinter early on formed part of a development proposal the novelist was offered (the only part he truly wanted), but the deal fell through.[1] That the match was eventually made is something of a little drama of its own, and it is worth recording some of this history before going on to a consideration of the screenplay itself.

Fowles's experience as a screenwriter for the adaptations of his own novels had, even before *The French Lieutenant's Woman,* already made him something less than confident in his ability to translate word into image. He told one interviewer in 1981 that he no longer had any desire to write screenplays. "Not after *The Magus,*" referring to the movie version of his second novel for which he wrote the script he now considers a disaster. "Trying to adapt my own book, never again," he admitted as he stood near his home in Lyme Regis, the seaside town that provides not only the nineteenth-century fictional setting for *The French Lieutenant's Woman,* but the place where the movie was shot, as it were, on location. "I would only be interested in writing for film if I could direct it myself. It's a kind of egocentricity, really. In a prose text, you have complete control. Of course, a lot of writers enjoy this feeling of community in art. I was watching them film here. Everything was discussed. They all supported each other. I do feel a tiny envy for that."[2] In his introduction to the published version of Harold Pinter's screenplay, Fowles took the opportunity to expand upon the same point:

The business of proper domain is one reason I am no longer in the least interested in scripting my own fiction. To assemble a book with a considerable and deliberate number of elements you know cannot be filmed, and then to disassemble and reconstruct it out of the elements that can, is surely an occupation best left to masochists or narcissists. Nowhere can there be a clearer case for a fresh and outside mind on the job. The second reason is that I know I am, like most novelists, far too corrupted by and addicted to the solitary freedoms of prose fiction (where the one megalomaniac plays producer, director, all the cast *and* camera) ever to be any good at a team art—or team anything, for that matter. The third reason is that true script-writers are a race apart in a craft apart. It is only vanity that makes other writers believe that anyone can turn a hand to it. I believed so myself once. Then one day I persuaded Sidney Carroll to give me a copy of the superb scenario he wrote, with Robert Rossen, for *The Hustler*; and recognised (as I do again here) a league I shall never be in.[3]

Fowles had initially been driven to this foreign "domain" of scripting *The Magus* because he had been disappointed in William Wyler's interpretation of his first published book, *The Collector*, even though the movie sale, on top of his profits from the epistolary novel's healthy distribution, freed him to devote his full time to writing.[4] The vagaries, not to mention the politics, of an English writer trying to make movies in Hollywood, where life in the fast lane frustrates and finally disillusions the title hero of *Daniel Martin* (published in 1977), convinced Fowles that his third venture into movies demanded a new course. He could not do the screenplay himself, but this time he would retain veto power over director and writer:

Before the book was even published, and knowing I was less than happy with two previous films drawn from my novels, Tom Maschler (who was to prove as gifted an impromptu film agent as he is a publisher) persuaded me that I must this time insist on something that no producer happily grants: not just the usual token say in the choice of who shall direct, but a definite power to veto anyone I did not like. (We insisted on this—more than once at the cost of otherwise attractive offers—in all the dealings that were to come.) We also agreed that we would if possible have no truck with the ridiculous system whereby the finished script goes in search of a director, rather than the other way round.[5]

Fowles's insistence on a congenial team, collaborators who would be faithful to his novel and at the same time come up with something original, results from his long-standing concern that film not "overstamp" fiction. "What I like about the novel," he observed, "is that the reader actually supplies images. And so no one line will ever be read the same, even if it's from *War and Peace*. Of countless millions of readers, each will visualize it from his own memory stock. And so, one thing I'm a little suspicious of in the cinema is that, although you have to imagine in terms of motivation and psychology, the actual images are given to you."[6] "Novelists," he wrote, "have an almost archetypal fear that illustration will overstamp text, more precisely that their readers' imaginations (a vitally *creative* part in the total experience of the

book) will be pinned down and manacled to a set of specific images."[7]
For *The French Lieutenant's Woman* Fowles therefore wanted a director
sympathetic to the dangers the project might run into should text become
submerged in the process of making a film. Would the novel be forgotten
when the audience remembered the film instead? And would the entire
project degenerate into Victorian melodrama without the invention of some
counterpart to the novel's discursive style and allusive texture? *The French
Lieutenant's Woman* seemed to defy filming, especially when added to
these problems was the practical one of persuading a producer to spend
thousands of pounds for this property when there were dozens of authentic
Victorian stories waiting around to be filmed for free.

Fowles and Tom Maschler originally hoped to attract Karel Reisz to the
project, especially since they were impressed by the strong directorial hand he
had shown in such films as *Night Must Fall, The Gambler, Morgan,* and *Saturday Night and Sunday Morning*, the last based on the angry-young-man novel
by Alan Sillitoe. Fowles first showed Reisz his novel in 1969 when it was still
in manuscript, but the director was reluctant to begin another big "period"
picture so soon after reconstructing the early twentieth century in *Isadora*.
Besides, Reisz felt that he needed to work on a film that would garner him
something else besides critical praise; his last box-office success had been with
Morgan, back in 1966. Reisz reluctantly turned the project down.[8] Thereafter, as Richard Corliss pointed out so succinctly in *Time*, "the options
multiplied, the screenplays accumulated, the frustrations mounted."[9] At one
point Fred Zinnemann, whose films include *From Here to Eternity* and *A
Man for All Seasons*, held the rights to a script by the distinguished British
television for writer, Dennis Potter. Zinnemann, however, could not find
the right actress for the part, although at the time of this shaky negotiation
Fowles remembers that his own particular preference was for Vanessa Red-
grave. Zinnemann's plans eventually fell through, as did a subsequent
attempt by Mike Nichols and yet another one by Franklin Schaffner. "A
Hollywood scriptwriter came over to do that one," recalls Fowles. "I'm
told he had a nervous breakdown after six weeks."[10] Robert Bolt also declined to do the script but insisted with friendly honesty on explaining why:
in his view the book was, and would always remain, unfilmable. Another
well-known writer, one Fowles refuses to identify, also turned the script
down—"this time on the grounds that he could not help propagate a story
so biassed to the female side." Peter Ustinov became casually interested
in the idea of filming *The French Lieutenant's Woman* when he ran into
Fowles strictly by chance at the Beverly Hills Hotel. His idea for the film fell
in line with the popular previous answer proposed as an extension of a device
used in the book, "the creation of a character who was tacitly the author
and also a part in the Victorian story," someone who could both join the
action from within and stand back and comment on it, much as Anton Wal-
brook did in Max Orphuls's film *La Ronde*. Ustinov's project never got further than the discussion stage, though Fowles has admitted that he was the only

"narrator" who might have been able to bring this device off. Finally, after another overture from Maschler in 1978, Reisz said he would reconsider the project if he could persuade Pinter to collaborate with him by providing a script. For two weeks Pinter discussed the possible solutions with Reisz and then, as Fowles triumphantly relates, a "miracle" happened: "we found ourselves with the writer and director we most wanted."[11]

Pinter spent the next ten months working out a concept initially suggested by Reisz: setting the love story of Charles and Sarah within another, the "location" romance of Mike and Anna, the actors presented as portraying them. The modern love-affair, in Peter Conradi's telling summary, "then acts as an acoustic chamber within which the Victorian affair can resonate, amplifying and ironizing some of its meanings. It is a brilliant device."[12] The fourteen scenes detailing Mike and Anna's relationship are purely Pinter's invention, while the rest of the movie consists of Pinter's streamlining of Fowles's novel. The screenplay therefore switches back and forth between 1867 and 1979 in a clever juxtaposition of manners, plots, and social and sexual mores. Past comments on present, present comments on past. In several screenplays before *The French Lieutenant's Woman* Pinter used similar juxtapositions of time and place to establish startling contrasts, transitions, and tonalities.[13] In *Accident,* which Pinter adapted in 1967 from the novel by Nicholas Mosley, the action begins with a scene near the end of its "story," then flashes back to a scene furthest in time—from which point the scenes move forward chronologically with several brief flashbacks until a point in time close to where the flashback (the bulk of the film) began at the conclusion of the opening scene. *Accident* therefore features backward movements embedded in a forward movement that is in itself a flashback. In the filmscript of *Accident,* moreover, Pinter changed the entire narrative point of view. In Mosley's novel the bulk of the story, the entire flashback, is narrated from the perspective of its main character, Stefan. But Pinter did not choose to present these episodes from an introspective, private, or subjective point of view. He fixed the action, instead, in real, objective time rather than in psychological time. As Pinter later explained, the attempt to match images to every turn of Stephan's thought would result in an overwrought film, far too literary in the sense that everything would be overexplained. In a much quoted interview with John Russell Taylor, Pinter discussed his decision to strip *Accident* of its highly subjective form:

At first we thought of perhaps trying to do it the way the book does, to find a direct film equivalent to the free-association, stream-of-consciousness style of the novel. I tried a draft that way, but it just wouldn't work—anyway, I couldn't do it. You see, suppose a character is walking down a lane.... You could easily note down a stream of thought which might be perfectly accurate and believable, and then translate it into a series of images: road, field, hedge, grass, corn, wheat, ear, her ear on the pillow, tumbled hair, love, love years ago.... But when one's mind wanders and associates things in this way it's perfectly unselfconscious. Do exactly the same thing on film and the result is precious, self-conscious, overelaborate—you're using absurdly complex means to convey something very simple. Instead you should be able to convey the same sort of apprehension not by opening out, proliferating, but by closing in, looking closer and closer, harder and harder at things that are there before you.[14]

In *The Pumpkin Eater,* which Pinter adapted from the novel by Penelope Mortimer in 1964, time is manipulated much as it is in *Accident.* The opening scene is in the present. Then without dramatic preparation the next scene flashes back ten years. The following eight scenes move backward and forward within the ten-year flashback before reestablishing the "story" in the present, as in the opening scene. *The Go-Between,* from the L. P. Hartley novel, employs a much simpler time framework. Here we begin in the present, flash back to the past (where things take place chronologically), and then return to the present for the final brief scene of the film. *The Go-Between,* in addition, shows Pinter in full command of Hartley's late Victorian ambiance: "The past is a foreign country," we hear in a voice-over as the film opens, "They do things differently there."[15] The film script translates from novel to screen the tensions between the entrenched upper class and the emerging educated proletariat, the same class conflict from which Fowles draws his star-crossed lovers in *The French Lieutenant's Woman.* What Pinter highlights in both screenplays, however, is the contrast between a romantic, painful past and the remorseless, workaday present.

In each of these screenplays Pinter has displayed an enviable talent for concision, an ability to turn complex and at times baroque fictional worlds into the limited time frame movies demand. Nowhere is this technique more apparent than in *The Proust Screenplay,* where Pinter aims to achieve visually what Proust accomplishes verbally: the wonder of a fragment that only slowly reveals itself as a small part of a comprehensive canvas.[16] *The Proust Screenplay,* which Pinter wrote in 1972–73 for Joseph Losey, with whom he had worked previously on *The Servant, Accident,* and *The Go-Between,* is still unproduced and likely to remain so, especially since a French production team has completed a different project based on *À la recherche du temps perdu, Swann in Love.* Dismissing the notion of producing a film centered around only one or two volumes of Proust's seven-novel network, Pinter was determined "to distill the whole work, to incorporate the major themes of the book into an integrated whole."[17] In *The Proust Screenplay* Pinter moves quickly from scene to scene as the past, dissected and fractured, moves before us in a vast panorama of terse visual statements. Proustian narration is reduced to essential cinematic images; the architecture of the film script is based on two main and contrasting principles: "one, a movement, chiefly narrative, toward disillusion, and the other, more intermittent, toward revelation, rising to where time that was lost is found, and fixed forever in art."[18] Fowles, familiar with Pinter's reputation as a writer who can achieve maximum potential from minimal effects, observed: "He's got a very frugal mind. That kind of frugality in art is very, very rare. Most artists are much too ... talkative."[19]

Pinter's screenplay for *The French Lieutenant's Woman,* like much of his
earlier work in film, entails a search for metaphor rather than literal reproduction. For the latter, as Fowles suggested, "Go to television and ask for an
eight-hour serial. I think what you want in cinema is a good metaphor."[20] The
"excitement" in scripting *The French Lieutenant's Woman* exists, in Pinter's
own words, "in finding out how it can properly live in film." "It was a
question," the playwright continued, "of how to keep faith with Fowles's
complexity without being tortuous in film terms":

...the technical demands are, to use a cliché, a great challenge to solve. But
also it's entering into another man's mind, which is very interesting ... to try
to find the true mind.... there are boundaries, proper limitations, that you
have to adhere to, otherwise you are distorting, playing about, and having
your own good time, which is not the idea. But there remains within that the
freedom of the medium. And that is the whole point.... I don't really feel ...
any kind of constrictions. I always work—and certainly in the case of "The
French Lieutenant's Woman"—from a substantial respect for the work
itself.[21]

Pinter freely credits Reisz with the idea for the modern subject, though its
elaboration was his own. "Suppose we had a modern relationship that started
in bed and went from there?" the two agreed soon after embarking on the
project.[22] The screen version of *The French Lieutenant's Woman* would then
be a film-within-a-film about the making of a film, expanding upon the device
used previously by François Truffaut in *Day for Night.* By the end of 1979
Pinter had finished the weaving together of the two stories and the two centuries, and the proper metaphor was complete. "The novel is a science
fiction," said Reisz, "a Victorian story and a modern speculation about
fiction. Take away that acknowledgement of the 20th century, and the story
doesn't add up. Our sense of Sarah's sexual awareness is a modern thing;
inside her head, during the story, she jumps from the 19th to the 20th
century."[23]

Pinter's screenplay, moreover, takes for granted an audience familiar with
Fowles's story, and a knowledge of the book is tacitly assumed from the outset. The first scene is set at the Cobb in the Victorian town of Lyme Regis. It
is dawn, 1867: "*A clapperboard. On it is written:* THE FRENCH LIEU-
TENANT'S WOMAN. SCENE 1. TAKE 3. *It shuts and withdraws, leaving a
close shot of* ANNA, *the actress who plays* SARAH. *She is holding her hair in
place against the wind.*"

VOICE *(off screen)*
All right. Let's go.
    The actress nods, releases her hair. The wind catches it.
VOICE *(off screen)*
Action.
    SARAH *starts to walk along the Cobb, a stone pier in the Harbour of
Lyme. It is dawn. Windy. Deserted. She is dressed in black. She reaches
the end of the Cobb and stands still, staring out to sea.*   (P. 1)[24]

In the opening scene Pinter's adaptation is particularly apt, since it seems to harken back to the origins of the novel itself. Fowles has described in a valuable account of the novel's genesis how he got the idea for this story in the first place: he was imaginatively solicited by the mysterious figure of a woman staring out to sea from a deserted quay. "She represented a reproach to the Victorian age—she declined to belong to another epoch—and is an outcast."[25] The intrusion of the modern-day film world, which begins with the slap of a clapperboard, prepares us for the fact that this is not one featured story, but two: one modern, one period. Yet our awareness comes only gradually, for the first shot of the movie crew is followed by 25 consecutive period scenes. Only in scene 27 are we back in 1979: "*Dim light. A man and a woman in bed asleep. It is at once clear that they are the man and the woman playing* CHARLES *and* SARAH, *but we do not immediately appreciate that the time is the present*" (p. 8). Pinter means for us to be disoriented, just as we are when we try to separate truth from speculation in the process of reading Fowles's novel. "It's a kind of distancing, isn't it?" Pinter admits. "I remain very, very interested ... as to whether a given audience will find the presence of the modern scenes undermining to the Victorian tale. But I'm not a theoretician. I work mainly by instinct and sense of smell, as it were."[26]

The modern tale inserted into *The French Lieutenant's Woman* is all the more Pinteresque once we consider its relationship to the playwright's recent work for the theater, for Mike and Anna's story is a tale of upper-middle-class adultery, the sad litany of infidelity Pinter portrays in *Betrayal*. Whereas Fowles's nineteenth-century lovers are forced to meet in secret after passing a note carefully sequestered in a tea-party serviette, Pinter's wanton pair use the more mundane system of telecommunication. Yet in Pinter's world the telephone is both friend and betrayer. Mike will use it to ring up Anna after she travels to London to meet with her husband. When David answers the phone instead, Mike hangs up, but not before Anna's husband has the chance to hear children's voices in the background. When Mike calls again, almost too soon—this time to invite them to a party hastily arranged primarily so that he can see Anna again—David is no longer in the dark. Sonia, the other injured party, is not so innocent either: when Anna tells her in the garden of Mike's family's Victorian house (a nice Pinter touch there!) that she really envies her, Sonia answers in characteristic English understatement:

> ANNA
> It's a great garden. Who looks after it for you?
> SONIA
> I do.
> ANNA
> What, all on your own?
> SONIA
> Mmn. More or less.
> ANNA
> What about Mike? Doesn't he help?
> SONIA

Oh, when he's here. A bit. He's pretty lazy, actually.
    ANNA *smiles*

ANNA

I really envy you.

SONIA

Envy me? Why?

ANNA

Well, for being able to create such a lovely garden.
SONIA (laughing)
Oh, I wouldn't bother to envy me, if I were you.
Have some more wine.
SONIA *goes toward a table for a bottle.*   (Pp. 95–96)

Earlier, in scene 27, Anna had been momentarily upset when the telephone abruptly rang in her hotel room early in the morning and Mike lifted the receiver:

ANNA

Did you answer the phone?

MIKE

Yes.

ANNA

But then—they'll know you're in my room, they'll all know.
MIKE
In your bed.
    He kisses her.
I want them to know.

ANNA

Christ, look at the time.
    He holds her.

ANNA

They'll fine me for immorality.
    He embraces her.
They'll think I'm a whore.

MIKE

You are.   (Pp. 8–9)

Anna uses the word "whore" almost casually. Contrast Sarah's use of the same word in her set speech before Charles Smithson when she meets him by stealth at the undercliff:

I did it ... so that I should never be the same again, so that I should be seen for the outcast I am. I knew it was ordained that I could never marry an equal. So I married shame. It is my shame ... that has kept me alive, my knowing that I am truly not like other women. I shall never like them have children, a husband, the pleasures of a home. Sometimes I pity them. I have a freedom they cannot understand. No insult, no blame, can touch me. I have set myself beyond the pale. I am nothing. I am hardly human any more. I am the French Lieutenant's Whore.   (P. 45)

This is precisely the kind of irony Pinter's film script has been designed for us to appreciate. Nor does Pinter let the matter drop here. In scene 49 (Mike's hotel room in Lyme) Anna reads from a book: "In 1857 the Lancet estimated that there were eighty thousand prostitutes in the County of London. Out of every sixty houses one was a brothel." The figures make her suddenly realize the impact she is meant to have when she recites Sarah's lines from the script of *The French Lieutenant's Woman* she now holds in her hands: "If I went to London I know what I should become. I should become what some already call me in Lyme." Mike, who has been reading the sports page of a newspaper, takes out a pocket calculator:

MIKE

The male population was a million and a quarter but the prostitutes had two million clients a week?

ANNA

Yes. That's what he says.

MIKE

Allow about a third off for boys and old men... That means that outside marriage—a Victorian gentleman had about two point four fucks a week.

(Pp. 18–19)

Pinter will heighten such irony by inlaying the past with the present in other ways as well. In scenes 72–74 the "actors" Mike and Anna will use the lines of their "script" to refer to their own situation in the present.

CHARLES

May I accompany you? Since we walk in the same direction.
She stops.

SARAH

I prefer to walk alone.
They stand.

CHARLES

May I introduce myself?

SARAH

I know who you are. (P. 24)

In the scene that follows, set in Anna's caravan on the set, Mike and Anna will play with the same "text," but the nuances they interject foreshadow the end of their affair:

ANNA

Hello!
MIKE *comes in.*

MIKE

May I introduce myself?

ANNA

I know who you are.
They smile. He closes the door.

MIKE

So you prefer to walk alone?

ANNA

Me? Not me. Her.

MIKE

I enjoyed that.

ANNA

What?

MIKE

Our exchange. Out there.

ANNA

Did you? I never know ...

MIKE

Know what?

ANNA

Whether it's any good.

MIKE

Listen. Do you find me—?

ANNA

What?

MIKE

Sympathetic.

ANNA

Mmn. Definitely.

MIKE

I don't mean me. I mean him.

ANNA

Definitely.

MIKE

But you still prefer to walk alone?

ANNA

Who? Me—or her?

MIKE

Her. You like company.
He strokes the back of her neck.
Don't you?

ANNA (*smiling*)

Not always. Sometimes I prefer to walk alone.   (Pp. 25–26)

Pinter has made the dialogue serve both his "modern" and "period" ends. So much emotion—and so much irony—has been grafted into this exchange that when Mike and Anna do another "take" of the same Victorian scene from another camera angle, the tableau they have been trying to sustain breaks down completely. Reality intrudes into cinematic illusion:

CHARLES

May I accompany you? Since we walk in the same direction.
She stops.

SARAH

I prefer to walk alone.

CHARLES

May I introduce myself?

SARAH

I know who you are.
She collapses in laughter. He grins.

VOICE (*off screen*)

Cut! (*With bewilderment.*) What's going on?   (P. 26)

Here Mike and Anna's irony is intentional, as it will be again when Mike talks about "having" her in Exeter, where the actors are scheduled to shoot the crucial scene from Fowles's novel set in Endicott's Family Hotel. But Mike is destined to "have" Anna only in fiction. Anna, sensing the impossibility of the affair, has come down to shoot the scene in Exeter only for the day, leaving her husband behind in London.

MIKE

I'm losing you.

ANNA

What do you mean?

MIKE

I'm losing you.

ANNA

What are you talking about? I'm just going to London for—

MIKE

Stay tonight.

ANNA

I can't.

MIKE

Why not? You're a free woman.

ANNA

Yes. I am.

MIKE

I'm going mad.

ANNA

No you're not.
She leans through the window and kisses him.

MIKE (*intensely*)

I want you so much.

ANNA (*with mock gravity*)

But you've just had me. In Exeter.
She bursts into laughter. He grins slowly.... The train moves out of the station. She remains at the window. He remains on the platform.
(Pp. 73–74)

Other points of contrast between the modern and period stories will be noticed by the audience, and more particularly by the reader of Pinter's screenplay. In the nineteenth century "fiction" it is the man, not the woman, who must return to London. A favorite set piece of Victoriana, the almost obligatory scene at a glass-enclosed railway terminal (in this instance the one in which Sam greets his master on his return from London) is thus made to balance the parting shot of Mike and Anna played out before the sterile efficiency of British Rail. Scenes 113 and 118 point toward the same asymmetry. In the first Mike "*is lying on a sofa, staring at the ceiling. Jazz is playing from a transistor radio*" (p. 46). In the second, Charles is lying on the sofa in dressing gown, staring at the ceiling: "*Same set-up as shot 113*" (p. 47). Pinter makes us see that Mike's affair, despite the jazz, is becoming as complicated as Charles Smithson's. Anna, too, has been subjected to the same rigorous discipline. As she lies on the beach at Lyme Regis with Mike, plastic containers and thermos at their sides, and as she evades his questions about looking sad, her gaze turns almost inevitably to the undercliff, the place where she acts out her role of poor "Tragedy." She is thinking of her husband, her own French lieutenant, as she did almost subconsciously earlier in the film script when Mike woke her in the middle of the night and she murmured, almost mechanically, "David." In the modern story she is the center of the triangle: David/Anna/Mike replaces Ernestina/Charles/Sarah. And, just as Sarah will prepare her costume (a shawl) for her fateful sexual encounter with Charles (just as Ernestina had done for the proposal scene), so too will Anna arrive in her white Mercedes at the mews house of the film's costume designer in London. Draping a length of material across her, she looks at herself in a long mirror. "Yes," she says. "I think I'm going to like her in this" (p. 88). "This" is the fabric of the dress she will wear as the star in the final scenes of the movie to be shot at Windermere.

Foremost, however, among the many parallels between the past and present is the business Pinter has invented concerning how this movie the company is making is going to end. Mike answers David's question about this one way, Anna quite another. Pinter has made subtext paramount here in familiar "lines with no words" in them at all.[27] What everyone is really talking about is the end of Anna's affair with Mike. And that it is going to end sadly should come as no surprise: Pinter has been preparing us for that all along. "Good luck for the last scene," Sonia tells Anna when they say goodbye in scene 221. "We'll need it," Anna replies as the door closes (p. 95). Yet the special chemistry Mike and Anna have displayed in the scenes in which they portray Charles and Sarah changes once the crew moves to the Lake District. The acting isn't nearly so naturalistic as it was before. When "Charles" flings "Sarah" away in scene 233, he does so just a little too violently: *"She falls to the floor, hitting her head. He stops. She sits up, holding her head. He stares down at her. She looks at him. She smiles"* (p. 120). This scene will have to be reshot. Mike and Anna are "acting" badly—and in both senses of the word. Mike is using Charles to get at Anna through Sarah. Their affair, as we have seen, is on the rocks.

That is why the "final" two romantic shots of Charles and Sarah are all the more painful: they embrace, they kiss, followed by the slow dissolve to the lake boathouse at evening. Sarah sits in the prow, Charles rows, and the boat "glides out into the calm evening water" (pp. 102–3). But the lush tranquillity of Windermere is not for the likes of Mike and Anna. Rock music invades the Wordsworthian landscape; we make an all-too-abrupt switch to the present. The unit party is in full swing in the New House garden. Pinter, with characteristic nerve and originality, has found a striking cinematic analog for the novel's ambiguous ending. Anna is supposed to have an assignation with Mike, but when she retreats to her dressing room, she stares at herself in the mirror, as we have seen "Sarah" do in several memorable shots before. Mike, as full of anticipation as the Charles he has been portraying, rushes in, only to discover that the room is empty. Suddenly we hear the sound of a car starting up: "MIKE *runs to the window and looks out*" (p. 104), just as he did in scene 2, where we first meet him as Charles in the film he is making of *The French Lieutenant's Woman.* A white Mercedes is driving toward the gate. Anna is gone. But Mike calls out for Sarah.[28] Mike, a method actor, has been carried away by the figure he portrays. Pinter fixes Mike's passion, as he has done with Marcel's in *The Proust Screenplay,* forever in art, the movie he has just made.

"You and Harold go off and do what you like," Fowles told Karel Reisz, "But just don't explain Sarah."[29] Pinter has come up, instead, with two interlocking and intersecting stories, one a slimmed down version of Fowles's Victorian drama, the other an original tale that bears a tempting resemblance to his own work for the theatre. "What the project needed above all else was a demon barber," the novelist admitted, "In politer terms, someone sufficiently skilled and independent to be able to rethink and recast the thing from the bottom up."[30] The "long haul" of adapting this book points out once again Pinter's expertise in the medium of film. "Any original idea I may have," he continued, "I don't have very many of them ... always seems to go immediately into ... theater."[31] Yet in his adaptation of *The French Lieutenant's Woman,* a fleshing out of a director's unusual concept, Pinter opens up the story to accommodate a pair of modern lovers he has invented. The lines he has written for Mike and Anna read like familiar Pinter dialogue, the territory where menace lurks in the background of everyday speech when recited by characters wearing masks in seemingly "polite" conversation. In this screenplay Sarah remains the same "remarkable" person she says she is in Fowles's novel, for in the playwright's hands she becomes Anna/Sarah, as enigmatic as any woman we encounter in his repertory. Any view of Pinter that disregards his important work in cinema therefore misses one of the major sources of his dramatic imagination. As he said recently of *Betrayal,* "It was originally written for the stage in a kind of cinematic way, with a structure that possibly owes something to the films I've worked on for the last 20 years.... My early plays started at the beginning and went to the end; they were linear. Then I did more and more films, and I felt that 'Betrayal' —even the stage version—comes as much out of film as it does out of the stage."[32] A close examination of how Pinter's films have influenced the overall structure of his drama, and vice versa, would clearly support his candid assertion. But that is more properly the subject of another essay.

Notes

1. See John Fowles's Foreword to Harold Pinter, *The French Lieutenant's Woman: A Screenplay* (Boston and Toronto: Little, Brown, 1981), pp. viii–ix.

2. Leslie Garis, "Translating Fowles into Film," *New York Times Magazine*, 30 August 1981, p. 48.

3. Fowles, Foreward, in Pinter, *Screenplay*, p. x.

4. Richard Corliss, "When Acting Becomes Alchemy," *Time*, 7 September 1981, p. 48.

5. Fowles, Foreward, in Pinter, *Screenplay*, p. vii–viii.

6. Garis, "Fowles into Film," p. 49.

7. Fowles, Foreward, in Pinter, *Screenplay*, p. xiv.

8. Garis, "Fowles into Film," pp. 48–49; Fowles, Foreward, in Pinter, *Screenplay*, p. vii ff.

9. Corliss, "When Acting ... Alchemy," p. 48.

10. Ibid., p. 49.

11. Fowles, Foreward, in Pinter, *Screenplay*, p. vii ff.

12. Peter Conradi, *John Fowles* (London and New York: Methuen, 1982), p. 100. See also Conradi's article "*The French Lieutenant's Woman:* Novel: Screenplay: Film," *Critical Quarterly* 24 (Spring 1982).

13. For an elaboration of this point, see Enoch Brater, "Cinematic Fidelity and the Forms of Pinter's *Betrayal,*" *Modern Drama* 24 (December 1981): 503–13.

14. Harold Pinter, quoted in John Russell Taylor, "Accident," *Sight and Sound* 35 (1966): 183.

15. Harold Pinter, *Five Screenplays* (London: Methuen, 1971), p. 287.

16. Enoch Brater, "Time and Memory in Pinter's Proust Screenplay," *Comparative Drama* 13 (Summer 1979): 121–26.

17. Harold Pinter, *The Proust Screenplay* (New York: Grove Press, 1977), p. ix.

18. Ibid.

19. Garis, "Fowles into Film," pp. 48–49.

20. Ibid., p. 48.

21. Ibid., p. 51.

22. Corliss, "When Acting ... Alchemy," p. 49.

23. Ibid.

24. Quotations from the screenplay in my text are from the edition cited in n. 1.

25. Conradi quotes from the novelist's "Notes" to *The French Lieutenant's Woman* in his *John Fowles*, p. 59.

26. Garis, "Fowles into Film," p. 51.

27. Martin Esslin, in *Pinter: A Study of His Plays* (New York: W. W. Norton, 1976), p. 124, quotes from Pinter's unpublished novel, *The Dwarfs:* "But tell me this. What do they do when they come to a line with no words in it at all?"

28. It was John Fowles who suggested that the film's final line of dialogue be "Sarah!" See Corliss, "When Acting ... Alchemy," p. 50.

29. Garis, "Fowles into Film," p. 48.

30. Fowles, Foreward, in Pinter, *Screenplay*, p. viii.

31. Garis, "Fowles into Film," pp. 50, 51.

32. Leslie Bennetts, "On Film, Pinter's 'Betrayal' Displays New Subtleties," *New York Times*, 27 February 1983, sec. 2, pp. 1, 23.

12

After *No Man's Land:* A Progress Report

ARNOLD P. HINCHLIFFE

No Man's Land opened on 23 April 1975 and marked the culmination of twenty years' work in the theatre, work interspersed with other kinds of writing—poetry, plays for radio and television, adaptations and film scripts—and other kinds of work—acting and directing. The longest gap between stage plays was that between *The Caretaker* (1960) and *The Homecoming* (1965), but during that time Pinter produced plays for television and two, if not three, film scripts. In short, Austin Quigley is probably correct when he suggests that of all the dramatists who came to the fore in the middle fifties in the British theatre only Pinter has consistently maintained a momentum of achievement:

Where Osborne, Wesker, Simpson, Arden, and even Beckett have gradually faded as playwrights, Pinter increasingly attracts the attention of scholars, critics and audiences alike.[1]

The plays for the theatre were, it is true, getting shorter. Pinter confessed in 1969 that all he seemed to write were one-act plays: "I doubt if I will ever write something memmoth."[2] *Old Times* (1971) was certainly not *mammoth,* if that word implies five acts and a large canvas; nor, for that matter, was *No Man's Land,* but the texture and complexity of both rendered them formidable experiences in the theatre. *No Man's Land,* in particular, seemed to gather together in its bleak fashion the strands of Pinter's previous work—a room, power, violence, sex, memory, and language—in such a way as to leave us with the question: where can Pinter go after this? There was, of course, some difficulty in separating the play from the performance, since Sir Ralph Richardson and Sir John Gielgud could make anything memorable. Was it, after all, only, as Peter Thomson suggests, "an elaborate spoof"?[3]

In the period after *No Man's Land* Pinter worked on the film script of *The French Lieutenant's Woman,* which took over a year to write. Film scripts have nourished his stage plays, and filmic effects have been noted in *The*

Homecoming and *Old Times*. *No Man's Land* itself surely owes much to *The Go-Between*. But film scripts, however rewarding, are time-consuming and, however distinguished, are works of translation rather than creation. The opening of *Betrayal* at the National Theatre on 15 November 1978, was, therefore, more than usually interesting, particularly as, for the first time, the title of the play was ominous rather than cozy. The play was striking in other ways too. In it, for the first time, Pinter abandoned the use of a single set in favor of several sets. The nine scenes require seven sets, which the National Theatre solved with a rather clumsy and very cramped revolving stage. The use of sets rather than a single, composite set had hitherto been restricted to the more fluid medium of television. Second, the nine scenes were all dated, and the play begins in 1977 and moves backward to 1968, an arrangement that is listed in the program (the alternative would have been, presumably, Brechtian slides announcing time and place, which might have been difficult since a revolve was being used). Each scene also has a season as well as a time and place.

Betrayal opens in the spring of 1977 in a pub where Emma has asked Jerry to meet her. Emma runs an art gallery and has been married to a publisher called Robert for more than fourteen years. Jerry is also married, though his wife, Judith, a doctor, never appears in the play. Both couples have children, and Jerry, a literary agent, has been Robert's best friend and best man since they were both at college (Jerry at Cambridge and Robert at Oxford). Emma had a seven-year affair with Jerry, which had ended two years ago (scene 3), may be having an affair with a writer-artist called Casey (whose name is actually Roger), and has asked Jerry to meet her not so much to recall old times as to tell him that her marriage is now finished, that Robert has been betraying her for years with other women (as she and Jerry betrayed him for years) and that it is now all out in the open. So she has told Robert about her affair with Jerry.

Jerry immediately calls Robert (scene 2) only to discover that Emma told him about the affair four years ago (scene 5). Jerry is upset and points out that he and Robert have seen one another a great deal over the last four years (though, as Robert observes, they have never played squash). Jerry tries to recall their relationship by saying that he is reading Yeats but has to remind Robert that he read Yeats at Torcello four years ago (scene 7). Scene 3 is set in the flat in Kilburn in the winter of 1975 when the affair is ending. It has proved difficult to get away to make love in the afternoon!

The play now catches up on the relationship between these three characters at crucial points in the story: the summer in Venice (1973) when, according to Emma, they did not go to Torcello and according to Robert he did, when Emma is trapped by a letter and discloses all about her affair with Jerry but insists that their son is Robert's; followed by Emma's meeting with Jerry in the flat after the Venice holiday when she mentions nothing about the discovery (though Jerry, too, has had a fright concerning a letter and thus offers her the opportunity to tell him); and a scene between Robert and Jerry in a restaurant, also after the Venice trip, when Robert does not mention Jerry's affair with his wife. Scene 8 is the summer of 1971 and shows the beginning of the affair in the flat at Kilburn when Emma assures Jerry that her son is Robert's, not his, and throws in the suggestion that Jerry's wife is not always at the hospital when he thinks she is. Finally, in scene 9, we see the true beginning of the affair, in the winter of 1968, when a drunken Jerry declares his love for Robert's wife and Robert accepts that Jerry, as his oldest friend and best man, can do just that.

The play is as loaded with detail as the room in *The Caretaker* is cluttered up with objects, but are any of the details significant? Is squash a game you only play with friends (does Robert stop playing squash with Casey because Casey is having an affair with Emma?)? Who is Casey? Who is Ned's father? In Judith, that busy doctor, busy betraying Jerry? What significance can we attach to the novel by Spinks that is read in Venice and that may be about betrayal ("not much more to say on that subject, really, is there?")? Is the journey to Torcello, if it took place, a clue—and should it recall Ruskin or even *Howard's End*? And during the discussion on Venice in the restaurant is there some clue in the fact that Robert orders Corvo Bianco, a wine from Palermo? But such questions seem rather teasing than resonant.

Critical reception was puzzled, too, and on the whole disappointed. Robert Cushman, in *The Observer* (19 November 1978), retitled the play "Harold Pinter's Revenge" because here was a dramatist who has always been accused of giving us no details about his characters now giving us everything and it does us no good:

We learn a lot about the world of the three characters, and Mr. Pinter is as adept as ever in slipping immensely suggestive details on to a bland canvas. These details, however, are merely sociological; we learn almost nothing about the characters as individuals and thus—since their situation is hardly original—can take no very lively interest in them.

B. A. Young, in *The Financial Times* (17 November 1978), found "no complexities in the straight-forward tale of multiple adultery and the object of it seems to be to put forward the rival claims of wife and mistress." The characters were uninteresting presumably because Pinter wanted them to be uninteresting, and the colorless performances were, presumably, as Peter Hall required. Milton Shulman (*The Evening Standard*, 16 November 1978) also found nothing difficult or obscure in this Chinese box of deceit and thought that many women's magazines would be prepared to print it without changing a line. Noting that Pinter's concerns have gone up in the world, he suggested that the play was about something more important than the betrayal of a husband by his wife or vice versa—it was about "man's betrayal of his best friend." John Barber (*The Daily Telegraph*, 16 November 1978) came out feeling that he had seen "an intricate and unimportant machine" rather than a play, while Michael Billington, in *The Guardian* (16 November 1978), was distressed by "the pitifully thin strip of human experience it explores and its obsession with the tiny ripples on the stagnant pond of bourgeois-affluent life." Here Pinter has betrayed his talent "by serving up this kind of high-class soap-opera (laced with suitable cultural brand-names like Venice, Torcello, and Yeats) instead of a real play." Billington conceded that there was technical finesse in starting the play in the present and running it backward, but though he felt this would make for interesting discussions in a drama faculty it provided thin pleasure for the playgoer.

Bernard Levin, in the *Sunday Times* (19 November 1978), has never been an admirer of Pinter's very small talk—indeed he describes the Pinteresque elements in *The Caretaker* as "nothing but devices which cover a desperate poverty of thought and feeling"! Levin, therefore, was disheartened to find that he did not like the new, plain Pinter either. Here Pinter has written "a real play instead of a series of trivial dramatic acrostics" but he found "the content empty, and on its surface, dull":

There is no sign of any interest, on the part of Mr Pinter, in these people, their lives or their feelings; not surprisingly, they therefore arouse no interest of their own.

He concluded that Pinter's new ground turns out to be a quicksand into which he sinks without a struggle.

Was this a new, plain Pinter? Martin Esslin asks that question, too (*Plays and Players*, January 1979), pointing out that here was a realistic account of adultery in London middle-class intellectual circles with one unusual feature—the story is told backward, and the sting is in the tail:

Throughout the first eight scenes we might still have believed that it was the end of a great tragic passion that we witnessed at the beginning. Here it is revealed that it arose casually, out of drunkenness, and, above all, that the husband who burst into the room just as it was happening not only remained blind to what was going on but actually encouraged the affair by taking the confession of his friend's affection for the wife as no more than politeness and withdrawing leaving the two together.

The colorlessness of the characters is according to Esslin the point of the play. There is very little human emotion between them—the relationship on "a personal, intellectual, spiritual plane is shown as totally arid, in fact, nonexistent. That, to my mind, is the point the play is making. And it is by no means a trivial point. It is central to the sickness of our society." Possibly; but we cannot have the impression of a great tragic passion if the characters are colorless and uninvolved.

The play, it seems to me, is more suited to television. The clumsy revolve at the National Theatre may have been intended to suggest a roundabout (as in *La Ronde*), but it reduced the sets to one cramped space losing the distinction between the spacious elegant surroundings of their married lives and the narrow conditions of adultery. The actor Daniel Massey, in fact, was far from colorless, and the text supports his knowing, ironic treatment of his character. Robert may not "give a shit," but he is a man who enjoys the violence of squash and who gives Emma "a good bashing" once or twice *because* he feels like it. He is also witty. Penelope Wilton made what she could of Emma, which is not very much, while Michael Gambon caught exactly a Jerry who doesn't know very much about anything and runs round trying to find out without being found out. But it is a comedy Pinter could have written any time before or after *No Man's Land;* it boils the pot nicely, and resonances may emerge with time. Reading the text again in 1982, I no longer found that the word *dull* applied.

Pinter's next play was no indication of the route he would take, either. *The Hothouse* opened on 1 May 1980, but according to Martin Esslin it was a play written for radio in 1958 and discarded in favor of the style and methods of *The Caretaker,* which incorporates some of its material. Another episode from the play appears as the revue sketch "Applicant." In an interview with Laurence M. Bensky in 1966 Pinter explained why he had discarded it:

It was heavily satirical and it was quite useless. I never began to like any of the characters, they didn't really live at all. So I discarded the play at once. The characters were purely cardboard. I was intentionally—for the only time I think—trying to make a point, an explicit point, that these were nasty people and I disapproved of them. And therefore they didn't begin to live.[4]

Perhaps, however, in the mechanical world of *Betrayal* such characters struck their creator more sympathetically? At any rate, in an interview with John Barber (*Daily Telegraph,* 23 June 1980), he said that he had come across the script in 1979, read it as a stranger, and found himself laughing a lot: "Nothing about it seemed to be 22 years old. I could have written it yesterday, so far as I could see." He also added that it was more pertinent now than in 1958:

... when we didn't know anything about the Russian psychiatric hospitals, did we? Now we do. But then, it might have been dismissed as fantasy. No, I certainly had no special knowledge of such things. Of course I knew Koestler's "Darkness at Noon" and so on, but in 1958 I don't think there was general knowledge that these things were being refined, as they are to this day. Not that I consider this play to be a grim piece of work. I don't think it is. An odd mixture of "laughter and chill" if you like.

Again we must qualify the comment about special knowledge with the comment in the *Radio Times* for the television production of the play:

Way back in the 50s, Pinter became a guinea-pig in a psychiatric hospital, subjected to a test for "ten bob a time." And that was an experience, involving electrodes in the head, which stayed with him ever since.[5]

This would certainly explain material that runs through *The Hothouse* (1958),

The Dwarfs (1960), and *The Caretaker* (1960).

The Hothouse is a psychiatric hospital run by the Ministry and staffed with characters who have names like Roote, Gibbs, Lamb, Lush, Tubb, and Lobb (Hogg, Beck, Budd, Tuck, Dodds, and Tate are also mentioned). It is Christmas Day and the snow is falling fast as Colonel Roote and his deputy, Gibbs, discuss the problems of the institution, one of which is the death of 6457 (patients have no names, only numbers). Does Gibbs want to replace Roote as Roote may have replaced his predecessor? Certainly Roote's hesitant use of the word "retired" seems to suggest that it does not exactly described what happened to his predecessor. The lights fade and come up on another part of the establishment, suggesting that Pinter did not need film work to write the opening scene of *Old Times* and that the text as we have it was certainly not written for radio. Lamb has just played a game of table tennis with Miss Cutts (as in *Tea Party*?). Although Lamb has been at the hospital for over a year he has made no contacts nor has he realized his ambitions for promotion, so he is delighted to meet Miss Cutts and play with her. We are also told that his job is to go round and round the hospital checking that all gates and doors are locked. The scene fades back to Roote's office where the second problem is being discussed: 6459 has given birth to a baby boy! Miss Cutts enters and having noted that Gibbs seems frightened of her proceeds to comfort Roote and ask him whether he finds her feminine enough (as in *The Lover*?). Gibbs, meanwhile, is playing patience! Lush enters and challenges him about paternity and death, but he responds by summoning Lamb to the No. 1 Interview Room where he can assist at an experiment (as his predecessor did). Lamb is fitted up with earphones and electrodes, interrogated, and left there.

Act 2 opens again in Roote's office. It is night, the snow is turning to slush, and the heat is intolerable (though higher up in the building, we are told, it is very cold). Roote is drinking with Lush, who challenges him (as he challenged Gibbs) and gets a violent response. Gibbs arrives to announce that Lamb is the father of the child (though as *virgo intacta* this can hardly be true), and over the intercom we hear the sounds of the understaff's Christmas raffle in which all the prizes go unclaimed (including the duck won by Lamb). Tubb arrives with a cake for the Colonel and a request that he will give his Christmas address. Before that happens, however, we have a series of scenes: one between Miss Cutts and Gibbs who is trying to offer him the same "comforts" that she gives to Roote, provided that he kills Roote; a scene in which Roote insists that Gibbs has come to murder him, and the three men (Roote, Lush, and Gibbs) draw knives and circle one another (as in *The Collection*?); and, finally, a scene in which Miss Cutts arrives for bed wearing a negligee given to her by 6459, when it is strongly suggested that Roote is the father of the baby. After the Christmas address, which is suitably platitudinous, the stage is filled with the murmur of madness and the lights go up on an office at the Ministry where Gibbs is offered Roote's job. It appears that all the staff have been killed when the patients escaped—possibly because the locktester was absent. Roote, as Gibbs says, was unpopular because he had murdered 6457 and seduced 6459. But all the staff have not been killed: the final scene of the play reveals locktester Lamb still sitting in Room 1 wearing electrodes and earphones and as if in a catatonic trance.

The Hothouse was played in a composite set from which most of the color had been drained—it was unnerving to see the familiar *Sunflowers* by van Gogh painted in creams and browns. Clearly, too, the play has been quarried for subsequent work.

James Fenton, in the *Sunday Times* (4 May 1980), asked the obvious questions: why reject the play in the first place and why resurrect it now? The answer to the second question he finds easy: it is a work of comic invention that clearly occupies an important transitional role in the development of the writer. The answer to the first question lies in the faults of the play:

There is too much here which yields, or seems about to yield, to the more intrusive spirit of criticism. At the centre is the struggle between the two men, but at the periphery there are distracting figures and scenes waving to attract our attention.

When Pinter says in his program note that he put it aside and then went on to write *The Caretaker,* this shows, Fenton remarks, that he already knew he could do better. Robert Cushman, however, in *The Observer* (4 May 1980), sees Pinter as a major talent producing minor plays and suggests that this play shows that *The Caretaker* was not progress but rather "a glorious sidetrack." *The Hothouse,* he points out rightly, looks forward to *The Collection* and *The Homecoming* and beyond, where "the honing gets finer, and the people thinner." The theme is state-subsidized terror: "It isn't a particularly interesting statement, but the author is clearly more hooked on the mechanics anyway." The play was directed by the author and televised on 27 March 1982. The composite set was replaced by a large mansion with an enormous, bare, classical staircase, long whispering corridors, and snow falling against leaded panes of glass. Pinter is reported to be happier with this version than with the stage production. Certainly in the theatre I found the play less funny than the audience seemed to find it, mainly because so much in it had been done better in subsequent plays. The television version was remarkably gray and unfunny: more chill than laughter—and the power struggle between Roote and Gibbs was intensified by making the nervousness of Gibbs clear. The close-up of his face wearing a genuinely haunted look when he says that something is happening and he cannot define it suggested that he will be as unstable as Roote when the time comes and matched the bleak passionless atmosphere of the play—even sex takes place in the control room of the interrogation center! A play, here, then, as unnerving as *The Homecoming* and as unlikeable as *Betrayal.* Pinter said that he did not like any of these characters, and it showed.

Pinter's next play, *Family Voices,* was written for radio in 1980. It was first broadcast by the BBC Radio 3 on 22 January 1981 and later given a concert

performance at the National Theatre. Radio has always been a favorite
medium for Pinter—it was radio that rescued him after the disaster of *The
Birthday Party*—so in writing this play Pinter felt that he was coming home.
In the *Radio Times* (17 January 1981) he spoke of the purity he finds in writing for the radio: "It reduces drama to its elemental parts and enforces the
sort of restraint, simplicity and economy I strive for anyway." *Family Voices*
is a dialogue between a young man and his mother. The young man has left
his home (somewhere by the sea) to live in a boarding house in a big city run
by a Mrs. Withers. Although the dialogue begins as a series of letters, the
letters are never sent and, indeed, since the third voice is that of his father
who speaks from the grave, the whole play may take place in the mind of
the protagonist. The mother misses her son and wonders what is happening
to him—and with reason, for as the boy explores the house and meets its
strange inhabitants, he grows more and more uncertain. His mother, on the
other hand, grows more and more angry until she finally threatens to denounce him to the police as a spineless character who has fallen into the hands
of underworld figures who use him as a male prostitute. At the end the boy
announces his homecoming, but if it takes place it will be too late since his
father is dead and what he had to say can never be spoken. The son may be
happy or unhappy, he may seduce the landlady's daughter or be seduced by a
homosexual policeman in a house that may be charming and aristocratic or
little more than a bawdy house. Such uncertainty is Pinter at his enigmatic
best, and we would no more trust this young man than we would trust Stanley in *The Birthday Party*. For this family play about a homecoming (and as
disturbing as *The Homecoming*), Peter Hall directed a splendid cast with
Peggy Ashcroft, Mark Dignam, and Michael Kitchen, who captured this experience of knowing nothing, expecting much, and fearing everything splen-
didly. With a different cast, *Family Voices* was included in a triple bill at the
National Theatre on 14 October 1982 under the title *Other Places*.

The second sketch, *Victoria Station,* is short and comic, but comic only in
the surreal sense that, say, *The Hothouse* was comic. A radio-car controller is
trying to get hold of car 274 to go to Victoria Station to pick up a passenger
coming from Boulogne. This passenger is an old friend of the controller, a
Mr. MacRooney, who has a limp and a feather in his hat, is carrying fishing
tackle, and wants to go to visit an old aunt at Cuckfield who will probably leave
him all she possesses. So the trip would be worthwhile. But, 274 seems to be
in a fog and neither knows nor cares about Victoria Station but thinks he is
stuck outside Crystal Palace. The controller tries to humor him, then gets
angry with him, but finally admires him and threatens to join him for a nice
celebration, for 274 confesses that he has a Passenger On Board, a girl with
whom he has fallen in love. We cannot see a girl on the back seat so, like the
Matchseller in *A Slight Ache*, she may not exist or 274 may have killed her
and kept her body on the back seat. Pinter leaves the sketch open and vague.

By contrast, *A Kind of Alaska* is founded on fact and gives us another
country where, indeed, they do things differently. A note to the text acknowl-

edges that the source is a book called *Awakenings*, published by Oliver Sacks in 1973, recounting his experiences as a doctor with a new drug, L-DOPA. Between 1916 and 1917 there was an epidemic of sleeping sickness, and fifty years later those still alive were treated with L-DOPA and "erupted into life once more" after a sleep that had lasted in some cases for twenty or thirty years. Pinter's play dramatizes the awakening of Deborah after her first injection. Deborah fell asleep when she was sixteen and awakens after 29 years at the age of 45, caught between an adult body and an adolescent mind. Critics compared the play to Luigi Pirandello's *Henry IV*, but Pinter eschews both melodrama and fancy dress, allowing the play to happen only as Deborah can tell it. She speaks, of course, with remarkable fluency and presents the memories the playwright needs to recapture her lost world. When she awakens she meets her doctor and her younger sister Pauline, who are married. But Pauline calls herself a widow because her husband has devoted his life to caring for the sleeping Deborah, keeping the body supple and ready to move should awakening take place. Deborah now has to adjust to her new world. She sees her sister as some old aunt who has come to visit her and keeps asking about her boy friend Jack or whether her elder sister Estelle married the ginger boy from Townley Street. She has been away, in a kind of Alaska, an arctic territory not unlike no man's land, which she recalls as "a vast series of halls. With enormous interior windows masquerading as walls. The windows are mirrors, you see. And so glass reflects glass. For ever and ever."[6] Shall I tell her lies or the truth, asks Pauline. Hornby, her husband, suggests that she tell Deborah both. So Pauline says that the family is away on a world cruise and has stopped off at Bangkok. But Hornby tells Deborah that her mother is dead, and her elder sister never married because she has had to look after her father who is blind. And Pauline married him so that he could look after her. Martin Esslin claims that Deborah adjusts to and accepts her new reality, but at the end it is Pauline's version of reality that she chooses.

James Fenton, reviewing this triple bill in the *Sunday Times* (London; 17 October 1982), noted how difficult it is to distinguish between Pinter the gag writer and Pinter the poet. The whole experience of *Other Places* was, somehow, greater than the parts—a disturbing experience, though one that could as well take place on the radio as in a theatre.

At this stage we can, therefore, offer only an interim report. Martin Esslin sees *Betrayal* as something like a new beginning: a realistically told tale of trivial adultery among the London literary establishment. Jerry, a literary agent, has an affair with Emma, the wife of his best friend, Robert, which starts in 1968 and ends in 1975. Emma yields to Jerry because she resents Jerry's relationship with her husband and what she sees as a betrayal leads to a whole series of betrayals. The special touch, apart from the factual background each character is given, is that the tale is told backwards so that we see each "truth" happening after the "truth" that followed it. The idea of a collection of "truths" is not new (*The Collection,* after all, dates from 1961), and characters have always been free to invent any past or memory that suits them. Linguistically, too, nothing about *Betrayal* is new. The characters now are socially superior to the characters in the early plays and are both intelligent and literate, but whether it is Robert from *Betrayal* or Gus from *The Dumb Waiter* who is talking, the result is still just chatter. *Betrayal* may demonstrate that causality is fictititous, or that facts about characters are useless, but the characters here are, for Pinter, unusually empty. Adultery produces no resonance of guilt. What went wrong in the lives of Stanley or Davies is replaced here by an oddly anodyne feeling. The play is certainly the first that has been directly aimed at the audience that Pinter can expect at the National Theatre and turns out to be his most commercially successful play in America. The film, directed by David Jones and starring Jeremy Irons, Ben Kingsley, and Patricia Hodge has, apparently, been very successful in America and will, presumably, be so when it opens in England. A production of *Betrayal* at the Greenwich Theatre showed, in 1983, that it could sparkle in a Noel Coward sort of way, though one wonders what the Chinese made of it since this production was sent in 1982 as part of a British Council Tour and was the first modern Western play seen in China since the Cultural Revolution. Presumably, it confirmed their worst suspicious about Western society, for the characters are shallow and seem to be exclusively preoccupied with sexual relationships, which are shown to be casual and superficial. Esslin contends that this aridity is deliberate and satiric. Pinter presents us with a sardonically bitter portrait of the world of literary commerce and ladies who manage art galleries, none of whom have any deep commitment to culture, literature, or art. This, he suggests, is mature and distilled Pinter.[7] Certainly, Pinter after *No Man's Land* is distilled. The qualities that he most admires and strives for—restraint, simplicity, and economy—are strongly evident in all his recent work, and it is tempting to see him writing for radio and theatre in a deliberately spare verbal way to balance his work for films, where his words (often translations after all) exist only as part of an opulent whole. He certainly preserves the distance and anonymity of the camera.

All the more pleasing, then, to end with *Players,* which opened at the National Theatre on 7 September 1983. A dramatic monologue delivered by Edward de Souza gave us Pinter's memories of Anew McMaster and Arthur Wellard. The cliché "fondly remembered," used in the advance publicity, was, for once, quite accurate. Here Harold Pinter celebrates the two games in his life, acting and cricket, and recalls, with great affection, two old timers.

Notes

1. Austin E. Quigley, *The Pinter Problem* (Princeton: Princeton University Press, 1975), p. 273.

2. Harold Pinter, *The Times* (London), 11 April 1969.

3. Peter Thomson, "Harold Pinter: A Retrospect," *Critical Quarterly* 20 (Winter 1978): 21–29.

4. The interview with Lawrence M. Bensky was for the *Paris Review*. It is printed in *Writers at Work: The Paris Review Interviews,* Third Series, ed. George Plimpton (1967). It is reprinted by Arthur Ganz in *Pinter: A Collection of Critical Essays*, Twentieth Century Views (Englewood Cliffs, N.J.: Prentice-Hall, 1972), pp. 19–33. This quotation appears on p. 28.

5. *Radio Times*, 27 March–2 April 1982.

6. "A Kind of Alaska," *Other Places* (London: Methuen, 1982), p. 39.

7. Martin Esslin, *Pinter the Playwright* (London: Methuen, 1982), pp. 214–16.

13

Family Voices and the Voice of the Family in Pinter's Plays

KATHERINE H. BURKMAN

Although Harold Pinter has claimed as the territory for his plays a place in which his characters exist "at the extreme edge of their living, where they are living pretty much alone,"[1] he also writes and has always written plays about living in families. Since his first play, *The Room* (1957), in which Rose is summoned home by her father's emissary, until this more recent play, *Family Voices* (1981), in which a young man writes his mother about a newfound family, Pinter has dwelt on the family; even the sole character in Pinter's television play *Monologue* (1973) has fantasies about family life. He would die, the man in *Monologue* insists, for his friend/rival's unborn children, whose uncle he imagines himself to be. In *Family Voices*, initially performed on BBC Radio 3 in January of 1981 and then as a "platform performance" by the National Theatre in London in February of that year, Pinter has made explicit what has been implicit in all of his previous drama—the agonized isolation of the individual "living pretty much alone" at the same time that he lives in the midst of family, in this case a newfound family and his original one.

Pinter interweaves the voice of the young man, Voice 1, telling his mother about his new family, with the voices of the young man's mother, Voice 2, and of his father, Voice 3, dwelling on their relationship with him in such a way as to make the connection between the two families clear. Benedict Nightingale, in his review of the play for the *New York Times*, considers the young man's original home life to be "bloodless." "No wonder the boy escaped," he writes, "and no wonder he is attracted by these sinister, unsettling Witherses [his new family]. Their household is sexy, inscrutable, frightening and fascinating, where his old one was sexless, predictable and dull."[2] But as Nightingale himself perceives, the boy has not really escaped—the original family voices are ever present, even if he does not appear to hear them. While he seems, at play's end, to be caught between old and new fami-

ly, as motionless, despite his announcement to his mother that he is returning
to her, as the tramps who decide to leave are at the end of Samuel Beckett's
Waiting for Godot, he is really imprisoned in what is fundamentally one family situation. The Withers family is not so different, it turns out, from his own.
There is, in fact, as with the *Godot* tramps, no escape—no place to go.

The counterpoint of past and present in *Family Voices* reveals the love-hate
relationships in the family that are typical of Pinter's other dramas. The
young man, who writes with ostensible love to his mother, is, according to her
voice, which he does not appear to hear, completely out of touch with her and
has not even responded to news of his father's death. All three of the characters demonstrate their ambivalent feelings by juxtaposing clichéd statements
of affection with outbursts of hostility.

The young man, for example, says that he is planning to meet a nice girl to
bring home to his mother, but then he goes on to tell her of the far-from-
"nice" girl he has met, Jane. Jane, whom he supposes to be Mrs. Withers's
fifteen-year-old granddaughter, despite her dedication to homework—"She
keeps her nose to the grindstone,"—tends to keep her toes in the young
man's lap. And despite her dedication to homework, Jane apparently does
not go to school since no one, except Mr. Riley, leaves the young man's new
home, and Mr. Riley does so only rarely. Invited to have tea by Lady Withers, probably Jane's mother, though he wonders whether mother or sister, a
lady who wears red dresses (one turns out to be pink) and who entertains
people at night, he tells his mother of Jane's behavior. "Her stockinged toes
came to rest on my thigh," he explains, though later the toes became "quite
restless, even agitated" (p. 287). The young man's desire to offer himself as
Jane's tutor is fraught with sexual innuendo. "She possesses a true love of
learning," it seems. "That is the sense of her one takes from her every breath,
her every sigh and exhalation. When she turns her eyes upon you you see
within her eyes, raw, untutored, unexercised but willing, a deep love of learning" (p. 288).

The young man not only juxtaposes his ostensible desire to meet a respectable girl with his descriptions of Jane and her acrobatic toes, he also describes
himself alternately as drunk and as a teetotaler. He first disclaims his drunken
habits by pretending he was joking about them:

When I said I was drunk I was of course making a joke.
I bet you laughed.
Mother?
Did you get the joke? You know I never touch alcohol.   (P. 282)

Several lines later, however, he indicates that his relationship with his landlady, Mrs. Withers, is one of drunken comradery:

I get on very well with my landlady, Mrs. Withers. She tells me I am her
solace. I have a drink with her at lunchtime and another one at teatime and
then take her for a couple in the evening at the Fishmongers Arms. (P. 283)

Similar contradictory attitudes emerge from Voice 2, as the mother alternates effusive expressions of love with ferocious attacks of hate. She tells of her fantasy of living with her son and his "young wife," the nice girl she expects him to marry, and speaks of her longing and love for him and of his father's affection as well: "Darling. I miss you. I gave birth to you. Where are you?" (p. 284). Shortly thereafter, however, she speaks of him as a monster whom his father cursed on this deathbed. In one speech she makes, her alternation of attitudes comes together as she apparently recognizes her isolation, not just in her present deserted state but in her past state when her son was home and the family seemed to be intact:

Sometimes I think I have always been sitting like this. I sometimes think I have always been sitting like this, alone by an indifferent fire, curtains closed, night, winter.... What I mean is that when, for example, I was washing your hair, with the most delicate shampoo, and rinsing, and then drying your hair so gently with my soft-towel, so that no murmur came from you, of discomfort or unease, and then looked into your eyes, and saw you look into mine, knowing that you wanted no-one else, no-one at all, knowing that you were entirely happy in my arms, I knew also, for example, that I was at the same time sitting by an indifferent fire, alone in winter, in eternal night without you.
(Pp. 289–90)

What the mother intuits, of course, is that she will have no place in her son's life with a nice wife. He is, she later asserts, depraved and has doubtless become a male prostitute. "I have declared in my affidavit," she informs him, "that you have never possessed any strength of character whatsoever" (p. 295). Women, she asserts, were his downfall; witness their French maid or his governess. Jealousy of her son is the paramount emotion that emerges. Far from sexless or bloodless, the mother seeths with sexual jealousy and prophetically fantasizes the worst, ensuring the realization of those fears with her domineering and repressive character.

Equally ambivalent is the allegedly dead father, who protests when his voice emerges quite late in the play, that he lives and then admits that he is dead. Alternately cursing his son for wishing him dead and expressing his love for him—"Lots of love, son. Keep up the good work" (p. 294)—the father has the play's last word. "I have so much to say to you. But I am quite dead. What I have to say to you will never be said" (p. 296).

In the context of the play, the suggestion is that the father has never been able to speak to his son; he has always, in the sense of communication, been the living dead. Now that he is dead, it makes little difference. Like Beckett's improperly born characters, the prototype being a child Mrs. Rooney refers to in *All That Fall,* because he has not been fully born, he cannot fully die.

The father, however, makes himself well understood through the young man's alternate fathers, Mr. Withers and Mr. Riley. When the young man asks Mrs. Withers to clarify her relationship to the bald, retiring man who, someone has told him, is called Benjamin Withers, she evades the question by calling the young man her pet and apparently offering him an embrace—"Sometimes she gives me a cuddle, as if she were my mother" (p. 286). But if the mother would ignore the father and possess the son, the father will not permit this to happen. Mr. Riley disposes of the original mother and Mr. Withers warns the young man away from the three Withers women with their provocatively sexual ways.

It is while bathing that the young man learns from the intruding Mr. Riley that his mother and sister have been sent on their way. From the outset, the bathroom has taken on symbolically surreal importance to the young man as the room the inhabitants of the house all brag of to everyone they meet because of the pleasant baths they may take in it "quite naked." Significantly, what the people brag about is the baths in the bathroom "we share." One gets the feeling that what is shared in his new family is a form of nakedness or exposure, one that worries the young man so much that he must assure his mother of the pleasantness of the room and bath four times in one brief description.

Mr. Riley is able to come through the bathroom door, which the young man thought he had locked, to inform him both of his dismissal of his mother and sister and of his own homosexual leanings. Denying any knowledge of the young man, Mr. Riley has sent his relations, in hilarious fashion, on their way. "I can smell your sort a mile off," he has apparently informed them, "and I am quite prepared to put you both on a charge of malicious mischief, insulting behaviour and vagabondage, in other words wandering around on doorsteps knowingly, without any visible means of support. So piss off out of it before I call a copper" (p. 289). The young man reacts to this outrageous treatment of his family and to the homosexual pass that Riley proceeds to make at him by commenting on his father's absence. "It interests me," he notes, "that my father wasn't bothered to make the trip" (p. 289). The father is both absent and ominously present in Mr. Riley, who later, having invited the young man to his room, dwells again on his homosexual inclinations, which he says he restrains only to keep on "the right side of God." He could, he asserts, crush the young man with his love.

I'm a big man, as you can see, I could crush a slip of a lad such as you to death, I mean the death that is love, the death I understand love to be.
(P. 292)

Sexual love, historically so often associated with death, is explicitly related to it here, but we have seen the dangers of love tinged with death throughout the play.

The other father figure appears with threatening warnings just as the young man prepares to settle into his new family. "I took a seat," he says, describing an elegant evening with the three Withers women. "I took it and sat in it. I am in it. I will never leave it" (p. 290). Almost immediately after so settling, the young man appeals to his mother for advice, worried by Mr. Withers's summons to his room and his seemingly senseless and mystifying speech. "Don't mess about," is one of his clear messages, and he informs the boy that he is in a "diseaseridden land" (p. 291). "I'm the only saviour of the grace you find yourself wanting in," he assures the young man, who, when asked to look at him and does, finds the experience "like looking into a pit of molten lava" (p. 291).

The young man collapses before the claims of the two father figures, the one threatening him away from women if he is to receive salvation, the other threatening the damnation of a crushing, homosexual love. To whom does he turn, then, when so threatened by the men but to his mother, to whom he decides to return. Back in his original home, at least in fantasy, he accuses his mother of doing away with his father. A final wish? A half-feared, half-anticipated fantasy?

The final irony of the young man's plan to return home, which is expressed in counterpoint with his mother's decision to give up on him and with his father's admission that he cannot reach him, is heightened by the audience's realization that the young man has clearly never left home. In essence, his two families, the new and the old, are one. The women are sexually available and possessive while the men are threatening, uncommunicative, and also sexually available. And so the young man's paralysis—he does not move—is given full psychological explanation. The family is a wasteland in which any move is fatal, and not to move, though safe, is stultifying.

Family Voices bears some resemblance, as Nightingale points out, to *The Homecoming*; the Withers family attract the young man because they act out the dark sexuality that is repressed in is own home, even as Ruth is attracted by her intellectual and repressed husband's unrepressed family.[4] Ruth, however, elects to stay with her new family, who provide much more of an alternative for her than the young man finds in his new family. At the end of *The Homecoming* Ruth is not only at home but well in command of her situation. The young man, in contrast, seems quite lost at the end of *Family Voices* and is certainly not self-possessed.

Family Voices harks back more clearly to an early Pinter play, *A Night Out* (1960), in which another young man attempts unsuccessfully to break away from his mother. "Your father would turn in his grave if he heard you raise your voice to me,"[5] Albert's mother tells him when he wishes to spend one night "out." "You're all I've got, Albert. I want you to remember that I haven't got anyone else. I want you ... I want you to bear that in mind" (p. 6). When Albert does go out, he identifies a girl he picks up with his mother. The girl poses as a mother but is actually a prostitute. "You're all the same, you see, you're all the same, you're just a dead weight round my neck" (p. 43), he complains to her.

While the images are richer and fresher in *Family Voices* than they are in this earlier play, the drama suffers from the same tendency, rare in Pinter's canon, to make something of a case history of its protagonist. Although the same oedipal tensions emerge in many of Pinter's plays, the characters and

situations, however bizarre, do not give the impression of aberration or mental illness; they tend, instead, to suggest universal struggles for dominance, love, and identity, with the voice of the family operating as the ground on which the characters work out their salvation or suffer their damnation.

In most of his plays, as much as Pinter cares for some of his individual characters, he is as concerned with the family or the "tribe" as he is with those who make it up. Rarely involved with the kind of caricature that he played with in *A Night Out* and possibly *Night School* (1960), and that he has partially returned to in *Family Voices,* Pinter does not always give us three-dimensional characters, but he does, more often than not, create characters with archetypal resonance. The ritual rhythms and structures of his plays suggest Pinter's concern with the survival not just of the individual, but of the family within which the battle for survival and salvation takes place.

We have a touch of this universalizing tendency in *Family Voices* when Mr. Withers reportedly suggests himself to the young man as the source of salvation ("I'm the only saviour of the grace you find yourself wanting in" [p. 291]); focus remains, however, on the young man's psychology. Mythical overtones are clearer, however, in *No Man's Land* (1975), a play about a lost old man, in which Hirst, like the lost young man of *Family Voices,* cannot deal with his sexuality—Alan Jenkens has aptly titled his review of *Family Voices* "No Man's Homecoming."[6] Focus here is less on individual psychology than it is on a ritual struggle for renewal with Spooner, as Hirst's double or inner potentiality, playing out his spurious savior role until his, and consequently Hirst's, final defeat at the play's conclusion. In *No Man's Land* the disease-ridden land of *Family Voices* partakes of the mythical dimensions of T.S. Eliot's wasteland as Hirst becomes the wounded fisher king whose impotence Spooner diagnoses—"Do forgive me my candour. It is not method but madness. So you won't, I hope, object if I take out my prayer beads and my prayer mat and salute what I take to be your impotence?"[7]—and would cure—"I offer myself to you as a friend. Think before you speak" (p. 33). Spooner, whom Hirst has picked up at a pub, and who may be his old friend and sexual rival, Charles Weatherby, offers himself not only as Hirst's friend but as his secretary, cook, companion, and warrior; he will even "accept death's challenge" (p. 89) in his behalf. The form of renewal Spooner offers is a literary reading, to which young and old will flock, actually a literary revival.

Hirst seems to find this invitation as absurd as it sounds, coming, as it does, from a man who is clearly down and out and desperate to make Hirst his benefactor. But the eternal winter that Hirst's henchmen, Foster and Briggs, provide for him as an alternative—"The subject is now winter. So it'll be winter forever" (p. 92)—is a condition that Spooner has at least desired to expel. Not only has he offered a vision of a reading that will summon young and old, he has also earlier offered to go through Hirst's photograph album in an effort to bring the past to life to quicken the dead. And he has described a scene of renewal to Foster and Briggs that is central to the struggle for renew-

al in the play. In this scene in an Amsterdam restaurant, a fisherman's triumphant catch, held aloft, is enjoyed and greeted with the happy laughter of a little girl, kissing lovers, and an applauding waiter, all watched by a whistling man sitting at a table in shadow. Spooner has not, as he has planned, painted the picture of the scene, but his vision has all the connotations of a restored people celebrating their now potent fisher king. If it is his fate to remain like the whistler, in shadow, Spooner has made every attempt to share with Hirst the several possibilities he envisions for a return to spring.

What makes this battle between winter and spring a family drama is Spooner's claims on Hirst as a family man and his particular kind of sexual rivalry. "He has grandchildren. As have I. As I have. We have both fathered. We are of an age. I know his wants. Let me take his arm. Respect our age. Come, I'll seat you" (p. 47), Spooner says, playing his role of understanding family man. Both men evoke a pastoral family past in which their wives have served tea on lawns. The sexual rivalry that surfaces—Spooner taunts Hirst with the suggestion of a straying wife and Hirst claims to have cuckolded Spooner—is always part of the Pinter family drama in which oedipal conflict is ritualized into a battle for renewal: in Frazerian terms, the battle of the old god with the new, both for the kingdom and for its fertility-goddess queen.[8]

As in so many of Pinter's dramas, the past is uncertain in *No Man's Land*. The women are absent, and one does not know whether the sexual rivalry is based in fantasy or reality. Verification, however, is irrelevant because that rivalry is dramatically present.[9] Because Spooner is Hirst's double, that rivalry also becomes something of a challenge to Hirst, whom Spooner attempts to awaken and restore as an artist and as a man, so, too, restoring himself.

While the young man in *Family Voices* is bound by his psychology in a family prison, the old man of *No Man's Land* elects his doom and ultimately defeats not Spooner but himself. Unable to accept his mortality (he refuses to accept his recurrent dream in which someone, either himself or Spooner, is drowning), he is beyond the possibilities of renewal.[10] Indeed, Pinter's male characters, like Hirst, are rarely able to accept the opportunities that they are given for renewal; witness the Matchseller, who rises as Edward falls in *A Slight Ache* (1959), driven more by Flora's needs and the fatalities in his situation than by any visible choices he may elect to make. Richard in *The Lover* (1963) is a rare exception as he attempts to integrate the several roles he plays with his wife but is defeated by her need to continue to relate as a series of fragmented selves.

While women in Pinter's early plays are often caught as completely as the men are in the destructive nature of family relationships (Rose in *The Room* [1957]; Meg in *The Birthday Party* [1958]), Flora makes her tragicomic choice for renewal in *A Slight Ache*; and Ruth in *The Homecoming* (1965), Kate in *Old Times* (1971), and Emma in *Betrayal* (1978) are all women who take charge of their lives. Taking charge of her life, for Ruth, in what may remain Pinter's most significant family drama, involves the exchange of one family for another and the wresting of the rule of her new family from a weekend

patriarch, Max.

Ruth moves into a position of power in her husband's family by assuming the role of their absent wife and mother, Jessie. Like Jessie, she is regarded by the men as mother, wife, and whore; and she derives her strength from the ability to play all roles at once but also from her need to do so. Teddy loses the right to his homecoming by a refusal of involvement. "You're just objects," he tells his family. "You just move about. I can observe it. I can see what you do. It's the same as I do. But you're lost in it. You won't get me being ... I won't be lost in it."[11]

Ruth, on the other hand, by losing herself in the family, not only offers a potential renewal to them but finds it for herself as well. America with her intellectualizing husband has been a place of dryness for her, a desert of insects and rocks. Draining the glass of water that Lenny offers and then would take away, Ruth confesses her thirst and proceeds to use the demands of the family to fulfill her own needs. She will stay on as a part-time prostitute, but she will decide the terms of the contract. "She'll use us, she'll make use of us, I can tell you!" (p. 81), Max complains, groveling at the end of the play for a kiss. But when she withholds sexual consummation from Joey, he is strangely satisfied; "Sometimes you can be happy ... and not go the whole hog. Now and again ... you can be happy ... without going any hog" (p. 68), he explains to his family. Receiving her final blessing at the end of the play—"*She continues to touch JOEY's head, lightly*" (p. 82)—Joey, whose oedipal conflict with Max has been dramatized throughout, would seem to be the new king who has won his new mother/wife's love. For the play, despite its seeming cynicism, is about love[12] and about the way a family regroups around the woman who promises it new life even as their needs promise new life for her. Because the men express themselves in harsh and brutal terms, and because Ruth seems so capable of success in playing their jungle games, one is tempted to see the play in terms of a savage power struggle. Beneath the mask of the pimp, however, Lenny is the sensitive, questioning philosopher that Teddy, the professional philosopher, fails to be. And beneath the laconic comments of Ruth, one can sense how she suffers her victories. True heir of the biblical Ruth, Pinter's Ruth arrives as an alien and stays to bring forth new life. The play's rituals, as Vera Jiji points out, "allow for the expression of aggression and the reaffirmation of love."[13] And above all they allow for the reaffirmation of the family.

The self-possession of Kate in *Old Times* is achieved, like the self-possession of Flora and of Ruth, by discarding a husband, an effete, middle-aged artist, though in this case there is no new king-god to take his place. Kate must come to terms in this play, not only with the failure of her marriage but with a past self who comes back to haunt her in the form of an old roommate, Anna. Victorious but alone at the end of the play, Kate moves away from the kind of possessiveness that characterizes family relationships at their worst in Pinter's dramatic world. "And someday I'll know that moment divine,/ When all the things you are, are mine" (p. 27), Deeley sings in vain to his wife. Unlike the young man of *Family Voices,* Kate is able to deal with the voices of the past; "But I remember you. I remember you dead" (p. 71), she says in an annihilating speech to Anna. Startlingly and somewhat agonizingly alone at the end amid the ruins of her past, Anna and Deeley, Kate is, in contrast to *Family Voices's* young man, quite free.

Emma, too, in *Betrayal* is able to deal with the voice of the family, and though she does not take on the matriarchal tasks of *The Homecoming's* Ruth, like Ruth, she plays out the roles of mother, wife, and whore within the family circle. Like *The Homecoming, Betrayal* is a play that would seem to shatter the family structure irreparably; yet it, too, has its homecoming—its celebration and affirmation of the family.

In the backward movement of the play, which begins with Emma's meeting with her ex-lover, Jerry, to tell him of the end of her marriage to his best friend, Robert, and ends some years earlier with Jerry making his first pass at Emma, we discover betrayal within betrayal within betrayal. Emma has betrayed Robert with Jerry, Robert claims to have betrayed Emma, and he has betrayed Jerry by concealing his knowledge of the Emma-Jerry affair from him. Since Emma and Robert have a child during the course of her affair with Jerry, Robert points out to her that she has betrayed Jerry as well.

Why, then, is a play suffused with sexual betrayal a family-affirming drama? Partly because the characters care very much about each other as family. Their very betrayals, wounding as they are, are desperate attempts at cummunication; they betray one another, paradoxically, to find that which is authentic within the family.

The theme of betrayal as communication appears much earlier in *The Collection* (1961), a play in which Stella clearly tells her husband, James, of a passing affair with a fellow dress designer, which may or may not have transpired, in order to get his full attention. Just as Stella fails to win her husband's affection with her tactics—James, instead, develops a homosexual interest in her alleged lover—so Emma finds herself rejected by both men, whose relationship, it appears, Emma has actually interfered with from the beginning.

In the oedipal rivalry of the men over Emma, she becomes something of an object. They are less about her than about their rivalry—a case, perhaps, of what René Girard would call triangular desire. What occurs is that one man (Jerry, in this case) desires another's woman (Robert's) because the other man desires her. This particular case of imitative desire involves double mediation as Robert founds his own desire on that of his disciple/rival.[14] Jerry's hostile fantasies about Emma reveal how much he has aproached her in order to get at Robert somehow. Recalling that he was Robert's best man at his wedding, Jerry remarks to her, "I should have had you in your white, before the wedding. I should have blackened you in your white wedding dress, blackened you in your bridal dress, before ushering you into your wedding as best man."[15] And Robert, in his fury over the affair, quite openly states his feelings about Jerry. "I've always liked Jerry," Robert confesses to Emma. "To be honest, I've always liked him rather more than I've liked you.

Maybe I should have had an affair with him myself" (p. 87).

The hostility of the men toward Emma is, however, not necessarily based on a latent homosexuality that Robert comes to recognize. It is, rather, part of the family drama in which Robert as publisher-father vies with Jerry as agent-son over the mother. The ultimate betrayal is actually built into the family structure—the men simply cannot forgive the women who begot them by betraying them with their fathers, and that hostility carries over to their wives. The wife/mother, Emma, who chooses now the father, Robert, now the son, Jerry, is considered a whore by both men who have cast her in that role from the beginning.

Jerry has thrown Emma's daughter Charlotte up in the air and caught her in the midst of both families, an event that Emma and Jerry return to several times in the play and one of its central images. Since Charlotte apparently looks like Emma, the image comes to stand for Emma, who is herself thrown into a precarious position. That involves the two families. When Jerry and Emma break up the flat in which they have carried on their clandestine meetings, they note rather sadly that it was never a home with children. Still, whatever their affair was about involved the two homes that formed its backdrop. As in *Family Voices,* one may seem to move outside of the family—to betray it—but the family holds one.

The renewal of the family in *Betrayal* is suggested in the new triangle that emerges from the old. Robert, who considers himself a bad publisher because he hates books, especially the modern prose fiction Emma and Jerry seem to feel enthusiastic about, has not really lost Emma to Jerry, who is, after all, merely an agent. They both lose her, however, to Casey, a writer whose work Emma has not initially cared for, but either she or his work, she explains, "has changed." Jerry claims Casey as his "boy" since he has discovered him, so the new triangle of Robert/Jerry, Casey, and Emma is still a family affair, but one that will test the authenticity of Emma's or Casey's change. Emma's move to the creative source is still within the publishing family, but unlike Kate in *Old Times,* there is a creative source, at least off stage, toward whom she moves. She has found her freedom within the family. And just as she knows the book she has been reading in scene five is not, as Robert suggests, about betrayal, we come to see *Betrayal* as being less about betrayal than it is about the fidelity that may at last be found in the family.

The men, on the whole, in Pinter's family plays are trapped in their ambivalent family relationships. Several of the women, though, who as whores seem to betray all that is sacred in the family, tend to find their way to freedom and to an authentic voice that is still a family one. Because the oedipal rivalry that claims the young man as its victim in *Family Voices* is an inevitable part of the family dynamic that Pinter depicts, his family dramas always do have their victims. But in those plays in which the women, who are at the center of the rivalry, refuse to become either the possessive mother of *Family Voices* or the helpless victim of male wrath of *The Room,* they do sometimes find their way to a self-possession in which they accept their multiple roles as wife, mother, and whore, belonging to themselves and thereby offering new life to the family.

Notes

1. Quoted by Roger Manville, "The Decade of Harold Pinter," *Humanist* 132 (April 1967): 114.

2. Benedict Nightingale, "Pinter's New Play Evokes 'The Homecoming,'" *New York Times*, 1 March 1981, sec. D, p. 8.

3. Harold Pinter, *Family Voices* in *Complete Works: Four* (New York: Grove Press, 1981), p. 284. All subsequent quotations from the play are from this edition and are hereafter given parenthetically in the body of the text.

4. Nightingale, "Pinter's New Play," p. 8.

5. Harold Pinter, *A Night Out*, in *A Night Out, Night School, Revue Sketches: Early Plays by Harold Pinter* (New York: Grove Press, 1967), p. 6. All subsequent quotations from the play are from this edition and are hereafter given parenthetically in the body of the text.

6. Alan Jenkins, "No Man's Homecoming," *Times Literary Supplement*, 27 March 1981, p. 336.

7. Harold Pinter, *No Man's Land* (New York: Grove Press, 1975), p. 33. All subsequent quotations from the play are from this edition and are hereafter given parenthetically in the body of the text.

8. See my book, *The Dramatic World of Harold Pinter: Its Basis in Ritual* (Columbus: Ohio State University Press, 1971), for a discussion of how Sir James Frazer's *The Golden Bough* provides insight into the ritual structures of Pinter's drama.

9. In Harold Pinter's *Old Times* (New York: Grove Press, 1971), pp. 31–32, Anna states, "There are some things one remembers even though they may never have happened but as I recall them so thay take place." All subsequent quotations from the play are from this edition and are hereafter given parenthetically in the body of the text.

10. Water dreams, we are told by Freud, often suggest birth, and dreams that involve rescue from water suggest giving birth. See Sigmund Freud, *The Interpretation of Dreams*, trans. and ed. James Strachey (New York: Avon Books, 1965) pp. 435–37, 459.

11. Harold Pinter, *The Homecoming* (New York: Grove Press, 1965), p. 62. All subsequent quotations from the play are from this edition and are hereafter given parenthetically in the body of the text.

12. See Vera M. Jiji's discussion of love in *The Homecoming* in her "Pinter's Four Dimensional House: *The Homecoming*," *Modern Drama* 27 (December 1974): 441.

13. Ibid.

14. René Girard, *Deceit, Desire, and the Novel: Self and Other in Literary Structure*, trans. Yvonne Freccero (Baltimore: The Johns Hopkins University Press, 1965), pp. 9–10, 99.

15. Harold Pinter, *Betrayal* (New York: Grove Press, 1978), p. 135. All subsequent quotations from the play are from this edition and are hereafter given parenthetically in the body of the text.

14
The Pinter Surprise

LUCINA PAQUET GABBARD

After a quarter century of critical acclaim, Harold Pinter's position as a master playwright of the contemporary theatre needs no documentation. The desire to examine his techniques, however, grows with his fame. To sit in a hushed theatre engrossed in a Pinter play is to recognize that the heart of his theatrical success is his ability to hold an audience. Basic to this power is his use of the element of surprise. Pinter's plays abound in reversals that outwit expectation at every turn.

From the beginning his plays attracted attention because they reversed one of the fundamental premises of dramatic structure. The well-crafted play was supposed to make clear who its characters were, what was happening, and why. From the exposition in the first act to the resolution in the last act, everything was to be carefully explained. Pinter surprised his early audiences by ignoring this practice. Writing in *The Theatre of the Absurd* about Pinter's "personal style and idiom," Martin Esslin mentioned "the deliberate omission of an explanation or a motivation for the action."[1] Early questions raised by this technique are now so familiar they seem trite. Who is Riley of *The Room*? Is he Rose's father? Why does Bert kill him? Who is upstairs sending down orders in *The Dumb Waiter*? Did Ben know at the outset that Gus would be the victim? And, of course, who are Goldberg and McCann in *The Birthday Party*? What has Stanley done and why is he hiding? Pinter's justification of this technique in the program for the Royal Court Theatre's 1960 production of *The Room* and *The Dumb Waiter* is now equally well known. "The desire for verification," he explained, "cannot always be satisfied" because things are not necessarily real or unreal, true or false. Amplifying this statement, he added:

A character on stage who can present no convincing argument or information as to his past experience, his present behavior or his aspirations, nor give a comprehensive analysis of his motives is as legitimate and worthy of attention as one who, alarmingly, can do all these things.

Steven Gale cites "this concept" as "one of the most important elements" in Pinter's work,[2] and this absence of verification is certainly germane to Pinter's use of surprise. Since characters and events are not precisely defined, they can readily shift direction, leaving behind them the S-curves and "dangerous corners"[3] that create exciting theatre. Pinter's masterful use of this technique, however, lies in his honest approach to it. The unexpected in Pinter's plays is believable, not contrived, because it is dictated by the characters themselves. As Pinter told Henry Hewes: "Finding the characters and letting them speak for themselves is the greatest excitement of writing.... I find out what they are doing, allow them to do it, and keep out of it."[4] In other words, Pinter surprises his audiences because in the process of creation he has himself been surprised by his characters.

Within Pinter's plays surprises are created by various kinds of reversals; the most noticeable one is character shifts. Characters do not violate the rule of consistency; they are, rather, progressively revealed. A character will present one aspect of himself at the beginning of the play, but by the end he has presented other aspects that completely alter his image. Bert, in *The Room,* is the first example. He speaks not a word until his return at the end of the play; and since his wife, Rose, mothers and pampers him like a child, he appears to be quiet and harmlessly infantile. Upon his return from his run in his van, however, he reveals himself to be fearful and violent. As he enters, he announces almost triumphantly: "I got back all right,"[5] thereby disclosing his earlier unspoken anxiety about his trip. The sense of his paranoiac relationship to the world heightens with his description of bumping the car that would not move out of his way. "I got my road," he declares (p. 210). Then after regarding Riley for a moment, Bert erupts into violence, knocking the black man down and kicking his head against the stove until he appears to be dead. Another example of a character shift is Mick in *The Caretaker.* On his first appearance he is a sinister figure in black. On his next appearance his abusive treatment of Davies seems the more hostile compared to Aston's gentleness. Then, as he conspires with Davies against Aston, he seems deceitful and unfaithful. Ultimately, the audience is surprised by the discovery that Mick is actually very protective. Aston's shelter, food, pocket money, and job—all come from Mick, who has contrived to safeguard Aston from the treachery of the old tramp. Another outstanding example is Gibbs in *The Hothouse.* He begins as a subservient, respectful hospital employee and ends as the diabolical deviser of a massacre of the entire hospital staff. A variation of the pattern is Sally Gibbs of *Night School,* who reverses during the play from a domestic young schoolteacher to a nightclub dance girl. At the end she disappears, leaving behind a photo of herself, amid a group of schoolgirls, holding a netball. The photo delivers its surprise by complicating rather than solving the mystery of Sally's altering identity. Almost every one of Pinter's plays contains these character shifts.

Another form of character shift is the reversal of feelings; what a person appears to feel is the opposite of what he or she actually feels. Thus appearance and reality are literally turned inside out. In *The Homecoming* the men's behavior matches the play's animal imagery—Max and his sons bully, insult, and threaten each other, appearing to be callous and fearless. Actually, however, they are hiding their disappointments and insecurity behind a wall of bluster and boasts. Max, for example, once found his joy in horses. Whether his experience at Epsom was real or imagined, he longed for it to be true. He dreamed of a life on the paddock in the open air, but he explains: "I had family obligations, my family needed me at home."[6] Max had to go into the butcher shop and work to support a bedridden mother and some invalid brothers. Then he cared for a "crippled family" of his own—"three bastard sons, a slut-bitch of a wife" (p. 47). As a result, Max feels so sorry for himself that he would like to cry, but instead he shouts with anger. At the time of the play, Max is also desperately afraid of his declining strength. "You think I wasn't a tearaway?" he boasts, "I could have taken care of you twice over. I'm still strong" (p. 8). Yet he is so unsure of his strength that he carries a stick with him at all times, lifting it at the slightest threat. Lenny also attacks in self-defense. He brags of his exploits with women and his rough treatment of them; but having had his bluff called by Ruth, he admits: "We've got rocks. But they've frozen stiff in the fridge" (p. 61). Out of sensitivity to his own inferiority he challenges Teddy on philosophy: "Do you detect a certain logical incoherence in the central affirmations of Christian theism?" (p. 51). Joey is less alert and aware than Max and Lenny, but he shows reversal too. Like the others, only more overtly, he makes a grand display of seeking sex when his real desire is to be mothered like a little boy. Sam finds protection in withdrawal, but Max accurately characterizes Sam as always scraping up the leavings. Sam's compensation is the boast that he is the best chauffeur in the business.

The characters in *Betrayal* are also dominated by reversals of feeling. On the surface they are untouched by infidelity and rejection. Concerning the affair between his wife, Emma, and his best friend, Jerry, Robert states: "You don't seem to understand that I don't give a shit about any of this."[7] Yet the backward movement of time reveals that he has cared deeply about Emma. In 1974 Robert kisses and holds Emma lovingly, and in 1971 they have conceived a child. Jerry affects a casual air about a doctor taking his wife, Judith, out for drinks. Nevertheless, he insistently hangs on to his marriage to Judith throughout the five-year affair with Emma. Emma also feigns indifference. On her last rendezvous with Jerry in the flat, she states blandly: "I think we've made absolutely the right decision" (p. 58). But her actions betray her. She is unable to remove the key to the flat from her keyring and throws the keying to Jerry, forcing him to perform the final gesture. These reversals of feeling correspond to Pinter's statements about evasions in conversations. He maintains that "people fall back on anything they can lay their hands on verbally to keep away from the danger of knowing, and of being known."[8]

In many of his plays Pinter's reversals take the form of crisscrossing relationships. As one character loses control, his or her antagonist gains control; as the tormentor becomes threatened, he or she exchanges roles with the tormented. In *A Slight Ache* the pattern forms a simple "X." At the outset Edward is the affluent homeowner smothered with attention from Flora, his wife. The Matchseller is a homeless vagrant stationed outside Edward's garden gate. By the end of the play, Edward has suffered a complete collapse, and Flora has become attracted to the Matchseller. As she takes his arm to show him her garden, she leaves Edward holding the tray of matches. The men's positions are totally reversed. The Matchseller has traveled the rising leg of the "X" while Edward has traced the falling side. *The Basement* sets a seesaw in motion with a whole series of fast-paced reversals in which Law and Stott win and lose possession of Jane. At the start she is with Stott, and the two present themselves at the door of Law's basement apartment. At the end, Law has Jane, but Stott has the apartment.

In *The Collection* the seesawing is doubled and complicated. The entire action begins in Stella's tale of an affair with Bill while the two of them were showing their dress collections at Leeds. Apparently, Stella has been feeling neglected and unnoticed, so she tells her tale to James, her husband, in the hope of gaining attention. Instead of satisfying her need, James tips the seesaw by becoming threatened. Consequently, he goes in search of Bill to demand satisfaction. At Bill's he discovers a homosexual partnership, knowledge that he uses for revenge against Stella. He taunts her with threats of visiting Bill—after the fact. He hints at having his own latent homosexuality aroused. Stella, on the down side of the seesaw again, is near tears. Meanwhile, Harry is similarly threatened with the possibility of Bill's infidelity; thus he loses the control in their relationship. Bill and James appear to carry on a flirtation, first one and then the other rejecting and pursuing, Bill using as weapon a variety of responses to Stella's story. Harry goes to visit Stella and regains the upper hand over both Bill and James by claiming a cozy tête à tête with Stella in which she confessed the whole tale to be a lie. Bill retaliates with still another version of the Leeds affair, hurting and angering Harry and sending James home more perplexed than ever. Reaching his flat, he announces to Stella: "You didn't do anything, did you? ... *Pause.* That's the truth, isn't it?"[9]. Stella refuses to answer. Her end of the seesaw is up. She has him in the pit of anguish, and her enigmatic smile reveals her intention to keep him there.

Old Times presents still another variation of reversal by crisscrossing relationships. In this case the play ends as it begins, with Kate in control and Deeley slumped in despair—alienated and remote. The seesaw is set in motion by the intrusion of Anna, Kate's former roommate. In the first half of the play Deeley is threatened by Anna's visit and her reminiscences of past intimacies with Kate. As the two "lovers," husband and lesbian roommate, vie for control of Kate, she is silent—aware that their competitiveness gives her the upper hand. Then in act 2 the whole situation reverses. Pinter announces the reversal by his description of the set: "*The divans and armchair are disposed in precisely the same relation to each other as the furniture in the first act, but in reversed positions.*"[10] Along with the furniture, character relationships reverse as well. Deeley recounts the past attraction between himself and Anna. Anna's sexual identity changes from homosexual to bisexual, and Kate, remembering that Anna had once loved Deeley, becomes the threatened one. But Kate's end of the seesaw is only briefly in the down position. She eliminates Anna by recalling the symbolic death she had once inflicted by dirtying Anna's face. As before, Anna accepts the fate Kate deals out, and all elements of the relationship return to their original positions, represented by the characters' tableau. Kate, the victor, is sitting upright on one divan. Deeley, the loser, is slumped in a chair. Anna, the intruder, is lying on the other divan—symbolically dead.

Some of Pinter's most startling surprises are achieved by sharply reversing audience expectations that he has calculatedly appeared to foreshadow. A prime illustration occurs in *Night Out*. Albert is the docile, repressed son of a possessive widowed mother. Against his mother's wishes, Albert goes out to an office party where he is taunted and bullied. The final insult—being called "mother's boy"—blows Albert's fuse. His anger bursts forth into an exchange of blows with his tormentor. Upon his return home, his mother begins to lecture him, at which Albert picks up a clock and raises it above his head as if to strike her. The scene ends with "*a stifled scream from the mother.*"[11] The audience, recognizing that Albert's hostility is still out of control, wonders if he has killed his mother. In the next act Albert has gone out into the night again where a prostitute picks him up and takes him to her apartment. Once there she acts out her fantasy of being a respectable mother and begins to nag Albert. Associating her with her own mother, Albert seizes a clock from her mantelpiece and holds it aloft as he yells: "DON'T MUCK ME ABOUT!" (p. 42). She is terrified as he stalks her around the room stammering: "Watch your step! I've had—I've had—I've had—just about enough. Get it? ... You know what I did?" (p. 43). Moments later, however, he drops the clock and leaves the room. The audience is gripped. They suspect that Albert has indeed killed his mother and barely refrained from killing the prostitute. The opening of the next scene seems to confirm this suspicion. Albert saunters into his house wearing a slight smile. Uncharacteristically, he throws his jacket and tie across the room and flops into a chair. He stretches, "*yawns luxuriously, scratches his head with both hands and stares ruminatively at the ceiling, a smile on his face.*" Then—his mother's voice rings out from upstairs, "Albert!" (p. 46). The illusion is shattered!

An equally astonishing moment occurs in *The Lover*, but it is associated with sex rather than murder. The play opens in the apartment of a young couple—Richard and Sarah. Richard is leaving for work and questioning Sarah about her lover: "Is ... [he] coming today?" "What time?" "Will he be staying long?"[12] Sarah's answers seem mockingly honest: "Mmnn," "Three," "Mmmnnn ..." (p. 5). The audience concludes that Richard is either an ultrasophisticate or an injured husband hiding behind his pride. In the next scene

Richard is returning from work at the end of the day. His questions—
"Pleasant afternoon?" "Your lover came, did he?"—and her answers—"Oh
yes. Quite marvelous," "Mmnn. Oh yes" (p. 7)—build the image of a docile
husband tormented by a boldly faithless wife. But then Richard reveals a new
aspect by retaliating that he has visited his mistress that afternoon and reminding Sarah that "frankness at all costs" is "essential to a healthy marriage" (p. 12). In a later scene Sarah is dressed in a revealing low-cut black
dress and high-heeled shoes; the doorbell rings. The audience naturally expects to meet Sarah's lover. She answers the door. It is the milkman! Sarah
quickly finishes her business with him and closes the door. The doorbell rings
again. Suspense has built. This must be the lover. Sarah opens the door and
coos, "Hallo, Max" (p. 19). Then Pinter pulls his surprise. Richard walks in!
He is the lover! The remainder of the play discloses that Richard's and
Sarah's affairs are fantasies acted out with each other to keep sexual excitement alive.

The surprise of *The Lover* is doubly sharp because it has been set up not
only by the dialogue of the play but also by the title itself. Seeing the title on
the program, the audience is predisposed to expect a lover, not a husband.
The title of *The Caretaker* operates in a similar fashion to intensify the effect
of the reversal set up by Mick's character shift. Warned to expect a caretaker,
the audience watches for one. By rescuing and bringing home Davies and
explaining his job in the old house, Aston seems to fill that role. When he and
then Mick invite Davies to be caretaker of the building, the old tramp appears
to be the title character. By the end of the play, however, the revelations of
Mick's character and intentions hold the surprise that he, the most unlikely
one at the outset, is the caretaker.

Pinter frequently upsets audience expectations by reversing the conventional attitudes that society demands. In *The Dwarfs,* for example, the tradition of cherishing one's friends and nourishing one's family roots is discarded,
and Len dispossesses himself of his friends, his parental attitudes, and his
entire heritage. *The Lover* ignores the traditional response of the jealous husband. Thus it delivers its first surprise at the opening of the play as Richard
accepts so amiably his wife's afternoon rendezvous with adultery. *The Hothouse* reverses the age-old axiom "Crime does not pay," as Lobb commends
Gibbs and places him in charge of the hospital—whose entire staff Gibbs has
managed to eliminate.

The outstanding example is, of course, *The Homecoming,* in which the
reversal of conventional behavior moves past surprise and shocks the audience. Even a sophisticated critic like Margaret Croyden called the play
"hideous" and "grotesque." Explaining these adjectives she commented:

... the characters ... move from the rational to the unpredictable, from the
mundane to the savage, so that the characters' life styles appear shocking and
incomprehensible. But what may seem to be reversals of form and order and
unconventional attitudes to sex, marriage, and the family can be traced

to primitive ritual—dramatized within the framework of the middle-class comedy of manners.[13]

These reversals of convention become more appalling as the play progresses. At first, Max and his sons reverse the polite practice of being outwardly cordial to each other while feeling inwardly hostile. In addition, they violate society's dictum that sons shall honor their parents. Lenny tells Max, "Why don't you shut up, you daft prat?" (p. 7); and as a pimp, Lenny shows disrespect for his mother's sex. Teddy's welcome is little more than an affront; and Ruth, Max's new daughter-in-law, is greeted as "a stinking pox-ridden slut" (p. 41). Relatives, in particular father and brothers, normally consider it dishonorable and incestuous to make sexual advances to each other's wives. Teddy's family unabashedly set out to take Ruth; she is to serve not one but all of them. This family even lacks respect for the dead. When Sam, Max's brother, collapses on the floor, no one shows either concern or grief. Max shouts: "A corpse? A corpse on my floor? Get him out of here!" (p. 78).

Indeed, *The Homecoming* is a complex structure of reversals within reversals. Operating inside this pattern of reversing convention, Teddy and Ruth display both character shifts and a crisscrossing relationship. They arrive at Teddy's family home behaving conventionally. Teddy shows concern for Ruth's comfort; he offers her a drink, asks if she is cold, tells her not to be nervous. He speaks fondly of his family: "They're very warm people really. Very warm. They're my family. They're not ogres" (p. 23). (A minor reversal of Teddy's expectation is set up here and completed by the family's subsequent insults.) Ruth worries that the children might be missing them. An undertone of tension between husband and wife foreshadows coming shifts, but their conduct, at this point, accords with expected patterns. When Lenny makes his first advance to Ruth, she rejects him with decorum. Very quickly, however, Ruth and Teddy reverse themselves. Ruth's about-face begins when she offers Lenny a sip from her glass and then forces him to drink the water. As Steven M. L. Aronson points out: "The glass of water that she makes Lenny drink is the realness of her own sexuality, exploited now for the first time, in the presence of a highly anxious male...."[14] Ruth's character shift is completed in act 2 when she calls attention to her leg. Lenny has been trying to have a philosophical discussion with Teddy about a table: "All right, I say, *take it, take* a table, but once you've taken it, what you going to do with it?..." Max throws in: "You'd probably sell it." Lenny retorts: "You wouldn't get much for it." Ruth interrupts, deliberately associating herself with the table:

Don't be too sure though. You've forgotten something. Look at me. I ... move my leg. That's all it is. But I wear ... underwear ... which moves with me ... it captures your attention. Perhaps you misinterpret. The action is simple. It's a leg ... moving. My lips move. Why don't you restrict ... your observations to that? Perhaps the fact that they move is more significant ... than the words which come through them. You must bear that ... possibility ... in mind.   (Pp. 52–53)

Ruth has made her move. By reversing conventional practice and acknowl-
edging publicly the sexual attraction that people usually note privately, she
has announced to all her character shift. She has assessed the family; she has
perceived their desire as the key to her gaining control. She has put up her
shingle! The family members respond with a reversal of their own: they are
silent—until Max maneuvers their withdrawal. Ultimately, Ruth completes
her reversal, going upstairs to bed with Joey and agreeing to be the family's
communal prostitute. In turn, Teddy's tense conventional concern transposes
into cold, unfeeling withdrawal—a reversal of feeling that conceals his vulnerability. Such complex structures of reversals are responsible for the
surprise—shock, affront—of audiences who come unsuspectingly to see *The
Homecoming.*

For the informed Pinter fan, surprise operates not only within the plays but
also between them. As Steven Gale has noted, "Harold Pinter's plays are
complex collections of interrelated themes."[15] As a group of Pinter plays circles around an idea, each adopting a slightly different perspective, a variety of
reversals are evident. For example, Bert's need to kill in *The Room* and the
calculated murders of Ben's organization in *The Dumb Waiter* soften to an
unfinished gesture in *Night Out,* an act of riddance in *The Caretaker,* and a
psychic purge of feelings in *The Dwarfs.* These are subtle reversals, however.
More distinct are such reversals of character and situation as occur between
The Birthday Party and *The Dumb Waiter. The Dumb Waiter* focuses on the
idea of hired killers, which was introduced by Goldberg and McCann in *The
Birthday Party.* Ben and Gus, like Goldberg and McCann, arrive in a strange
town, move into a rented room, take care of a victim, and move on the next
day. In *The Birthday Party* the hired killers terrify their victim, Stanley.
However, *The Dumb Waiter* "reveals the terror of the terrorists."[16] In this
second play the killers are themselves anxious and afraid, and one of them is,
in fact, the intended victim. Individual reversals of character occur also. In
The Birthday Party Goldberg talks a great deal and gives orders while
McCann, more quiet and frequently absorbed in tearing up newspapers,
carries out the commands. In *The Dumb Waiter* Ben, the quiet one usually
absorbed in reading the newspaper, is the senior man who gives the orders.
Gus, the talker, is the doer. The idea of stale marriages and infidelity is
treated in both *The Collection* and *The Lover.* In *The Collection,* however,
Stella merely spins a fantasy about infidelity with Bill at Leeds. In *The
Lover* Richard and Sarah act out shared fantasies of infidelity with each other.
Tea Party and *The Homecoming* both deal with carnal desire. In *Tea Party*
Disson tries to suppress his desire for his secretary, Wendy, and remain re-
spectably loyal to his society wife, Diana. As his lust for Wendy grows,
however, he projects it outward onto Willy, Diana's brother, and suspects
him of making sexual advances to both Diana and Wendy. The effort at sexual
repression ultimately leads Disson to mental collapse at a party given on the
first anniversary of his wedding. *The Homecoming* totally reverses Disson's
psychopathology. Teddy's family exposes all feeling. No one suppresses his

lust for Ruth, and she allows and accepts their advances at a would-be party in honor of her husband's first homecoming since their marriage.

Over the years Pinter also reverses the pattern of time in his plays. From *The Room* to *The Homecoming* the action onstage always moves forward. Characters are affected by their past, but onstage, time unfolds in straightforward chronology. Then in *Landscape, Silence,* and *Old Times,* Pinter achieves another coup. He has his characters look backward through memory; instead of inverting the movement of time through the usual flashback, however, Pinter makes time stand still, blending the past and the present into simultaneity. *Landscape* is essentially a pair of monologues. Beth and Duff occupy the same space, but each exists in a different time zone. They flashback in memory, but these memories are not acted out; they do not happen in stage time. They are spoken as private memories. Beth mingles her present with the memory of a gentle lover. Duff speaks of more recent times. Recited in counterpoint, their excursions into the past explain the loneliness and stagnation that pervade their present. *Silence* complicates the time pattern of *Landscape* by presenting three people rather than two. Ellen, Bates, and Rumsey are all on the same stage but separate and isolated from one another. Each is stilled in a different phase of life: Ellen in her twenties, Bates in his thirties, and Rumsey in his forties. In memory they move both backward into youth and forward into old age. Pinter seems to suggest that "in their memories they remain the same age forever."[17] In their minds time has stopped—present and past are all one. Pinter's directions for achieving this effect on stage are starkly simple: "*Three areas. A chair in each area.*"[18] However, the imaginative scene designer, John Bury, added mirrors and accomplished a strikingly appropriate representation of memory playing back and forth through three separate minds becalmed in three separate worlds. Simon Trussler has described Bury's set as "an elaborate confusion of mirrors at once multiplying angles of vision and entrapping the reflected images in a maze of memory."[19]

Old Times blends past and present in yet a different way. Deeley, Kate, and Anna are not isolated; they address each other in the same room and at the same stage moment. Some slight movement of time seems to transpire within the play because the furniture reverses order between acts 1 and 2. The movement is brief, however, perhaps only a quirk of mind in keeping with Pinter's Royal Court program statement: "there are no hard distinctions between what is real and what is unreal." In this case, Pinter gives at least two indications that the entire happening may be as much imagination as reality. At the outset he places Anna onstage—a shadowy, silent figure—while Deeley and Kate discuss her, suggesting thereby that Anna is present even in her physical absence. Second, Pinter begins and ends the play with almost identical tableaux. The only change is in Anna's position, which could represent merely a new image of the relationship in the minds of Deeley and Kate. In between the tableaux the characters occupy themselves by recreating the past through conflicting memories and deliberate fantasies. At times memory is so sharp and absorption in it so complete that the past comes to life again onstage.

Such an instance occurs at the end of act 1. Deeley and Kate are questioning Anna about her life in Sicily when Anna stares at Kate and a silence falls. When dialogue resumes, Anna and Kate have mentally removed themselves to another time. They are still in Deeley and Kate's house; the physical space is the same. Deeley is still present, but he is outside their awareness. They have stepped into a time warp where they are reliving a moment from their youthful days as roommates in London. They discuss whether to stay home or go out, whether to take a walk in the park of invite someone over—Charlie or Jake. They plan what Kate will wear the next day. Then a pause brings them, just as suddenly, back to the present, and Kate moves offstage for her bath.

In *No Man's Land*, also a memory play, Pinter surprises his followers by another configuration of present and past. In this play the movement of time has ceased for only one character—Hirst. He exists in a still point, "the blur between drinking and passing out."[20] He confuses people of today with people from yesterday. Spooner, the shabby man whom Hirst has brought home from the pub, engages in memory play with Hirst, but he uses Hirst's confusion to advance his own need. Foster and Briggs live very much in the present, as caretakers to Hirst. Furthermore, within the play time does pass. Act 2 opens after a period of sleep for Hirst and Spooner, but the past intrudes on the present through Spooner's déjà vu as well as through memory. Spooner, through a character shift, turns out to be Charles Wetherby, Hirst's intimate friend from the past, who is now down on his luck. He pleads with Hirst to take him in as an all-around servant and public-relations man. But Hirst refuses—coldly, revealing the still point in his heart where time was snagged on hurt and has stagnated in unforgiveness. Hirst lives in a timeless no man's land because of his need not to remember pain and guilt—the roots of his alienation from life.

Finally, in *Betrayal* Pinter completely overturns chronology and starts his play at the end and moves almost unswervingly into the beginning. Scene 1 takes place in 1977, two years after the close of Emma's affair with Jerry. The final scene, scene 9, takes place in 1968 in the bedroom of Robert and Emma's house. Robert and Emma are having a party. Jerry ambushes Emma in the bedroom, tells her he is crazy about her, kisses her—and begins the affair. The intervening scenes move in a backward path through the decline and blossoming of Emma and Jerry's relationship, crisscrossing it with the deterioration of Emma and Robert's marriage and the alterations in Robert and Jerry's friendship—tracing all through layers and layers of betrayals.

The surprises wrought by these various patterns of reversal have two significant results besides that of holding audience attention. First, within the individual plays the unexpected intensifies the impact of the endings. The full force of *The Dumb Waiter*'s intent only hits the audience in that final moment when Gus stumbles in, stripped of his upper clothing and his revolver. His shocked silence and his stooped body cry out his bewilderment and fear. He and Ben stare at each other. And in the silence that follows, the meaning and direction of the play fall into place for the spectator. Finally, they realize that

Gus is the victim for tonight, to be silenced because of his insistent questioning. The audience experiences the pleasant sensation of sudden enlightenment. Similarly, the full extent of Gibbs's culpability and cunning bursts upon the audience in the last scene of *The Hothouse*, when Gibbs makes his report to Lobb at the Ministry. Until then the audience is slightly confused. Then with Gibbs' declarations, the pieces of the puzzle come together: "The whole staff was slaughtered" (p. 148); the patients did it; they escaped because their doors were not properly locked; the lockster was absent from duty; he is nowhere to be found; his name is Lamb. Then after Lobb has congratulated Gibbs, the office blacks out, and the lights rise on Lamb. He is still in the soundproof room where Gibbs has earlier locked him. He still wears the electrodes and earphones that the audience saw Gibbs attach to him. "*He sits quite still, staring as in a catatonic trance*" (p. 154). At that moment the curtains close, and the audience knows for the first time that the play has been the unfolding of the motivation and execution of Gibbs's scheme to gain control of the hospital. The realization packs a stronger wallop because of its suddenness.

The final result of the Pinter surprise is a lingering provocativeness. Images and final tableaux, in a sense, haunt the thoughtful spectator, causing him to contemplate the meaning of what he has seen and to arrive at thematic statements that lie behind the characters and events. In retrospect, the spectator perceives in *The Dumb Waiter* statements about man's sense of powerlessness in an uncertain world, about his fear of the unknown, and about his acceptance of violence as the partner to his fear. He understands the analogy of the mental hospital and the hothouse—both being shelters for the bizarre flora of life. He intellectualizes the hospital as a metaphor for contemporary society and absorbs the notion that control can pass from the inadequate, like Roote, to the criminally insane, like Gibbs. He appreciates the play's ability—in the true spirit of black comedy—to make the audience laugh at the dangerous absurdities of the twentieth-century world.

The scholar can pause in between the plays and, studying their relationships, observe such continuing Pinter themes as the fear of dispossession, the struggle for dominance, the unknowability of truth, the fluidity of human character, the vagaries of memory, and the uncertainty of life. Thus, Pinter's habits of oblique statement and refusal to moralize are transmuted in the minds of his readers and playgoers into revelations about the human conditon—a final reversal.

Notes

1. Martin Esslin, *The Theatre of the Absurd* (Garden City, N.Y.: Doubleday, 1961), p. 199.

2. Steven H. Gale, *Butter's Going Up: A Critical Analysis of Harold Pinter's Work* (Durham, N.C.: Duke University Press, 1977), p. 28.

3. This phrase is intended to borrow meaning from J. B. Priestly's play of that name.

4. Henry Hewes, "Probing Pinter's Play," *Saturday Review*, 8 April 1967, p. 56.

5. Harold Pinter, *The Birthday Party and The Room* (New York: Grove Press, 1961), p. 119. Subsequent references to these plays will be to this edition and will appear in the body of the text.

6. Harold Pinter, *The Homecoming* (New York: Grove Press, 1966), p. 10. Subsequent references to this play will be to this edition and will appear in the body of the text.

7. Harold Pinter, *Betrayal* (London: Eyre Methuen, 1978), p. 41. Subsequent references to this play will be to this edition and will appear in the body of the text.

8. Lawrence M. Bensky, "Harold Pinter: An Interview," in *Pinter: A Collection of Critical Essays,* ed. Arthur Ganz (Englewood Cliffs, N.J.: Prentice-Hall, 1972), p. 26.

9. Harold Pinter, *Three Plays: A Slight Ache, The Collection, and The Dwarfs* (New York: Grove Press, 1962), p. 80. Subsequent references to these plays will be to this edition and will appear in the body of the text.

10. Harold Pinter, *Old Times* (New York: Grove Press, 1971), p. 47. Subsequent references to this play will be to this edition and will appear in the body of the text.

11. Harold Pinter, *A Night Out, Night School, Revue Sketches: Early Plays* (New York: Grove Press, 1967), p. 33. Subsequent references to these plays will be to this edition and will appear in the body of the text.

12. Harold Pinter, *The Lover, Tea Party, The Basement* (New York: Grove Press, 1967), p. 5. Subsequent references to these plays will be to this edition and will appear in the body of the text.

13. Margaret Croyden, "Pinter's Hideous Comedy," in *A Casebook on Harold Pinter's "The Homecoming,"* ed. John Lahr (New York: Grove Press, 1971), p. 45.

14. Steven M. L. Aronson, "Pinter's 'Family' and Blood Knowledge," in *A Casebook,* ed. Lahr, p. 74.

15. Gale, *Butter's Going Up,* p. 17.

16. Lucina P. Gabbard, *The Dream Structure of Pinter's Plays* (Rutherford, N.J.: Fairleigh Dickinson University Press, 1976), p. 64.

17. Ibid., p. 224.

18. Harold Pinter, *Landscape and Silence* (New York: Grove Press, 1970), p. 31. Subsequent references to these plays will be to this edition and will appear in the body of the text.

19. Simon Trussler, *The Plays of Harold Pinter* (London: Victor Gollancz, 1973), p. 169.

20. Gabbard, *Dream Structure,* p. 253.

15
Time after Time: Pinter Plays with Disjunctive Chronologies

WILLIAM F. DOHMEN

The past is a foreign country: they do things differently there.
                                        —**L. P. Hartley,** *The Go-Between*

In the quarter of a century during which Harold Pinter has been composing scripts for stage, screen, television, and radio, he has developed ever more sophisticated structures by which to dramatize his material; that material, however, has remained remarkably consistent. Characters are isolated by conflicting, self-serving perceptions of experience; the sexes are polarized by the failure of each to appreciate the other's needs; and most prominently, present action is inexorably influenced, submerged, even swept away by powerful currents from the past. Well before Pinter came to write a film script for L. P. Hartley's *The Go-Between* in 1969, he had shared that novelist's obsession with the "foreign country" of memory, both seductive and threatening, alternately a haven and a battlefield. Yet Pinter's perception of the effects of the past, and concurrently his means of dramatizing those effects, have matured, so that the playwright's own canon reflects the Proustian thesis, adopted explicitly in Pinter's later works, that "past" experience is timeless, omnipresent, but paradoxically only to be shaped and comprehended through the passage of time.

Until Pinter actually incarnated the past and brought it before the footlights in *Betrayal* (1978), that realm had remained remote, hazy, and ambiguous in his original scripts—though nonetheless influential. In the early plays the past appears ominous, a region to be denied, falsified, evaded—until its emissaries mysteriously appear or, more insidiously, its patterns of behavior reimpose themselves in the present. Messengers from their pasts deliver debilitating fears and guilts to Rose (*The Room* [1957]), to Stanley (*The Birthday Party* [1958]), and to Edward (*A Slight Ache* [1959]). The spectral Matchseller who

187

haunts Edward is perhaps the most surrealistic of these figures, early undetect-
able in the radio version but substantial on the stage, where he hovers, mute,
guilt inducing, inescapable as some long-repressed awareness emerging into
the light of consciousness. Edward's pose crumbles as he seems finally to recognize himself in this vacuous, pathetic figure, whom he acknowledges as "my
oldest acquaintance. My nearest and dearest. My kith and kin" (1: 196),[1] and
whose role he finally assumes, much as Rose takes Riley's blindness on herself. If the mysterious menace of these plays is that of the characters' own
pasts catching up with them, such is clearly the fate of those subsequent Pinter
protagonists who set out to forge new identities for themselves, only to be
crushed by the resurgence of previous roles they had sought to deny: inescapable pasts abort the fresh starts of Albert (*A Night Out* [1960]), Walter and
Sally (*Night School* [1960]), Davies (*The Caretaker* [1960]), Bill and Stella
(*The Collection* [1961]), and Teddy (*The Homecoming* [1965]).

Although the past may be a prison for many of Pinter's early characters,
trapping them in demeaning roles or crippling guilts they had sought to evade,
it is also a weapon in the hands of those who assert its influence. Goldberg in
The Birthday Party wields reminiscences and innuendoes as a skilled fencer
would handle his rapier, thrusting, parrying, feinting, keeping everyone off-
balance, while puncturing Stanley's identity until only a drained human cara-
pace remains. Max similarly manipulates the past, selecting and modifying
incidents for his own advantage in *The Homecoming*; his son Lenny masters
the family art as well, and even Sam attempts to drop a strategic bombshell
but succeeds only in demolishing himself. In *Old Times* (1971) and *No Man's
Land* (1975), the past is no longer just an invasive force but occupies the
entire field of combat, whereon characters pit their recollections against one
another.[2]

However, the first significant shifts in Pinter's treatment of the past appear
during the mid-1960s, particularly in his television play *The Basement* (1967)
and to a lesser extent in his stage play *The Homecoming,* but also in several
screenplays based on novels analyzing the interaction of past and present,
beginning with *The Pumpkin Eater* (released in 1964).[3] A minor work in itself, *The Basement* has proved seminal in light of Pinter's later career and, in
a sense, prefaces his entire career, since the script's origins can be traced to
the brief dialogue "Kullus," written by Pinter when he was nineteen. Surfac-
ing next as a poem ("The Task" [1954]), then a story ("The Examination"
[1955; 1: 251–56]), an unproduced film script (*The Compartment* [1963]), and
finally the television play (which eventually received its first stage production
in 1968), the characters and conflicts of *The Basement* suggest a stripped-
down prototype of the Pinteresque vision.[4] Two men, of superficially polar
but ultimately interchangeable personalities, whose friendship-rivalry extends
back into a misty past, periodically compete for possession of a room and a
woman. Both seem uncertain whether to pursue the excitement of a new
environment, a new affair, a new identity, or to settle into the security of reading alone by a familiar fireside, or finally to devote themselves to maintaining

the strained friendship that apparently has survived their alternating choices and periodic combats. If this situation seems familiar, it may be because it is essentially that of the more recent *Betrayal* (substituting Torcello for the fireside); it emerges in the reminiscences of *Monologue* (1973); and with variations, similar unstable triangles underlie *A Slight Ache* and *The Lover* (1963); where the competing males appear as aspects of one personality), *The Homecoming* (where Teddy's antagonist is his family), *Silence* (1969; where contact between the males is diminished), *Old Times* (where Anna replaces the usual male challenger), and *No Man's Land* (where the female part is submerged into memory).

Yet the characters in *The Basement* are undeveloped and insubstantial; what renders the play interesting are the devices Pinter employs to convey the timelessness and repetitiveness of the play's conflicts and of the characters' alternating, contradictory, and hence insatiable desires. Capitalizing on the freedom afforded by writing for the cinema and television, Pinter could finally seek a structure appropriate to a concept that had remained implicit in his earlier drama: the omnipresence of the past, the deceptiveness of time's flow. Some years later Pinter described his perception of time, a view already apparent in *The Basement*:

I think I'm more conscious a kind of ever-present quality in life.... I certainly feel more and more that the past is not past, that it never was past. It's present.... I know the future is simply going to be the same thing. It'll never end. You carry all the states with you until end.... But those previous parts are alive and present.[5]

Rather like Eugène Ionesco's *Bald Soprano*, the play concludes by repeating its initial scene, the male characters having exchanged roles. The dizzying alternations of setting, of decor in the room, and of time from winter to summer, night to day, defy any effort to impose chronology on the action, though the events themselves follow a relatively straightforward deveopment. When Stott requests music, for example, Law seeks, finds, and plays a Debussy record, while night and day replace one another four times, as do summer and winter (with appropriate changes in the characters' apparel), and the room undergoes three changes of furnishing.

Such deliberate disruption of time suggests the workings of the subconscious, and in fact the play can readily be interpreted as Law's fantasy,[6] rather like an enactment of Len's verbalized visions in *The Dwarfs* (1960). This perhaps explains Pinter's final choice of *The Basement* as his title, with its connotation of the subconscious, similar to that evoked by Riley's abode in *The Room*. Whether the action is viewed as a dream or as condensed reality, however, the disruptions of chronology, the role reversal, and the dialogue repetition create an impression of the action as archetypal, the eternal and ineluctable pattern of human behavior. Law and Stott fencing in a bare room with broken milk bottles while Jane placidly prepares their coffee suggest a pair of Neanderthals competing for a cave, a mate, or simply domination per se. If Pinter's earlier plays suggest that the past cannot be discounted, *The Basement* matches structure to concept by dissolving past into present so that in fact no distinction between them is possible. Despite its subsequent stage productions, however, such extreme devices are more amenable to film than to live action,[7] and Pinter continued to explore more conservative means to achieve a similar effect of the presence of the past on stage.

Between writing *The Compartment* film script and revising it for television as *The Basement,* Pinter composed *The Homecoming,* employing conventional chronology and yet stressing in new ways the inescapability of the past, a concept apparent even in the title. From the moment Teddy opens the door of his father's house after an absence of six years, the ominous silence and the heavy furnishings seem to engulf him in the childish, destructive behavioral patterns he had sought to escape. "Nothing's changed. Still the same," Teddy observes with ironic satisfaction (3: 38), and he almost immediately reverts to an immature pattern of withdrawal and detachment that sacrifices his wife's affections and his own dignity, while Ruth also, insofar as we can believe her hints, returns to a behavioral style she had dropped upon marrying Teddy.

Such reversion to past behavior, however, while a bit more realistic and circumstantial than that in *A Slight Ache,* is not substantially different from the withdrawal of Edward and the sexual reawakening of Flora. What contribute to the sense of inevitability, of time as wheel or gyre rather than linear progression, are the implications of repetition from one generation to the next, a sort of "curse" like that which dries up love relationships through the generations in *The Go-Between.* As the tenuous bond between Teddy and Ruth gives way, the reminiscences of Max and his brother Sam suggest that the younger couple is recapitulating the failure of Max's marriage to Jessie, and very possibly of that of Max's parents as well, for Max only remembers his mother as "bedridden," while his father cared for him and his disturbed brothers (3: 63, 35). So Max has been forced to raise his three sons since Jessie's infidelity, as the marital discord, lovelessness, and confusion of roles in each generation infect the next. Max exults at the sight of his superior son, Jessie's favorite according to Sam (3: 79), reenacting his father's doom as Teddy loses his wife and returns alone to America to raise his three sons, who, with no mother and an emotionally debilitated father, may perpetuate the pattern. Meanwhile, Ruth will stay behind as Jessie's avatar to dominate the remaining male clan, who as the curtain falls reenact the mingled resentment and dependence that have characterized Max's memories of his wife. Within *The Homecoming* the family becomes the agent for the transmission of the past,[8] exemplifying Pinter's conviction that "the future is simply going to be the same thing. It'll never end."

Meanwhile, Pinter's growing interest in writing for the cinema has provided greater latitude for experimentation with techniques for disrupting chronology and blending past with present. Indeed, most of the novels he has selected for conversion to screenplays have been remarkably similar, particularly *The Pumpkin Eater* (script written in 1963), *Accident* (1966), *The Go-Between*

(1969), *Remembrance of Things Past* (1972), and *The French Lieutenant's Woman* (1979). All involve crosscutting between two or more time periods, illustrating the inescapable links, patterns, and repetitions among events within individual lives, between generations, or even over centuries; all focus on the frustrations and failures of love or marriage, on the inexorable waning of hope, and on dreams' betrayals by time. Initiating Pinter's cinematic alterations of temporal sequence, *The Pumpkin Eater* intersperses brief glimpses of the day of Jo's nervous breakdown in Harrods with scenes ranging over the previous ten years, highlighting episodes which led to her collapse and prepare for her subsequent reacclimation to her pumpkin-shell marriage with Jake. Normal chronology is observed following Jo's collapse about one-fourth of the way into the film, although Pinter does experiment with over-laying dialogue on nonsynchronous action to compress the effect of a scene, a device he employs more frequently in *The Go-Between* and *Remembrance of Things Past* to establish thematic links between disparate time periods. Such superimposed dialogue and repeated alterations between time periods go beyond traditional film flashbacks to achieve an effect more of simultaneity than of simple regression in time, approximating an aim Piner expressed for *The Go-Between* of creating "an interrelationship between past and present so that they are almost happening at the same time."[9]

Accident follows a somewhat more conventional flashback structure, though Pinter occasionally crosscuts between snatches of dialogue for ironic effect, as between Stephen's conversations with his wife and with Laura.[10] This film's much more extensive portrayal of the past suggests that the "accident" may in fact have been fated by a complex web of relationships and irresolvable emotional needs. Past events also predominate in *The Go-Between,* but here the "current" events occur in a completely separate era. Unlike Pinter's earlier flashbacks, which eventually caught up to "present" action, Leo's boyhood episodes are half a century distant from his return visit as an old man. While Pinter could have adhered to the pattern of Hartley's novel (essentially that of *Accident*), framing the past with a prologue and epilogue occurring in the present, he chose instead to intersperse frequent and very fragmentary glimpses of Leo's reunion with Marian among the pre-dominating turn-of-the-century events, so that the audience is continually, if almost subliminally, reminded of the barren man Leo will become, particular-ly at the more traumatic moments of his boyhood summer.

Pinter's attraction to film has not wholly superseded his initial devotion to the stage, but it certainly has influenced his theatrical vision, intensifying his already evident interest in the strength of the past. It is a commonplace of Pinter criticism to note that his plays after *The Homecoming* lose much of their menace, and perhaps some vitality, in favor of a more reflective, elegaic, vaguely Chekhovian tone. The two short works *Landscape* (1968) and *Silence* evince Pinter's straying into a cul-de-sac of Beckettian meditations (and for all his merits, Pinter's talents are not Beckett's). Max's advice to Teddy and Ruth in *The Homecoming,* ironic enough in its original context, proves even more applicable to the remote denizens of Pinter's subsequent stage offerings: "Listen, live in the present, what are you worrying about? I mean, don't forget the earth's about five thousand million years old, at least. Who can afford to live in the past?" (3: 66). Yet the past is the exclusive residence of Duff and Beth, of Rumsey and Bates and Ellen.

Clearly, Pinter's characters had always sought to define themselves and affirm their identities—as we all must—by reference to past events, whether actual, modified by memory, or entirely fabricated. This is as true of the more aggressive characters like Goldberg, Mick, and Lenny as it is of the patently insecure Stanley, Davies, and Teddy; the former merely manipulate the past more effectively, though even they may occasionally glimpse the underlying void, as when Goldberg's patter runs down while he tries to affirm his credo (1: 88), or when Lenny's tactical story of his pox-ridden "lady" is outflanked by Ruth's logical question (3: 46–47). Past memories, however, are subjective, unverifiable, and so vulnerable to question and attack by others; thus a more secure sanctuary for an identity constructed on the past than retreat within a room is the impenetrable haven of a solipsistic mind. With the possible exception of Duff, the voices of *Landscape* and *Silence*—for they are little more than that, prefiguring *Monologue* and *Family Voices* (1981)—are of loners who have foregone external communication and affection for the peace of contemplation. Thus their identities, their dreams, their memories are untouchable, amenable to whatever shape and interpretation they themselves wish to impose.

An ideal solution to the anxiety of the previous Pinter protagonist? Not quite. Granted, the past now becomes a refuge to be defended rather than a threat to be evaded, but for all that, it still remains a dangerous terrain wherein a character's identity may easily be lost. Rather than an external force capable of disintegrating a personality, as in *The Birthday Party,* the past in these short works proves more insidious. These dreamers who renounce life in the present to wander in the mists of memory find their self-images dissolving like Beth's sand-people, who "didn't look like human figures. The sand kept on slipping, mixing the contours" (3: 188). Without ongoing external activity or contact, these characters are stranded beyond the flow of time. Like many of Beckett's plays, *Landscape* and *Silence* seem to occur outside time, which has become irrelevant: there is no action for it to measure. Yet identity is built through action in time: if the past is always present, conversely the present must continually contribute to accumulating the past. Once the past stops expanding, identity is frozen, as in Spooner's climactic description of "no man's land. Which never moves, which never changes, which never grows older, but which remains forever, icy and silent" (4: 153).

If this is Hirst's landscape, it is also Beth's, and that of *Silence.* Beth at least achieves consolation from her misty past, whereas Duff's memories are discontented, troubled by guilt, anger, and frustration, so that he occasionally speaks to Beth, offering conversation, an outing to the park, or just an airing of the drawing room—but all in vain. *Silence,* however, maintains a darker tone than *Landscape* and represents Pinter's most extreme presentation of the past's vertiginous power, an eddy in time's current that has drawn the play's lonely trio into a deadly whirlpool of repetitious but ever-contracting memories. The familiar cast of two men and a woman appear to probe the past in a futile search for the origin of that shadow that has fallen between them. As in *The Basement,* Pinter deliberately distorts the time frame, so that while the characters appear as they were in their remembered encounters, and even approach one another on the bare stage, their dialogue indicates that this minimal action portrays their reminiscences, the only existence remaining to them. Thus while Ellen is presented as being "in her twenties," she recounts her response to the curiosity of her elderly drinking companion: "I'm old, I tell her, my youth was somewhere else, anyway I don't remember" (3: 204).

Moreover, the play's verbal repetitions establish Pinter's notion of time as a Charybdis destined to spin this trio slowly downward to anonymous nonexistence, prefiguring the fates of such later Pinter characters as the man (Spooner, according to his own affirmation) drowning in Hirst's dream-lake, or Anna drained with the bath water out of Kate's past (4: 68–69; 109, 153). Repeated fragments of dialogue near the end of *Silence,* as characters recall memories already fossilized into formulaic phrases that themselves diminish with each retelling, achieve much the same futile, time-warp effect as does the final repetition of the opening scene of *The Basement.* Whether represented as an external or an internal presence, the past consistently returns in Pinter's theatre to doom his creatures, who, like children lost in a forest, retrace their aimless footsteps until they drop.

Barely surviving in the present, Ellen, Bates, and Rumsey have grown irretrievably apart, alone and introspective; without external affirmation, all sense of self and even the memories upon which identity rests are eroded. Of the three, Ellen most eloquently expresses the effect of such solipsism: "I couldn't remember anything I'd actually thought, for some time. It isn't something that anyone could ever tell me, could ever reassure me about, nobody could tell, from looking at me, what was happening"; "I'm never sure that what I remember is of to-day or of yesterday or of a long time ago. And then often it is only half things I remember, half things, beginnings of things" (3: 204–5, 214). Finally, the characters wind down like Krapp's last tape, their memories exhausted, emptied, and all that remains is the silence of the play's title: the appalling static world that marks the end of time.

But unlike poetry, the form wherein Pinter first exercised his literary talents, or even prose fiction with its greater versatility, drama is a genre that lives in time. For all their artistry, *Landscape* and *Silence* barely breathe on the stage. Pinter's only course was to return toward action, and hence some temporal progression in his dramas. Short memory pieces have continued to appear: *Night* (1969), *Monologue,* and *Family Voices;* in his three subsequent full-length works, however, Pinter has sought further devices to compress past into present so as to represent a world at once timeless and yet alive and moving in time, remaining true both to his temporal concept and to the inescapable nature of the theatre. Pinter's attempt to stage the experience of that elusive "moment in and out of time," as T. S. Eliot once phrased it,[11] has perhaps not been wholly successful, but it has produced some intriguing experiments with theatrical form. As Pinter acknowledged after writing *Old Times,* "The whole question of time and all its reverberations and possible meanings really does seem to absorb me more and more."[12]

For the most part, *Old Times* adheres to a linear chronology, and *No Man's Land* is even more conventional in that regard. Yet in both, the present is merely the arena where divergent visions of the past meet in mortal combat; whereas this does provide at least verbal conflict, the past remains omnipresent and omnipotent. Despite their renewed vitality as compared to *Landscape* or *Silence,* both dramas conclude with the stasis that characterizes Pinter's works of the later 1960s, and that has come to signal Pinter's curtain-tableaux. No matter how intense the combat, how lively the wit, Pinter's world remains a quicksand of subjective memories wherein characters are fated to betrayal by time. Now rather than merely running from their pasts, or even ensconcing themselves within a private barricade of memories (though Kate and Hirst remain closer to this behavioral mode), more often the characters turn instinctively to the past to seek and affirm their own identities, as well as to grasp and mold the elusive personalities of their companions.

But since, as Anna observes so memorably in *Old Times,* the past exists only as each of them chooses to re-create it in their conversation (4: 27–28), each character's being is subject to endless redefinition, not only by himself, but more alarmingly, by others. Anna and Deeley pit their reminiscences against one another to assert their possession of Kate and their personal supremacy, but their efforts to master the past prove as futile as their predecessors' hopes to escape from, or into, its domain. Similarly, Spooner's obsequious bravado in affirming an ambiguous past tie to Hirst is challenged by the inscrutable Foster and Briggs, and finally proves inadequate to faze Hirst's imperturbability. Kate and Hirst will only spar with their assailants, but ultimately they will not condescend to engage their pasts in open verbal battle. Deeley, Anna, and Spooner are thus reduced to nonentities, forgotten and denied as if they no longer existed, as if, indeed, they never had existed. Kate and Hirst remain icy, monumental, no longer subject to time and its alterations, rather like the less willingly petrified poet of Pirandello's *Quando si è Qualcuno* (*When One Is Somebody*), except insofar as their stony roles remain subject to the erosion that besets the denizens of *Silence.*

Structurally, *No Man's Land* shows little of that experimentation with circular, overlapping, or discontinuous chronologies that had begun to mark Pinter's scripts for both stage and screen. Here, Pinter allows repeated dialogue and patterns of imagery to carry the impression of time's immobility: faces in a photograph album, recurrent dreams, the fog induced by heavy drinking, allusions to painting and poetry, and Spooner's reiteration (echoing Prufrock as well as himself), "I have known this before" (4: 96, 117, 118,

126). Nonetheless, the "no man's land" across which these old men duel is that familiar Pinteresque landscape, the past—and from its desolation, no victor emerges.

The structure of *Old Times,* however, is a bit more adventurous: Anna's presence on stage even before her "entrance," the evident shift in time (from before to after dinner) marked only by her initial participation in the dialogue, and her seduction of Kate into their shared past so that by the end of act 1 Deeley has replaced Anna as the "absent" presence while the women reconstruct a conversation from their girlhood together in London—all help maintain the presence of the past and suggest that Anna is its representative, its mysterious embodiment in the tradition of Riley, Goldberg, or the Matchseller, come in this instance to eradicate Deeley. The women's literal immersion in the past recalls the dialogues of *Silence,* and in keeping with that work's outcome, act 2 demonstrates again that those who are sustained by the past must finally be extinguished by the past. Thus Anna is ironically trapped along with Deeley in a "memory" of her own making. When at the play's end Kate details a devastating variation of Anna's first-act "recollection" of a man in their room, Anna and then Deeley proceed to enact the scene, which in Kate's version amounts to miming their own dismissal, their virtual deaths, at least insofar as they may ever have existed for Kate (4: 28–29, 69–71). Thus both acts culminate in reversions to the past, and the play's end recalls that of *The Basement* by implying a circular, inescapable pattern to its characters' behavior.

The finale of *Old Times*, however, remains teasingly ambiguous: Anna's initial account of the scene is itself equivocal, following as it does her comment, "There are things I remember which may never have happened, but as I recall them so they take place" (4: 28). And as Anna fades back into silence and the past (whether actual or imagined) from which she had so miraculously arisen, so her very existence in the "present" of the evening's encounter, and with her the reality of the encounter itself, of the play's entire action, is called into question.[14] As is *The Basement, Old Times* is open to interpretation as a fantasy, conjured up by the initial conversation of Kate and Deeley, much as Stott and Jane may represent Law's dream. These figures may be no more than visualized counterparts of those presences conveyed verbally in other Pinter plays, such as that quiescent but attractive man who escorts Beth to her chosen timeless landscape and who there exists so vividly for her. Of course, *Old times* is less amenable to such a view, both because Anna would seem to be a joint illusion of two dreamers and because of the play's generally more realistic, chronological development; yet the fact that the interpretation has been offered testifies to Pinter's disruption of the theatre's normal temporal pattern. Whether as fantasy or memory, the past has once more erupted into the present to shatter characters' relationships by undermining the deceptively stable identities on which those fragile bonds had been constructed.

The more recent full-length play, *Betrayal,* marks a new step for Pinter: a step forward in technique by stepping backward into the past. It seems odd in view of Pinter's consistent preoccupation with time that he had never before staged events from the past. Rather, he had savored their ambiguities, depicting the past's influence upon the present as enhanced by its amorphous and mysterious nature. Yet, perhaps intrigued by structural possibilities he had explored while writing screenplays, Pinter does move back from the time of *Betrayal*'s first two scenes through five progressively earlier stages in its characters' ménage à trois. While the flashback technique is unusual in the theatre, where departure from conventional chronology is a more difficult logistical matter than it is on film or in print, still it is by no means a radical innovation. Arthur Miller's *Death of a Salesman* and Thornton Wilder's *Our Town* are classic examples, and a more recent and analoguous model of progressive stepping back through time is provided by a 1972 radio play by a member of Pinter's cricket team: Tom Stoppard's *Artist Descending a Staircase*. This play begins in the present, moves steadily backward through five subsequent scenes, and then (unlike *Betrayal*) returns through five more scenes to the present.

Why, then, did Pinter wait until *Betrayal* finally to sacrifice the uncertainty of the past for the advantages of its direct portrayal? His own answer is that his characters began by "talking about the past. So, I thought I'd better go back there.... The actual structure of the play seemed to dictate itself. When I realized what was going on, this movement in time, I was very excited by it."[14] This, of course, is a bit of an evasion; for one thing, every Pinter play since *The Basement* has focused on characters speaking about the past, yet at most he had permitted only indirect or verbal, and so equivocal and subjective, movements back into time.

Pinter's work during 1972 on the Proust screenplay, and to a lesser extent his previous film adaptation of *The Go-Between*, provide the clearest models for his new approach in the theatre. The latter film portrays the past almost to the exclusion of the present, revealing the aging Leo and Marian only enough to convey how unmistakably they and her grandson are the products of that summer half a century in the past. Here the past is not merely felt in the present, but is examined and relived in an effort to understand the failures of the present, and by explaining, perhaps to alleviate them: the past not only reaches forward to paralyze the present, but conversely, the present begins to probe back into the past, and by mastering it, to renew hope for the future. That hope has motivated Marian to summon Leo after so many years to be her "postman" once more, this time to her grandson: "I think he feels ... that he's under some sort of spell or curse, you see.... You know the facts, you know what *really* happened. Tell him, tell him everything, just as it was."[15] A reprise of past experience is no longer merely an inexorable doom, a haven from uncertainty, or a psychological tool for dominating an adversary, but has become a form of exorcism, whispering of salvation after wreaking its destruction. Whether the curse can be lifted from Marian's grandson, however, remains unknown; Marian and Leo are clearly too old to be revived.

However, in Pinter's greatest screen-writing achievement, *Remembrance of*

Things Past, Marcel, who in his early forties seems well on the way to becoming another Leo, cursed by memories of premature and frightening adolescent contact with destructive sex drives, is renewed by suddenly perceiving the shape of his past. True, his rebirth will not be as a lover, but unlike the shriveled Leo, he will create, transmuting the agony of memory into art, like Thomas Mann's Tonio Kröger at once blessed and cursed by his inability ever to be a Hans Hansen. Here a return to the past goes beyond even explaining and exorcising its painful influence on the present, for it is found to conceal a hidden beauty, an aesthetic shape that perhaps compensates for its earlier pain. To convey this complex vision of the past, Pinter's Proust screenplay disrupts chronology far more radically than any of his previous scripts, beginning with a montage of more than thirty fragmentary scenes, like scattered pieces of an enormous puzzle that gradually takes shape as Pinter skillfully assembles shards selected from four decades, until the script returns at the end to its initial scene (recalling Pinter's many other circular structures). Here at the house of the Prince de Guermantes, in the midst of a party whose guests embody time's most hideous and grotesque effects, Marcel suddenly experiences his epiphany and can "conclude": "It was time to begin"; or as Eliot would have it, "to make an end is to make a beginning."[16] "The subject was Time," Pinter bluntly affirms in his Introduction to the screenplay, and he points out its two opposing movements, the first being time's erosive nature so familiar in Pinter's canon, and the second its fresh promise of grace: "the architecture of the film should be based on two main and contrasting principles: one, a movement, chiefly narrative, toward disillusion, and the other, more intermittent, toward revelation, rising to where time that was lost is found, and fixed forever in art."[17]

Very possibly, then, these screenplays affected Pinter's decision to allow the past its hour upon the stage in *Betrayal*. The reversed chronology not only facilitates a recognition of causes and motives, endowing events with a fatalistic inevitability (since on stage the future has already happened), but also turns disillusion inside-out, and by revealing its pattern, encourages acceptance and converts anguish into art. The play's effect is akin to that of Leo Tolstoy's beginning with an account of Ivan Ilych's funeral: interest is directed less at the events of the plot than at its underlying movement and implications. The wisdom of hindsight permits attention to the significance of casual comments or apparent digressions. This is particularly useful in the theatre, where there is no opportunity to flip back to an earlier page to recall some half-forgotten reference; Pinter's structure obligingly does the "flipping back" for his audience.

After the first two scenes, set consecutively in 1977, an audience knows that both Emma's marriage to Robert and her affair with Jerry are finished, as well as when Robert knew of the affair, when Emma knew he knew, and when Jerry at last knew they both knew. This moderately confusing fund of knowledge does facilitate insight as the play shifts into reverse from despair to hope. That hope, of course, is dripping in dramatic irony provided by the inverse structure, so that one arrives sadder but wiser at the final 1968 scene of Jerry's excited initiation of an affair with Emma, his evident joy at his clandestine mastery of his friendly rival, Robert, and Emma's eagerness to establish another "home" wherein to share love while extending her domestic domain. Jerry's seduction speech, rather unusual even allowing for his inebriation and his literary bent, takes on ominous significance in view of the preceding scenes' subsequent events: "I'll be a cripple, I'll descend, I'll diminish, into total paralysis, my life is in your hands, that's what you're banishing me to, a state of catatonia ... where the reigning prince is the prince of emptiness, the prince of absence, the prince of desolation. I love you" (4: 266). Jerry is accordingly banished, ironically not by Emma's refusal but by her acceptance, and at the end of scene 1, Emma is in a similar state herself: "It's all gone.... It's all all over" (4:175–76). Another confrontation that gains resonance from the reversed sequence is the men's comical but superficially irrelevant conversation in scene 4 regarding the anxiety levels of boy and girl babies, which seems now to reflect their own discomfort with themselves and one another, while Robert's questions in particular convey implied criticism of Jerry's "boyish" restlessness that drove him to desire Emma. And Jerry's obsessive recollection of tossing up and catching Robert and Emma's daughter while both families were laughing together suggests a wistful longing for an idyllic innocence their families could have shared (4: 165–66, 175, 236–37).

Foreknowledge of these characters' futures also creates an impression that they are fated, their relationships doomed, that however willingly they betray their marriages, their lovers, their best friends, themselves, their careers, their ideals, and their dreams, they yet are all victims of the ultimate betrayer, time. In his screenplays and stage plays alike, Pinter has consistently shown the insidious, pernicious betrayals of characters' efforts to realize their dreams through time. Moreover, the fact that this play's triangular pattern of intertwining attraction and competition echoes *The Basement* and so many other Pinter scripts indicates that motifs from the past have haunted Pinter's entire career as surely as within each play they have shaped his characters' lives. If time's linear movement is a deception, then so is reliance on progress and lasting change: the wheel completes its revolution, the past returns, new beginnings are dashed by reawakened memories. (It is no coincidence that both men in *Betrayal* are fond of reading William Butler Yeats, whose belief in the wheels and gyres of history underlies his numerous poetic and dramatic portrayals of the recurrence of the past. In fact, *Betrayal*'s structure invites comparsion with Yeats's concept of "Dreaming Back," e.g., as experienced by the Old Man in *Purgatory*.) Time's reversal in *Betrayal,* the future foretold, merely reflects and clarifies the structure of experience as an endless repetition of familiar plots, threatening infinite regression like that of Casey, the protégé of Robert and Jerry who has left his wife and three children to write "a novel about a man who leaves his wife and three children and goes to live alone on the other side of London to write a novel about a man who leaves his wife and three children—" (4: 206). As in *The Basement* with its abrupt winter-summer transitions, the rotation through the seasons in *Betrayal* additionally stresses the cyclical nature of existence. The play's first two scenes occur in spring; its last, in winter, an inauspicious season for initiating an affair that already seems, as Jerry himself bemoans, to have begun too late: "I should have had you, in your white, before the wedding" (4:265).

Yet the play permits a double perspective; like the Proust screenplay, it has two opposing movements. In some ways Jerry comes at last to find himself in the position of the friend he had betrayed a decade before: he himself feels betrayed by discovering a confidence shared by Robert and Emma for four years without his knowledge, his wife is very possibly having an affair (on top of which his former protégé is having an affair with his former mistress), he profits from the career of a writer he cannot respect, while he now reads Yeats, as had Robert when he was first assimilating his experience of betrayal. The repetition of events, the males' approximate exchange of positions are familiar Pinter devices, but here as the past unfolds and reveals its shape, the possibility is suggested that Jerry may begin to see its pattern, like a vision from Yeats "transfiguring all that dread," much as Pinter's audience is here privileged to do. In chronological sequence, *Betrayal* would conclude with Jerry's comment at the end of scene 2 that he plans to spend the summer with his family in the Lake District—the very place to recollect emotion in tranquillity, if not to convert it into art like Marcel, at least perhaps to free himself from its curse as, it may be, Marian's grandson manages to do.

That these most recent scenes occur in spring may just be one more ironic note, or the season may affirm a deeper optimism beneath Emma's wistful observation, "It's nice, sometimes, to think back, Isn't it?" (4:159). This play comprises such thinking back, both for the characters whose memories are realized on stage, the pattern of their betrayals selected, focused, and artistically arranged, and for the playwright, who has given fresh shape to his familiar theme of a trio's bonds of love and rivalry, loosened by deceit, frayed by the weight of their past, broken by time. Pinter's earlier work illustrates the futility both of avoiding or manipulating the past and of renouncing life in the present. His latest scripts suggest that by employing that present to find meaning in the past, a future may be made possible. That Jerry is driven to understand and to reconcile his past is clear from scene 2, wherein he seeks out Robert to clarify all that has occurred; what he will make of his insight remains untold.

Like the Proust screenplay, *Betrayal* stresses that time's movement can be viewed from two perspectives, that inexorable disillusion and dissolution compose only one of its potential patterns, and that viewed in reverse, through the looking glass, an equally valid movement toward meaning may appear. The past in Pinter's drama remains "a foreign country," enigmatic and perilous, yet repeated expeditions have shown the risk of exploration to be well repaid by the benefits of charting its terrain. The adventurer's route lies upstream along Time's flow, a river swift to betray those who drift aimlessly or struggle hysterically in its current, yet liable also to betray its secrets to those strong enough to trace its course to the headwaters of their sorrows. To this goal Pinter has devoted a quarter-century of his art.

Notes

1. Parenthetical volume and page references to Pinter's stage plays are to his *Complete Works,* 4 vols. (New York: Grove Press, 1976–81).
2. Useful studies of the functions of memory in Pinter's dramas include Stephen Martineau, "Pinter's *Old Times*: The memory Game," *Modern Drama* 16 (1973): 287–97; Barbara Kreps, "Time and Harold Pinter's Possible Realities: Art as Life, and Vice Versa," *Modern Drama* 22 (1979): 47–60; and A. R. Braunmuller, "Harold Pinter: The Metamorphosis of Memory," in *Essays on Contemporary British Drama,* ed. Hedwig Bock and Albert Wertheim (Munich: Max Hueber, 1981), pp. 155–70.
3. Several plays that Pinter chose either to direct or to act in during this period further attest to his preoccupation with dramatic portrayals of the interpenetration of present and past: Jean-Paul Sartre's *No Exit,* Robert Shaw's *The Man in the Glass Booth,* and James Joyce's *Exiles,* wherein Robert baldly asserts, "The past is not past. It is present here now" ([New York: Viking Press, 1961], p. 84).
4. "Kullus," "The Task," and "The Examination" appear in Pinter, *Poems and Prose, 1949–1977* (New York: Grove Press, 1978), pp. 26–27, 51–54, 61–66. On *The Basement*'s links to its predecessors, consult Kurt Tetzeli v. Rosador, "Pinter's Dramatic Method: Kullus, The Examination, The Basement," *Modern Drama* 14 (1971): 195–204; and Martin Esslin, *Pinter: A Study of His Plays* (London: Eyre Methuen, 1973), pp. 41, 59–60, 162, 166–68.
5. Pinter, interviewed by Mel Gussow, "A Conversation [Pause] with Harold Pinter," *New York Times Magazine,* 5 December 1971, pp. 132–33.
6. Esslin, *Pinter,* pp. 165–68; and Kreps, "Time and Pinter's Realities," pp. 52–53.
7. The success of this script's eventual adaptation to the stage was debatable: John Russell Taylor praised set designs for permitting fluid scene shifts, while Irving Wardle found the effect of the transitions to be "only approximate and sometimes obscure." Taylor's review of the London production appears in *Plays and Players* 18 (November 1970): 36–39, Wardle's in *The Times* (London), 18 September 1970, p. 6.
8. The cyclic family behavior in *The Homecoming* has been well charted by Rolf Fjelde, "Plotting Pinter's Progress," in *A Casebook on Harold Pinter's "The Homecoming,"* ed. John Lahr (New York: Grove Press, 1971), pp. 102–5; and Bernard F. Dukore, "A Woman's Place," in *A Casebook,* pp. 111–15.
9. Pinter, quoted by William Wolf, "Wolf on Films," *Cue* (New York), 24 October 1970, p. 7.
10. Pinter, *Accident,* in *Five Screenplays* (London: Methuen, 1971), pp. 265–69.
11. Eliot, "The Dry Salvages," V. Braunmuller, "Harold Pinter," pp. 155, 167, has noted the increasing frequency of Pinter's allusions to Eliot; consult also John Bush Jones, "Stasis as Structure in Pinter's *No Man's Land,*" *Modern Drama* 19 (1976): 291–96; and Steven H. Gale, *Butter's Going Up: A Critical Analysis of Harold Pinter's Work* (Durham, N.C.: Duke University Press, 1977), pp. 188, 201, 207.
12. Pinter, interviewed by Gussow, "A Conversation," p. 133.
13. Alan Hughes suggests that Kate and Deeley fabricate Anna from their imaginations to mitigate their boredom, in "'They Can't Take That Away from Me': Myth and Memory in Pinter's *Old Times,*" *Modern Drama* 17 (1974): 468–70; Arthur Ganz argues that Anna represents the long-suppressed passional aspect of Kate, in "Mixing Memory and Desire: Pinter's Vision in *Landscape, Silence,* and *Old Times,*" in *Pinter: A Collection of Critical Essays,* ed. Arthur Ganz (Englewood Cliffs, N.J.: Prentice-Hall, 1972), pp. 173–76; while Esslin, *Pinter,* p. 188, hazards the possibility that the entire play might be "a nightmare of Deeley's."

14. Pinter, interviewed by Mel Gussow, "Harold Pinter: 'I Started with Two People in a Pub,'" *New York Times,* 30 December 1979, sec. 2, p. 5.

15. Pinter, *The Go-Between*, in *Five Screenplays*, p. 359.

16. Pinter, *The Proust Screenplay* (New York: Grove Press, 1977), p. 177; Eliot, "Little Gidding," V.

17. Ibid., pp. ix–x.

16
The Uncertainty Principle and Pinter's Modern Drama

JOHN FUEGI

The scene is a rather shabby apartment in Paris in 1932. A gangly young man is reading aloud to a somewhat older nearly blind man. The work being read aloud is Fritz Mauthner's *Beiträge zu einer Kritik der Sprache*. The reader is Samuel Beckett. The near blind listener is James Joyce. Their joint fascination with the regretably obscure Mauthner is extraordinary. On page after page Beckett reads off compelling examples of the manifest absurdity of much supposedly logical everyday use in all the major modern languages. Clearly, according to Mauthner, the revolution that has remade our post-Aristotelian and post-Ptolemian (not to mention post-Einsteinian and Heisenbergian universe) view of our entire universe, has totally outstripped "modern" language usage. The modern languages, according to Mauthner, remain frozen at a level of everyday usage that fails completely to recognize the achievements of the major physicists and astronomers who, since at least the time of Copernicus, have challenged and overturned many of the tenets of classical astronomy and classical physics. In a word, "modern usage" is in a basic way not modern at all, does not square with perceived reality, and is, therefore, inherently absurd. One can imagine the joy of Beckett and Joyce as they saw confirmed in Mauthner their own sense that it was their own work that was accurate and logical and that it was the general public that was busy denouncing Joyce as they later would denounce Beckett that was operating on inherently absurd principles.

The examples presented by Mauthner and enjoyed so much by Beckett and Joyce lo those many years ago still maintain their hold today. The television announcer assured me last night on all the channels available to me, and my *Washington Post* this morning reconfirmed last night's TV announcer, that the sun rose today at a certain time and that it will set today at a certain time. Now how much modern physics or even seventeenth-century physics do we really need to know most emphatically that the sun neither rose nor set today? Yet we make no adjustment to several centuries of scientific observation but simply repeat a forumla based on astronomical observations that predate by millennia the very creation of the so-called "modern" languages. Another example must suffice here to describe the widespread phenomenon of language being out of phase with other branches of human activity. In the modern languages, as in the classical tongues, we still say: "The tree is green." The fact that this is not so has not penetrated our linguistic consciousness. How many centuries is it likely to be before we will be able to bring ourselves to say something closer to the scientific fact, that is, "the tree greens me"?

The basic point that needs to be established here is one that is basic to scientists but has been too long ignored by humanists and artists *not* as well read as Joyce and Beckett. For most artists and certainly for most consumers of the arts, the revolutions of Copernicus and Galileo have not yet penetrated their consciousness, and the names of Albert Einstein, Werner Heisenberg, Kurt Gödel, and Max Planck may have associations with scenarios of horror, but seem to be largely ignored in everyday life. The world view of most people has, I submit, remained largely unchanged. It should not surprise us that a public enterprise such as the theatre should have remained largely at the level of that public rather than vigorously seeking to incorporate a world view almost universally accepted in the scientific community. Bluntly stated, with the few exceptions that I will enumerate below, the "modern drama" is about as modern in the main as the theory that the Earth is flat and the heavens revolve around a stationary Earth. Let me try and substantiate this rather blunt statement with some examples of what I shall call stability or certainty in the classical drama and a few examples of instability or uncertainty in the modern drama.

In the classical world it was possible for one person to be simultaneously a leading drama critic and a leading scientist because the world view expressed in the drama made sense to scientists. Aristotle the scientist did not need to be any less scientific when looking at the drama than he was when classifying various forms of life on earth.

The plays that Aristotle looked at are organized (to use a model derived from the Russian formalist Vladimir Propp) in the following manner: a problem is stated at the outset; the universe is organized, literally and figuratively, in a predictable way; Oedipus must do certain things even if he does not want to; by the play's end the predictability of the universe is confirmed. We have clarified all major factual obscurity. We know what's what.

Now I would go further to suggest that this structural model is characteristic of the drama (classical and most modern, comedy and tragedy, eastern and western). We begin with a problem, and at the play's end we have clarity and a sense of completion. Let me quickly describe three highly traditional (if not downright reactionary) plays using this model. *Hamlet*: problem on the battlements; who did in the king?; clarify the problem of Hamlet's father; do in the murderer; cleanse Denmark; enter Fortinbras to establish a new, more

secure rule (far from Hamlet's personal ambiguities); end the play. *Ghosts*:
problem in the middle-class living room; who is the villain?; clarify the problem of Oswald's father; Oswald suffers brain death; new clarity about the
problem of V.D.; end the play. *Mother Courage and Her Children*: problem
on the battlefield; will Courage, while living from war, save her children?
Answer: No. Play ends; war continues. To recap. In *Hamlet, Ghosts,* and
Mother Courage, the play materials fall into a highly predictable pattern. The
persons in these later plays, as in the plays of the Greeks, must do certain
things whether or not they want to; by play's end the rhythm or pattern of the
universe is reestablished for further mad princes, sick fathers, business-
minded mothers. The play ends. The world goes on. The play form is totally
unsynchronized with the discontinuities and ambiguities of a world where
everything does not run in this highly predictable way. I would suggest that
we extend the argument advanced by George Bernard Shaw when he con-
temptuously dismissed French nineteenth-century plays as "clockwork mice
set to run across a stage and then stop," and say that that description actually fits almost all plays (including those of Shaw himself). Using Shaw's own
provocative formulation and availing myself of Propp's *Morphology of the
Folk Tale* and extrapolating the morphology to the drama, I conclude that we
have only a very small sample of genuinely modern plays, that is to say, plays
that do not remain prisoners of a world view that is patently absurd. We issue
in paradox and we return to Joyce and Beckett. That body of work that is *not*
absurd from the viewpoint of modern science is that body of drama collected
by Martin Esslin under the general heading *The Theatre of the Absurd*. Bluntly stated, I believe that a strong case can be made for the contention that it is
only the absurd drama that is not absurd, for it is only the absurd drama that
seems sometimes to be aware of what has happened in the sciences since at
least the time of Copernicus.

In Harold Pinter's play *The Caretaker,* one person says to the caretaker
(who is not in fact a caretaker), "I can take nothing you say at face value.
Every word you speak is open to any number of interpretations." This sent-
ence can be used to describe any number of characters in any number of
Pinter plays. Typically in Pinter, instead of the audience being able to establish greater clarity as one of his plays proceeds, the audience, in fact, becomes
less and less sure of the truth of what is being seen and heard. In radical
contrast to the kind of drama I have described as classical or stable drama,
Pinter's play world is absolutely dominated very often by instability, ambiguity, uncertainty. Instead of things getting cleared up as the play goes forward
(who in fact killed Laius, or Hamlet's father, or who is responsible for
Oswald's condition, or what in fact will happen to Courage's three children),
that segment of space-time which is the core of the play is not reliably related
to other concerns. Whereas in *Oedipus* the guilt of the central character has a
direct bearing on the health of the whole city of Thebes, whereas in Hamlet
the rotteness revealed by the dead king must be rooted out before Denmark
can be returned to health, and whereas in *Ghosts* and *Mother Courage* one

sees a clear need for certain "middle-class values" to be abandoned before the world can be improved, where do you begin to get your hands on a definable problem let alone a soluble problem in Pinter? When we try to pin down the character of Davies in *The Caretaker*, we find that we can rely on nothing except the Planck constant of his unreliability.

In traditional drama one gradually learned more and more about a person and that person's environment. In Pinter, when you begin to rely on a character or you think you have "placed" a specific environment, you are often rudely shocked because other data points later in the play cannot be reconciled with the earlier data points. Characters in Pinter often do not inhere in a coherent system of space-time coordinates. We cannot place them with any certainty at any fixed point in space-time. They have the randomness of particles in the post-Einsteinian, post-Heisenbergian world view. When you try to illuminate the space-time coordinates of "the particles" in *The Caretaker*, they carom off in various directions. When you try to illuminate where "Davies" is coming from or where he is going to, you find that he is a totally unreliable narrator and perhaps does not even know where he has come from. He does not know his own name. He thinks he may have left some documents in Wapping that will establish his identity, but whether in fact he ever had such documents, whether they are in fact obtainable in Wapping, or indeed whether he will ever get there is never cleared up in the play. Our two other sources of information in the play are again examples of uncertainty or instability. One character proposes to build a woodshed, but our only certainty here is that it is uncertain that the shed will ever be built. The last character proposes to turn the dump of a room that is the play's locale into a palace of sorts, a triumph of the designer's art, a cover picture for *House Beautiful*. Does this character have the skills to make such a transformation? We don't know. If the character had the skills, would they be applied to these unlikely raw materials? We don't know. Where is this place anyway? It is upstairs somewhere. Where we do not know, for the room in which the action of the play takes place is never put into a contextual framework. It is constructive here to compare this deliberate lack of context of space-time with the time-space coordinates of a supposedly "modern" play, such as *Death of a Salesman*. The points of the Loman house are carefully related to one another. The relationship of the house to Willy's vast sales territory in New England is also what I would call space-specific. In this regard, *Death of a Salesman* is constructed on similar principles to those used in *Oedipus Rex, Hamlet, Ghosts,* and *Mother Courage*. The coordinates that place the relationship of Thebes to Corinth in Sophocles, of Denmark to Poland, England, and Sweden in *Hamlet*, of the Norwegian village to Paris in *Ghosts,* and the carefully mapped terrain of *Mother Courage* are all lacking in Pinter. Without contextual reference points it is virtually impossible to glean a reliable "meaning" from Pinter's text. It is like the extreme close-up photography of a section of human epidermis that looks very much like a shot of the surface of the moon or the Sahara Desert; we rely on the context to yield the "meaning" of the "text." Content *is* the text. In classical drama we have such a text because we are carefully given a context. In modern drama, we have an almost infinite variety of "texts" in any given play because we are not given a context to enable us to narrow down the choice as to what constitutes "the text." Davies simply is not a reliable part of a reliable context. He is indeterminate. The room in which we find him is indeterminate. He cannot be mapped or placed with any more reliability than the sub-atomic particles that constitute the physically verifiable base for the Uncertainty Principle in physics.

What seems to be true for Pinter's *Caretaker* seems equally true for *The Dumb Waiter*. Beginning with its very title the play redounds in multiple meanings while failing to provide any real context for where the two protagonists are and why they are doing what it is that they are doing. Who sent them? What are their orders? Are their orders any more certain or rational than the orders for even more exotic dishes that come down in the dumb waiter? Two men watch and wait. Are they in turn watched? If so, by whom One question begets another. Are we ourselves dumb to wait for answers?

To turn from Pinter's *Dumb Waiter*, it seems a ministep to the bleak landscape of other waiters: those characters of Sad Sam Beckett who are *Waiting for Godot*. Again the level of ambiguity in the form and the content of this play is staggeringly high. The road and the tree are probably somewhere in France because we know that Vladimir and Estragon have missed their chance to jump off the Eiffel Tower together. But this amounts to little more than the place name Wapping given in Pinter's *Caretaker*. The tree and the road of the play are kept at the maximum level of ambiguity. So are the inhabitants of this nonspecific space. Who are they? Where have they come from? For whom or what do they wait? In this landscape of the bereft, absurdity is played off against absurdity. Language and action is stripped down to a point where the absurdity of both language and action become manifest. Whereas in "the real world" language and action though manifestly absurd (as Mauthner showed Beckett) are nevertheless taken seriously, in Beckett's play such absurdities are vigorously underlined: when "the sun sets and the moon rises," it is done mechanically by a stagehand to underscore the fact that this is not to be viewed as the real, as the natural. In my view, what is being challenged here is our whole way of viewing, our whole way of hearing. We are being asked to face up to language as it is with all its quirks and illogicalities.

This is where I believe Beckett, and to a certain extent Pinter, are genuinely modern and scientifically rigorous. They do not reshape language to iron out its many illogicalities but allow it to be examined directly in a controlled setting, the theatrical space. To leaf back again to where we began, compare and contrast *Waiting for Godot, Endgame, Happy Days,* or *Krapp's Last Tape* with the premodern drama, which I earlier described as consisting of plays in which all major factual questions with which these plays begin are answered by the end of these plays. The premodern text presupposes the possibility of clarification and of reaching a solution. The genuinely modern drama does not do this and does not advocate this. With Beckett and with Pinter we enter a world where the principle of uncertainty is maintained in the form, structure, and language of the aesthetic construct itself.

In conclusion I would suggest that a genuinely modern world view is really quite at odds with the theatre as a social entity. For all the earlier success of a Pinter or a Beckett, I believe that the sheer weight of theatrical tradition and the form of organization of fixed theatrical space and ineluctable financial constraints work against the kind of experimentation so brilliantly advanced by Pinter and Beckett. As I read the more advanced and international theatre journals, I am led to the melancholy conclusion that the contemporary theatre is becoming less rather than more modern. As Beckett comes even closer to silence and Pinter devotes himself more and more to film, we see, I think, a theatre abandoned. My own sense is that we must seek modern thinking in the arts outside the theatres. Regrettably, the Uncertainty Principle has no real home in the modern theatre. The drama of uncertainty, despite the heroic efforts and considerable skills of Beckett and Pinter, appropriately enough faces an uncertain future. At its most modern the theatre is least certain of maintaining its existence. Perhaps Joyce, and Beckett, and Pinter, and Mauthner can all have a good laugh at that. Maybe we can join them. Maybe not. I confess a certain uncertainty. I am waiting. If there is any hope that I am wrong, Pinter and Beckett are most likely the two major contemporary playwrights who will supply the impetus for continuance. They are the only reason that I continue to wait at all.

A Chronological Index to *Harold Pinter: An Annotated Bibliography*

STEVEN H. GALE

In 1978 G. K. Hall published my *Harold Pinter: An Annotated Bibliography*. The volume contains 2,054 items listed in alphabetical order by author. In any project of this length, particularly one that is composed primarily of numbers and individual letters, typographical errors are bound to occur, and although I tried my best to avoid these, especially since accuracy is so important in a reference tool of this sort, some did end up in the published version. The name of one of the contributors to this present volume, for instance, was misspelled. More frustrating were the occasional errors that were caught, yet which still appeared in print. The spelling of Alrene Sykes's first name is a prime example. Professor Sykes's first name is spelled A-l-r-e-n-e, not A-r-l-e-n-e. I spelled the name correctly in the manuscript, but when I received the galley proofs, the copy editor had changed it. I changed it back, and made a note in the margin that I had reinserted the correct spelling. When the page proofs arrived, the Sykes entry was one of the first that I checked. Sure enough, the copy editor had again renamed Professor Sykes. This time I changed the spelling back, circled it in red, and wrote a note in inch-high red letters explaining that the name was Alrene, not Arlene. Check entry number 1798 to see how Professor Sykes will go down in history.

Unfortunately, errors of this kind will have to wait until a second edition to be corrected. However, there was one thing that can be changed with the publication of *Harold Pinter: Critical Approaches*. Because the format of the bibliography was alphabetical, and since I know that there are times when it is valuable for a scholar to be able to have quick access to all of the criticism written in one year, or to be able to compare critical reactions in say 1960 with those in 1980, I also included a "Chronological Index of Works on Harold Pinter" in the bibliography. Overall, I was very pleased with Hall, but it was very frustrating to learn, only after I had a copy of the published volume in my hand, that a last minute production decision had been made to delete this chronological index. I have managed to provide copies of the index to a few individuals who I knew would be interested in one; now I have the opportunity to make it available to anyone who can use it.

The format of "A Chronological Index of Works on Harold Pinter," which is herein titled "A Chronological Index to *Harold Pinter: An Annotated Bibliography*," is a referencing to the entries in the bibliography. For each year from 1957 through 1978 those publications which appeared in that year are listed by the number that corresponds to their entry number in *Harold Pinter: An Annotated Bibliography*. Since the numbers are in numerical order, this also means that they reflect the alphabetical order of the bibliography rather than any attempt to order them by month or day within a year (which would be impossible in many cases). Finally, there is also a listing of those entries for which no date was available. Since a second edition or a supplement of the bibliography is being planned, any information on any of these items that the reader can provide will be greatly appreciated.

A Chronological Index of Works on Harold Pinter*

Entry numbers are arranged in sequence across the page.

Year: *1957*

Entry number:
  1046

Year: *1958*

Entry number:

174	327	398	447	464	472
482	570	657a	662	688	932
1037	1045	1105	1106	1342	1374
1465	1466	1731	1866	1884	1922
1924	1988	1999	2015		

Year: *1959*

Entry number:

152	197	262	285	475	776
1177	1287	1634			

* An asterisk denotes reprints, revisions, or subsequent editions.

Year: *1960*

Entry number:

153	154	192	196	223	253
263	266	304	314	317	339
343	348	361	407	424	429
446	448	449	481	483	487
534	535	557	571	616	629
632	633	636	658	659	683
686	689	694	744	769	774
777	779	783	784	793	805
863	867	881	883	963	1009
1034	1035	1047	1048	1049	1053
1059	1089	1178	1179	1270	1273
1274	1290	1293	1299	1315	1317
1318	1334	1345	1385	1400	1403
1429	1430	1434	1439	1451	1453
1454	1455	1460	1473	1531	1548
1580	1581	1582	1585	1588	1599
1605	1613	1614	1618	1626	1627
1633	1635	1645	1656	1704	1706
1707	1756	1845	1853	1858	1859
1865	1868	1870	1872	1873	1880
1881	1892	1901	1912	1940	1973
1976	1981	1984	1989	2000	2005
2013	2022				

Year: *1961*

Entry number:

165	166	171	182	186	191
195	210	211	213	214	226
238	258	259	265	292	322
331	358	362	371	375	404
450	452	458	471	486	490
505	511	514	537	540	558
566	580	596	609	610	630
634	637	661	665	666	669
692	693	696	698	704	714
722	756	761	781	782	808
848	850	856	858	878	896
897	929	999	1003	1023	1033
1066	1067	1086	1125	1180	1185
1187	1233	1272	1275	1294	1302
1316	1325	1333	1336	1340	1344

1346	1354	1362	1383	1399	1407
1414	1423	1440	1459	1467	1478
1507	1536	1559	1589	1611	1616
1622	1657	1701	1705	1722	1732
1733	1736	1744	1750	1764	1806
1809	1841	1854	1886	1898	1946
1980	1983	2002	2004	2206	2023
2036					

Year: *1962*

Entry number:

190	209	212	242	286	291
299	302	312	315	342	346
359	378	403	477	479	503
507	517	536	572	581	601
622	633	667	697	707	709
718	732	748	791	816	845
849	887	894	986	993	1008
1010	1015	1051	1062	1069	1135
1170	1181	1186	1193	1225	1242
1276	1284	1305	1311	1327	1332
1350	1364	1410	1420	1457	1458
1471	1474	1508	1538	1628	1636
1658	1729	1734	1735	1757	1784
1790	1805	1807	1812	1813	1814
1832	1843	1860	1867	1871	1931
1950	1966	1977	1987	1995	

Year: *1963*

Entry number:

160	168	170	198	215	264
267	300	303	309	312	313
318	319	321	333	352	353
374	385	441	465	467	468
476	480	500	520	604	664
746	749	792	807	846	879
884	928	933	949	951	956
958	991	994	1036	1068	1093
1113	1126	1167	1200	1232	1240
1277	1291	1308	1314	1322	1347
1352	1373	1409	1476	1497	1504
1509	1532	1565	1583	1591	1617

1651	1709	1730	1812*	1816	1817
1831	1842	1857	1861	1885	1887
1897	1899	1915	1932	1937	1960
1964	1979	1991	2001	2003	2012

Year: *1964*

Entry number:

147	149	187	188	189	199
222	234	257	287	311	323
324	325	332	334	335	336
341	360	368	384	439	453
459	462	463	485	496	497
500*	506	513	526	532	533
543	582	583	600	607	608
613	614	618	621	640	641
645	657	660	668	671	685
690	699	702	711	737	751
763	786	790	797*	799	801
804	812	813	847	862	869
880	882	892	907	913	917
920	930	939	953	965	968
971	972	973	981	1000	1002
1012	1013	1050	1058	1076	1112
1150	1151	1152	1169	1171	1172
1191	1194	1195	1210	1227	1231
1241	1253	1285	1296	1312	1324
1326	1328	1341	1353	1363	1365
1367	1372	1378	1379	1406	1421
1436	1456	1469	1470	1498	1511
1520	1521	1522	1523	1526	1527
1529	1542	1560	1561	1566	1572
1584	1586	1597	1598	1606	1608
1609	1629	1639	1647	1659	1662
1663	1671	1681	1683	1687	1696
1728	1794	1808	1810	1824	1828
1834	1844	1847	1869	1891	1895
1907	1911	1917	1919	1920	1929
1942	1953	1954	1956	1967	1974
1986	1990	1993	1994	2011	2017
2028	2029	2033	2034		

Year: *1965*

Entry number:

141	157	159	205	221	239
243	270	277	302	305	313
316	326	347	369	399	411
426	433	438	451	456	474
484	489	499	504	510	512
514*	516	517*	519	521	525
550	559	562	568	598	617
627	648	651	670	673	703
743	754	761*	764	785	797*
802	806	851	854	855	876
931	941	957	962	1041	1054
1056	1064	1070	1212	1226	1244
1288	1292	1298	1323	1368	1371
1382	1404	1408	1411	1438	1448
1452	1477	1485	1501	1502	1515
1533	1590	1615	1642	1713	1720
1721	1724	1758	1788	1792	1796
1800	1804	1821	1822	1829	1835
1846	1855	1862	1864	1896	1924*
1982	2018	2021			

Year: *1966*

Entry number:

169	183	233	268	328	337
364	389	427	574	578	602
603	679	724	727	764*	778
840	853	1074	1107	1120	1137
1151*	1163	1204	1215	1224	1295
1380	1384	1401	1431	1445	1449
1480	1537	1604	1640	1690	1752
1785	1811	1876	1992	1997	2027
2030					

Year: *1967*

Entry number:

135	137	143	151	155	161
162	163	194	244	245	249
255	274	275	295	298	303
304	306	307	309	310	314

329	350	366	370	373	380
390	400	415	420	421	428
436	437	454.	460	461	470
515	523	531	534	549	560
561	565	567	573	579	584
585	597	605	611	615	620
623	625	635	639	644	649
650	687	708	720	721	726
750	768	771	789	796	800
860	865	871	875	885	890
891	893	895	912	915	926
942	948	959	964	974	976
978	995	998	1001	1005	1006
1011	1021	1024	1025	1027	1029
1030	1073	1114	1133	1134	1142
1164	1168	1182	1189	1196	1197
1201	1202	1208	1236	1247	1267
1300	1303	1306	1307	1313	1321
1337	1338	1348	1349	1355	1356
1360	1361	1381	1387	1388	1390
1395	1402	1405	1412	1419	1428
1443	1468	1472	1499	1524	1525
1543	1544	1550	1567	1573	1574
1587	1610	1612	1621	1630	1631
1632	1648	1655	1672	1675	1676
1677	1684	1686	1693	1708	1716
1741	1745	1749	1753	1754	1768
1772	1780	1782	1799	1819	1925
1840	1888	1905	1908	1913	1916
1918	1921	1947	1949	1963	1970
1971	1978	2008	2035		

Year: *1968*

Entry number:

144	150	164	175	181	200
217	218	235	241	246	251
273	300	330	351	357	382
383	416	457	466	469	499*
501	512*	530	541	547	586
619	643	672	695	700	706
710	749*	758	761*	775	850*
852	857	910	911	918	924
938	940	946	983	984	989

1022	1078	1085	1108	1109	1127
1132	1133*	1146	1198	1230	1238
1250	1256	1265	1268	1335	1339
1351	1370	1405*	1415	1416	1418
1430*	1435	1446	1479	1481	1483
1496	1514	1518	1546	1549	1551
1552	1553	1554	1574*	1575	1576
1579	1652	1665	1669	1673	1678
1688	1710	1742	1765	1774	1784*
1849	1850	1883	1889	1890	1903
1955	1958	1972	1985	2002*	

Year: *1969*

Entry number:

176	201	216	250	269	271
272	294	297	340	388	393
397	402	406	408	445	455
518	522	526*	527	542	544
555	577	599	612	652	653
678	680	715	736	741	743*
747	761*	798	841	859	861
904	919	921	923	967	969
970	985	997	1016	1017	1040
1061	1065	1082	1094	1118	1132*
1147	1148	1175	1197*	1199	1203
1205	1211	1218	1235	1237	1245
1246	1263	1264	1268*	1269	1278
1310	1331	1386	1389	1391	1393
1450	1475	1488	1490	1492	1494
1503	1557	1558	1592	1596	1602
1644	1674	1691	1692	1698	1714
1725	1726	1748	1767	1769	1770
1771	1783	1797	1801	1812*	1813*
1818	1833	1839	1856	1863	1875
1893	1905*	1927	1928	1936	2010
2019	2026				

Year: *1970*

Entry number:

134	139	145	156	202	276
305	308	355	394	396	401
423	431	518*	538	548	587

Year: *1971*

1820	1823	1838	1852	1878	1902
1906	1914	1925	1934	1939	1943
1944	1948	1952	1959	1967*	2009
2020	2031				

Year: *1972*

Entry number:

204	230	231	236	281	320
354	391	410	427*	430	442
498	502	601*	691	705	712
725	753	794	818	827	830
835	842	843	900	906*	955
961	1020	1043	1088	1111	1116
1123	1124	1188	1219	1239	1265*
1309	1330	1356*	1375	1417	1424
1434*	1441	1463	1482	1541	1544*
1545	1570	1650	1654	1664	1666
1759	1761	1774*	1780*	1793	1801a
1802	1826	1836	1848	1894	1923
2007					

Year: *1973*

Entry number:

146	167	185	193	219	220
224	225	282	284	293	317
363	381	386	387	435	440
494	495	545	552	593	628
655	701	729	730	733	742
755*	757	773	788	821	844
866	886	898	899	983*	988
992	1104	1110	1121	1128	1129
1144	1153	1162	1165	1166	1229
1259	1265*	1289	1297	1398	1413
1432	1444	1462	1495	1594	1620
1667	1668	1682	1695	1778	1830
1851	1877	1900	2014	2032	

Year: *1974*

Entry number:

| 138 | 140 | 179 | 184 | 206 | 237 |

240	365	372	478	492	528
556	575	576	628*	716	738
759	814	825	873	954	990
1019	1028	1077	1092	1096	1100
1102	1103	1115	1157	1174	1176
1214	1286	1343	1357	1394	1426
1427	1493	1519	1543a	1568	1569
1593	1637	1641	1670	1702	1760
1909	1968	2025			

Year: *1975*

Entry number:

142	177	178	208	232	254
260	278	279	280	288	295
298	301	318	338	345	367
392	417	508	539	551	553
554	590	595	631	654	656
681	723	731	745	765	766
770	901	908	937	952	982
1032	1038	1095	1097	1098	1101
1136	1155	1207	1216	1281	1282
1283	1359	1376	1484	1487	1535
1595	1625	1703	1751	1775	1777
1779	1781	1786	1787	1789	1930
1933	1962	2024			

Year: *1976*

Entry number:

136	158	207	289	290	413
418	419	422	432	434	491
546	591	592	626	642	719
728	735	739	757*	762	767
773a	815	833	839	870	872
943	980	1021*	1057	1075	1081
1087	1099	1122	1130	1139	1154*
1156	1159	1161	1192	1222	1248
1251	1255	1358	1369	1425	1461
1564	1603	1660	1685	1762	1766
1777*	1874	1938	1996		

Year: *1977*

Entry number:

261	296	319	379	425	478a
492*	554*	716a	817	820	823
829	834	836	960	983a	1021a
1069a	1209	1486	1638	1711	1717
1746	1747	1800a	1812*	1900*	1957
1969					

Year: *1978*

Entry number:
828

NO DATE**

Entry number:

172	173	734**	809	810	819**
822**	826**	831**	853	903	905
936	950	1173	1223	1433	1505
1528	1571**	1619	1623	1624	1624a
1646	1661	1719	1763	1882	1998

** A double asterisk denotes a piece in preparation.

Notes on Contributors

THOMAS P. ADLER received his B.A. and M.A. from Boston College and his Ph.D. from the University of Illinois. He is currently a professor of English at Purdue University, where he teaches drama and film.

Adler has published and spoken extensively on twentieth-century British and American drama, including three previous articles on Pinter.

ENOCH BRATER is a professor and graduate director in the Department of English Language and Literature at the University of Michigan. He has a number of publications on modern drama and on film to his credit, including articles on Samuel Beckett, Tom Stoppard, Friedrich Durrenmätt, Peter Nichols, Arthur Miller, and W. B. Yeats. Brater's work on cinematic techniques in Pinter's *Betrayal*, on the film version of *The Homecoming*, and on *The Proust Screenplay* have appeared in *Modern Drama* and in *Contemporary Drama*.

A. R. BRAUNMULLER received his B. A. from Stanford, and his M.Phil. and a Ph.D. from Yale. At present he is a professor of English at the University of California, Los Angeles, where he teaches Renaissance and modern drama.

Braunmuller has published and spoken on modern drama, including two essays on Pinter's drama (one on *Old Times,* the other on the metamorphic power of memory in the major plays). He has also published several essays on Shakespeare, editions of *A Seventeenth-Century Letter Book*, and of Brecht, of the anonymous *The Captive Lady*, and a critical study of George Peele's drama. He has received fellowships from the Folger Shakespeare Library, and the National Endowment for the Humanities, and he is an editor of *viator: Medieval and Renaissace Studies*.

KATHERINE H. BURKMAN attended Bryn Mawr College and received a B.A. from Radcliffe College. Her M.A. was conferred by the University of Chicago, and she also attended the University of Iowa and Indiana University. She was awarded a Ph.D. in Theatre from Ohio State University. As a teacher of English and drama, Burkman has taught in high school, at the University of Iowa, and at Butler University. She is currently an associate professor of English at Ohio State University.

Among Burkman's publications are several articles on Pinter, *The Dramatic World of Harold Pinter: Its Basis in Ritual* (1971), and *Drama through Performance: Shakespeare's Mirror and a Canterbury Caper* (1978). She has also received two grants from the National Endowment for the Humanities for projects concerned with dramatic performance, and she is on the advisory board of the Ohio State University Press.

WILLIAM F. DOHMEN received a B.A. from the University of Wisconsin and an M.A. and a Ph.D. from the University of Virginia. His teaching experience includes the University of North Carolina at Greensboro, the University of Virginia, Eastern Kentucky University, and the University of Pennsylvania. Currently, he is lecturing at Haverford College.

Dohmen has published several articles and delivered scholarly papers on Pinter at professional meetings, as well as publishing essays on James Joyce and Edward Bond. He is presently completing a book on contemporary British comedy. He has attened a National Endowment for the

Humanities Summer Seminar on tragedy, and he was awarded an English-Speaking Union scholarship for the study of modern British literature (with a drama emphasis) at the University of London.

BERNARD F. DUKORE received a B.A. from Brooklyn College, an M.A. from Ohio State University, and a Ph.D. from the University of Illinois. He is currently a professor of drama and theatre (and past chairman of the department) at the University of Hawaii at Manoa.

His many articles and books on modern drama include several on Pinter, including *Harold Pinter* (1982) and *Where Laughter Stops: Pinter's Tragicomedy* (1976). Among his other books are *American Dramatists 1918–1945* (1984), *The Theatre of Peter Barnes* (1981), *The Collected Screenplays of Bernard Shaw* (1980), *Dramatic Theory and Criticism* (1974), *Bernard Shaw, Playwright* (1973), and *Bernard Shaw, Director* (1971). He has been a Guggenheim fellow and twice an NEH fellow.

MARTIN ESSLIN was born in Hungary. He majored in English and philosophy at the University of Vienna and attended the Reinhardt (Theatrical seminar where he studied to be a director. A scriptwriter and producer for the BBC in London, Esslin was Head of Radio Drama for the BBC from 1963 to 1977. He is currently a professor of drama at Stanford University.

Esslin's major publications innclude *The Peopled Wound: The Work of Harold Pinter* (1970, rev. 1982), numerous articles on Pinter, *The Theatre of the Absurd* (1961, rev. 1969), *Brecht: The Man and His Work*, and *Reflections: Essays on Modern Theatre* (1971).

JOHN FUEGI is a professor and director of Comparative Literature at the University of Maryland. He has spoken and written extensively (in *Comparative Literature Studies*, *Shakespeare Quarterly*, *Modern Drama*, and *Educational Theatre Journal*) on drama. In addition, he is the editor of the Yearbook of the International Brecht Society (eleven volumes) and the author of *The Essential Brecht* (1972) and *Brecht the Director* (1984). He has also worked in documentary film and TV docudrama.

LUCINA PAQUET GABBARD received her B.A. from Louisiana State University, her M.A. from the University of Iowa, and her Ph.D. from the University of Illinois. She has taught at the University of Iowa, and she is currently a professor of English at Eastern Illinois University.

Among Gabbard's publications are *The Dream Structure of Pinter's Plays* (1976) and *The Stoppard Plays* (1982), as well as several articles on modern drama in *Modern Drama*, *Twentieth Century Literature*, *Forum*, and *The Journal of Evolutionary Psychology*.

STEVEN H. GALE was awarded a B.A. by Duke University, an M.A. by the University of California at Los Angeles, and a Ph.D. by the University of Southern California. His teaching experience includes the University of Southern California, the University of California at Los Angeles, the University of Puerto Rico, a Fulbright Professorship at the University of Liberia, and the University of Florida. Formerly a professor and head of the Department of English at Missouri Southern State College, he is currently Director of the college-wide Honors Program.

Among Gale's major publications are numerous articles on Pinter, and *Butter's Going Up: A Critical Analysis of Harold Pinter's Work* (1977) and *Harold Pinter: An Annotated Bibliography* (1978). His over fifty articles range over several national literatures, all four genres, and time periods from the sixteenth century to the present. Forthcoming are *S. J. Perelman: An Annotated Bibliography*, *S. J. Perelman: A Critical Study*, and *Encyclopedia of American Humorists*. He has received numerous grants, including a Danforth grant, and his work has been nominated for several literary awards. He is also the series editor of the *Contemporary American and British Drama and Film Series* for Peter Lang Publishers. Two of his one-act plays have been performed on radio, and he has directed little theatre and university players productions.

SCOTT GIANTVALLEY received his B.A. from Occidental College, his M.A. from California State University at Northridge, and his Ph.D. from the University of Southern California. He has taught at Los Angeles Harbor College, Los Angles City College, Occidental College, and the University of Southern California. He is currently a member of the Department of English at California State University, Dominguez Hills.

A published poet and author of *The Fair Lady Abroad: a Mock-Jacobean Tragedy* (staged at California State University, Northridge), Giantvalley has published *Walt Whitman, 1838–1939: A Reference Guide* (1981), assorted essays on contemporary poets and novelists, and an essay on John Guare, which will appear in *Critical Survey of Drama*. He has served as managing editor of *Humanities in Society* and *Quarterly Review of Film Studies* and has written theatre reviews for several Los Angeles newspapers.

FRANCIS GILLEN received his B.S. from Canisius College and his M.A. and Ph.D. from Fordham University. After a period of teaching high school English, he taught at Canisius College, Fordham University, and St. John's University. Currently, Gillen is a professor of English and director of the Honors Program (and the former chairman of the Humanities Division) at the University of Tampa. In 1982 he won the university's outstanding teacher award.

Among Gillen's many publications are several articles and scholarly papers on Pinter read at professional meetings. His drama essays have appeared in *Modern Drama*, *Twentieth Century Literature*, *The Arizona Quarterly*, and the *Dictionary of Literary Biograph*. Gillen has also published essays on E. M. Forster, Henry James, Virginia Woolf, Donald Barthelme, and Mary McCarthy. He is now working on a book-length study of Pinter's plays.

ARNOLD P. HINCHLIFFE is a senior lecturer in English Language and Literature at the University of Manchester. His publications include *Harold Pinter* (1967, rev. 1981), *The Absurd* (1969), *British Theatre: 1950–1970* (1974), and *Modern Verse Drama* (1977), as well as numerous articles on Pinter and modern drama. He has edited casebooks entitled *Drama Criticism since Ibsen* and *T. S. Eliot: The Plays* and is the author of the Twayne volume *John Osborne*. Presently, he is working on a short study of productions of *Volpone*.

CHRISTOPHER C. HUDGINS received a B.A. from Davidson College and an M.A. and a Ph.D. from Emory University. He has taught at Old Dominion University and Emory University. Currently, he is an associate professor of English at the University of Nevada at Las Vegas, where he teaches courses on dramatic literature and film.

Hudgins has published three previous articles on Pinter, and he is working on a book on Pinter's film scripts. He is also active in the theatre, most recently orchestrating the Nevada tour of Roadside Theatre, the "folk tale theatre" troupe from Whitesburg, Ky.

LEONARD POWLICK wrote his Ph.D. dissertation on Pinter at the University of Pittsburgh. He has taught at Wilkes College, and in the Cooperative Department of Communication and Theatre at the University of Notre Dame and St. Mary's College, where he specialized in both dramatic theory and practical theatre.

Powlick has published articles based on a phenomenological approach to Pinter in *Quarterly Journal of Speech* and *Modern Drama*. He has published essays on a number of other contemporary playwrights as well, and he is currently at work on a textbook on play analysis. He has also directed over a dozen stage productions.

AUSTIN E. QUIGLEY was born in England, where he received a B.A. at the University of Nottingham and an M.A. at the University of Birmingham. His Ph.D. was awarded by the University of California at Santa Cruz. He has taught at the University of Massachusetts, the University of Konstanz, the University of Genera, and the University of Nottingham. Currently, he is an associate professor of English and associate chairman of the department at the University of Virginia.

Quigley has published articles on Pinter, and he is the author of *The Pinter Problem* (1975). He has also written the forthcoming *The Modern Stage and Other Worlds* (1985) and several articles on modern dramatists. He has received a National Endowment for the Humanities Fellowship, and he is a member of the editorial boards of *New Literary History* and *Modern Drama*.

ALBERT WERTHEIM was awarded a B.A. from Columbia University and an M.A. and a Ph.D. from Yale University. Currently, he is a professor of English and associate dean for research and graduate development at Indiana University.

Wertheim's publications include co-editorship of *Essays on Contemporary British Drama* (1981) and *Essays on Contemporary American Drama* (1981), as well as many articles on classic and contemporary British and American drama. He has also received grants from the Newberry Library, the American Philosophical Society, and the German Exchange Service, and he serves as a member of the Executive Committee of the Modern Language Association "Drama Division," and as president of the Eugene O'Neill Society. He recently served as assistant to the directors of the Berkeley Repertory Theatre (California) under the auspices of a Lilly Faculty Fellowship.

Index

225